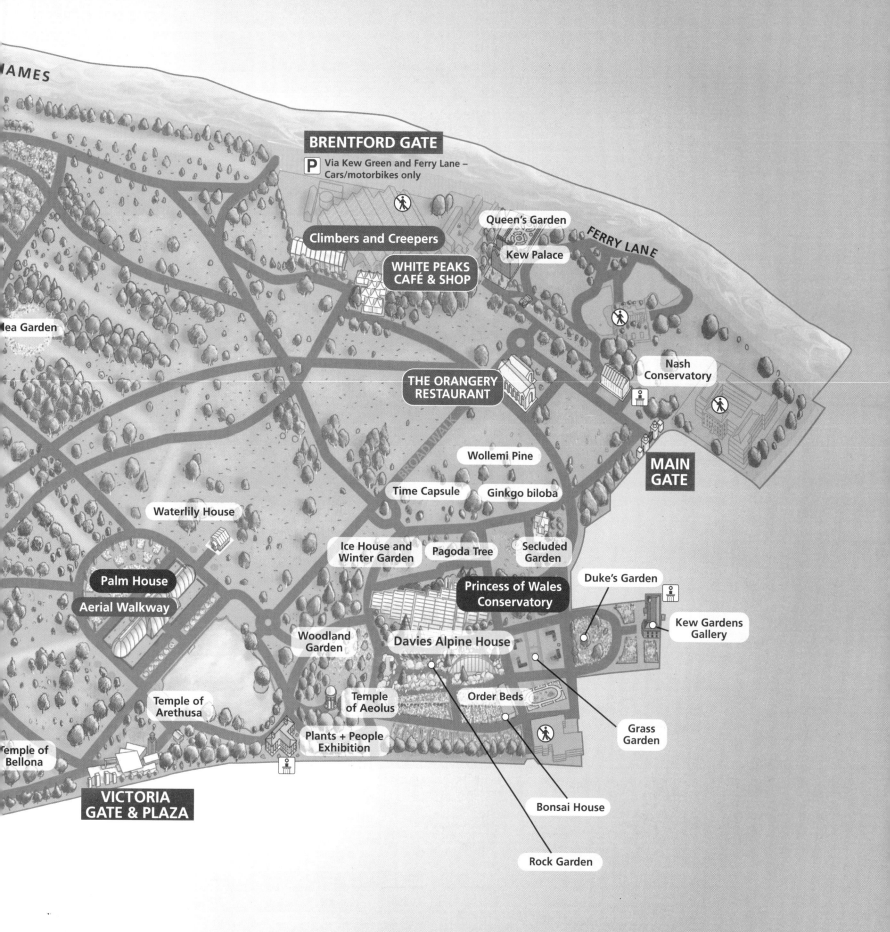

THAMES

BRENTFORD GATE

Via Kew Green and Ferry Lane –
Cars/motorbikes only

Queen's Garden

FERRY LANE

Climbers and Creepers

Kew Palace

WHITE PEAKS CAFÉ & SHOP

Nash Conservatory

ea Garden

THE ORANGERY RESTAURANT

MAIN GATE

Wollemi Pine

Time Capsule   Ginkgo biloba

Waterlily House

Ice House and Winter Garden   Pagoda Tree   Secluded Garden

Palm House

Aerial Walkway

Duke's Garden

Kew Gardens Gallery

Woodland Garden   **Davies Alpine House**

Princess of Wales Conservatory

Temple of Arethusa   Temple of Aeolus   Order Beds   Grass Garden

emple of Bellona   **Plants + People Exhibition**

Bonsai House

VICTORIA GATE & PLAZA

Rock Garden

THE GARDENS AT KEW

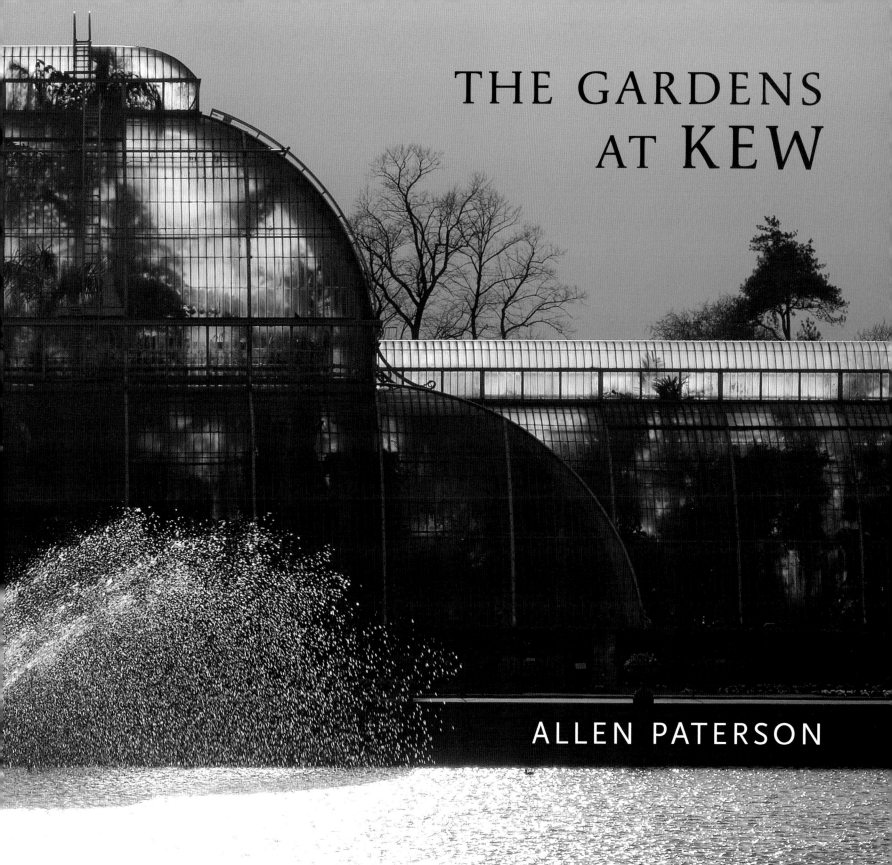

THE GARDENS
AT KEW

ALLEN PATERSON

F

FRANCES LINCOLN LIMITED
PUBLISHERS

Frances Lincoln Ltd
4 Torriano Mews
Torriano Avenue
London NW5 2RZ
www.franceslincoln.com

CONTENTS

Foreword

by Stephen D. Hopper FLS
Director, Royal Botanic Gardens, Kew

THIS BOOK IS PARTICULARLY WELCOME as the first major historical review of Kew by a former director of another botanic garden. From Allen Paterson's erudite pen flow insights of a practitioner deeply knowledgeable about the challenges faced by botanic gardens in our age. Allen is well-placed to provide fresh perspectives one-step-removed, given his long-standing contact with Kew: as childhood visitor, student horticulturist and colleague and respected peer in the global community of botanic gardens. Publication has been deliberately timed to coincide with Kew's 250th year in 2009. Such a milestone gives pause for reflection – honouring the past, enjoying the present, and charting the future. At no other point in history have plants been so critical to sustainable life on Earth. As the author so eloquently highlights, if we do not care for the world's plants and fungi, cease ongoing destruction of remaining wild vegetation, and repair and restore significant plant communities, the quality of life of billions of people, and the survival of millions, will hang on a tenuous thread indeed.

The history of Kew illustrates admirably a fundamental message of hope in a world where doom and gloom have become the currency of most mass communications. Kew is positioned to make a significant future contribution in helping deal with the environmental challenges we all face. This has and will occur via a combination of high quality problem-solving in plant science, applying the practical skills of able horticulturists and making best use of an inspiring global network of collaborative partners (illustrated, for example, by the Millennium Seed Bank Project).

From 2009, with partners around the world, Kew will embark on a ten-year Breathing Planet Programme, achieving a step-change in global conservation and sustainable use of plants. We must do this, for self interest alone, because of the scientific validity and veracity of Lord Stern's recent call to action that 'business as usual isn't an option' if we are to see our way through the worst aspects of looming climate change and loss of biodiversity. The time for action and fundamental change, supported by the best of scientific problem-solving, is upon us. Plants will play a critical role in helping us adapt to and mitigate environmental change in these unprecedented times.

Such serious work is an underlying theme and conclusion of the book. But there is much more along the way for the reader as Kew's history unfolds, enriched by the stunningly beautiful photography of Andrew McRobb. I never cease to be enthralled and intrigued by the human stories embedded in Kew's history, told with flair herein. The author has weaved an engaging narrative, highlighting major players and events, with an unusually keen eye for Kew's story in the broader context of British and global affairs.

I've enjoyed reading the book, learning much along the way as I explored its text and illustrations. All involved in its sumptuous production are to be congratulated. I commend *The Gardens at Kew* to anyone interested in botanical gardens, history, and the world heritage that is Kew, its plants, people and contributions, over a 250-year span.

The Temperate House in snow.

∽ Preface ∽

ANY HISTORIC INSTITUTION, be it a university college, for example, or a learned society, is bound to reflect and be reflected by those who lead it in good times and bad. The Royal Botanic Gardens, Kew, throughout its 250 years, demonstrate this wonderfully. From Sir Joseph Banks, the epitome of the talented aristocrat, its first Director in all but name, through the Hooker dynasty of Queen Victoria's reign, to the succession of eminent botanists of the twentieth century until today, all have left their mark upon Kew and the world of plants. It is perhaps unfortunate for modern-day directors that their early predecessors – Sir Joseph enveloped in a Maori cloak (never before seen in England) or in elegant court dress waiting upon King George III, and Sir William Hooker with a crinolined lady on his arm – are so inevitably used as illustrations to Kew's story. Chaps in modern suits and sober ties, however celebrated they be, are bound to lack the romantic image of the more distant past.

It is vital therefore to emphasise the extraordinary continuum that is Kew and to credit those twentieth- and twenty-first-century directors who, while being rightly proud of the Gardens' historical fame, promoted the forward thrust essential to a scientific establishment of global significance. Kew is no cosy heritage backwater reclining on its reputation. Neither is its beauty only skin deep.

In writing this book it has been fascinating to follow the story and discover the reasons why a private country retreat for a family of eighteenth-century royals famed, if anything, for their simple domesticity, should become a bastion of imperial expansion. And that in turn it should grow into an international centre of plant research and conservation.

In personal terms I feel rather proprietorial about the place. I was taken to visit as a boy and can still recall the excitement of seeing for the first time bananas ripening in the Palm House – and this at a time when the appearance of bananas in the shops provoked, if not riots in the streets, then certainly queues round the block. The student gardener course I joined in the 1950s had little of the sophistication and depth of the current diploma course but as a place for building up one's knowledge of plants Kew was unsurpassed as it is still is for today's students. It comes of something of a shock, however, to discover that, of the sixteen directors of Kew, including Sir Joseph himself who virtually began it all, I have actually known half; clearly I've only missed the Hookers by a hair's breadth. It is an honour that more recent incumbents have been dear friends and colleagues. How very suitable that, at this time of celebrating the 250th anniversary of the Royal Botanic Gardens, today's Director, Professor Stephen Hopper, is from Australia. Sir Joseph Banks, who linked Kew so strongly with that new-found continent, would surely have welcomed such a successor.

Any author is indebted to a host of people and I have been extraordinarily blessed, starting within my own family. My wife Penelope nobly typed up the nowadays almost antediluvian pencil-on-paper manuscript and our son Mark advised from the Eden Project in Cornwall. For facts about Kew everyone turns to Ray Desmond, Kew's historian and an old friend. Like the fabled Benjamin Jowett of Balliol College, what he doesn't know isn't knowledge. I am hugely indebted also to many members of staff at Kew and at Wakehurst Place especially those who were kind enough to read and offer advice on specific chapters. I am only sad that Anne Fraser of Frances Lincoln who started us off on this project was unable to see it through to completion because of ill-health.

Andrew McRobb's fine photographs speak for themselves. Gina Fullerlove, Head of Publications at Kew, has been a tower of strength and her colleague, Michelle Payne, an invaluable eagle-eyed editor. I thank them all.

Allen Paterson
Grovehill House, Dumfriesshire

The Xstrata Treetop Walkway, which opened in 2008.

Introduction

THE 300 ACRES of riverside land that today comprise The Royal Botanic Gardens, Kew epitomise, in that evocative phrase, Our Island Story. Over the centuries the area has held rough arable fields, poor pasture, the plots of local cottagers, country house estates and, by the early eighteenth century, a royal playground. The royals developed carefully designed landscapes and formal gardens with collections of exotic plants, animals and birds – those animated cabinets of curiosities by which the rich showed their taste and fashionable scientific interests. Royal emphasis on their plant collections at Kew are the key to what is there today and over time caused this little Thames-side village to become a promoter and supporter of the empire, with worldwide effects. In a post-imperial age the descendants of these collections and the expertise that cultivates and studies them is of even greater significance. They make Kew a hub of global conservation activity, an icon across continents.

The story begins simply enough. From the crossing-place of the still-tidal River Thames, between the parishes of Brentford (to the north) and Kew (on the southern bank), roads led to Richmond, Kingston and on into the deep English countryside of chalk downs, clay vales, heath and forest. The roaring A30 of today is the same Roman road that ran from Londinium to the provinces of the south west almost 2,000 years ago, passing close to Kew's sandy scrubland which provided subsistence living for a peasant community.

For centuries little changed but eventually London, less than ten miles away and capital of a gradually more settled and prosperous country (Barons' Wars, insurrections and religious conflicts notwithstanding), began to have its effect. Upwind and upriver – water providing a safer and more satisfactory means of transport than any roads well into the eighteenth century – the banks of the Thames became the most desirable place of residence for prosperous merchants, the gentry, nobility and even royalty.

In the seventeenth century, Chelsea, much closer to the city, was famously described as 'a village of palaces' and virtually every riverside community could claim such a title. There were royal residences at Kew, Richmond, Hampton Court and, another twenty miles further on, at Windsor. Although today the vast

The unseen river Thames keeps Brentford's twenty-first-century tower blocks and factories at bay. Kew Palace and the Orangery look south from the north-west corner of the royal estate.

ABOVE Syon House, a seat of the Dukes of Northumberland. This east front, castellated by Robert Adam in 1761, closes the long vista from Kew's Palm House across the river.

suburban sprawl that is south-west London has spread over most of these once elegant estates, enough great properties remain to evoke that fashionable and prosperous past: Osterley, Ham, Marble Hill, Chiswick House and hosts of substantial, if smaller, houses as well.

Only at Kew Reach, however, do both banks fully retain today their old aristocratic validity. On the north is Syon, the great palace of the Dukes of Northumberland, which still boasts private parkland and traditional water-meadows sweeping down to the river as if in the depths of the country. These, though species-rich in English terms, look across to the almost unimaginable diversity of the plant collections that have been assembled at the Royal Botanic Gardens opposite: endangered flora exists on both banks. Kew, in turn, aligns one of its main vistas over the river to that distant stiff-tailed Percy lion above the castellations of Syon House.

But while Syon continues as a bastion of aristocratic privilege, wonderfully fending off the worst depredations of the twenty-first century with walls and woodland screens, Kew, with similar origins, works practically to repair such depredations across the world. No two estates sharing a common boundary could differ more.

In the eighteenth century, when Kew's story really begins, Kew and Syon were typical of great patrician land holdings around the country. Syon was originally a monastic property which was passed to the Percys, Earls of Northumberland – 'a family' it was said, 'nobler than Kings' – who had virtually ruled the north-east of England throughout the Middle Ages. It became their London out-of-town retreat and they developed around it the usual assembly of ornamental gardens, landscaped parkland and, in the nineteenth century, great conservatories and an arboretum.

All this was paralleled across the river at Kew. In 1718 the Prince and Princess of Wales (who succeeded to the throne as King George II and Queen Caroline) began to live at Richmond Lodge, and over the next few years assembled further lands and buildings. Their son, and their grandson – who became King George III – used Kew as a convenient family rural retreat, though with less grandeur than that at Syon. Fashionable eighteenth-century interest in landscape gardening (or place-making as it was known) developed conventionally with the laying out of walks and flower gardens and the building of follies to act as eye-catchers and so on. But it was King George's mother, Princess Augusta, whose passion for plants took her collections into the category of botanic garden and laid the foundation of what exists today.

ABOVE Kew as royal playground. The Swan Boat *Augusta* was launched in 1755 for the Prince of Wales's birthday. It held ten people and was 4.5 metres high – but how was it propelled?

1

A PROSPECT OF KEW
A Landscape with Royals

THE THUNDERING A316, on its way to cross the Thames, cuts off a corner of Kew Green. The lost corner, holding a few fine houses and the Coach and Horses Hotel (once a posting inn on the London–Richmond road), puts on a brave front against the south London suburbia that crowds in for endless miles behind. Across the road, in spite of the racket and the fumes, is another world – a world of English country gentility in which Miss Austen or Anthony Trollope would have been immediately at home. Especially, perhaps, early on a summer Sunday morning when the twenty-first century is at its least insistent. The commuters' cars, the trails of trucks, even the jets bound for Heathrow airport are quieter, and the bell of St Anne's on the Green calls the parish to 8 o'clock communion.

Further across the Green someone will soon bring out the roller to prepare the wicket for this afternoon's match. Later it will be back to St Anne's for Matins, then pre-lunch drinks at the Crown before the first batsmen walk out. Great trees and elegant flat-chested Georgian Houses, a few with Regency balconies added, preside over the archetypal scene. It is a scene that is repeated again and again across the country, an essentially English

LEFT Carved stone and gilded wrought-iron proclaim the entrance to a great estate. The Main Gates at the end of Kew Green.

RIGHT The roar of jet planes bound for Heathrow Airport is a constant reminder of the modern world.

idyll doing its best to come to terms with the pressure of the present.

Through the trees beyond the cricket pitch high stone pillars and vast gates can be glimpsed. These are obviously an entrance to the parkland of what must be Kew House, ancestral home of the Lord of the Manor, patron of the Vicar of St Anne's, honorary president of the cricket club, owner of most of the houses around the green and the farmlands and woodlands beyond. But here fact differs from expectation. For Kew House read Kew Palace, for Lord of the Manor read Sovereign of the Realm. The gates do indeed open into parkland and lead to Kew Palace but they are also the main entrance to the Royal Botanic Gardens, more than 300 acres that comprise, with its glasshouses,

BELOW The mainly eighteenth-century St Anne's Church on Kew Green, parish church for the village and final resting place for many of Kew's botanists and gardeners.

museums and laboratories, the most significant scientific garden in the world. And a joy for its myriad visitors.

In spite of its present name and the fact that Kew Palace is the oldest building within the estate, the Crown's involvement with these Thames-side lands did not begin here. Indeed, it is a rather surprising survivor of more than a hundred years of acquisitions, adaptations, building, rebuilding and demolition of half a dozen royal residences at Kew as need, convenience and fashion waxed and waned throughout the eighteenth and early nineteenth centuries.

It all began at the other end of what is now Kew Gardens. There had been a royal palace at Richmond only a mile or so upstream since the sixteenth century and bits of rosy Tudor brick remain on the south side of Richmond Green with the charmingly named Maids of Honour Row near by. (Maids of Honour are also a local speciality that can still be found in adjacent patisseries.) In the royal park, halfway between Richmond and Kew, stood a house that King James I had used as a hunting lodge. In the 1690s

William III (Dutch William) had it enlarged for more frequent use and began to work on the landscape. Avenues were planted back to Richmond town in one direction and to the river and its terrace walk in the other. Rides were cut through the woods and great formal gardens were considered, but then in 1702 King William died.

The Duke of Ormonde, who leased the house from Queen Anne, renamed it Ormonde Lodge and continued to improve the grounds. But after unwisely supporting the anti-Hanoverian Jacobite rebellion of 1715 he was forced to flee abroad, forfeiting his estates here and elsewhere.

Ormonde Lodge reverted to the Crown and in 1718, under the name Richmond Lodge, became home to the Prince and Princess of Wales, son and daughter-in-law of King George I. Princess Caroline was an enthusiastic garden-maker in the formal fashion of the time – plantsmanship at Kew was still some time in the future. At the time she was brought up (she was born in 1683), the fame of Louis XIV's gardens at Versailles and that of

his gardener André Le Nôtre were spreading throughout Europe. Le Nôtre-style gardens, with their avenues, bosquets, parterres, fountains, cascades and statuary, sprang up, it seemed, around every schloss, château and palace on the continent, wherever sufficient land and money were available together. Even insular England was not immune, as Bramham Park in Yorkshire and Melbourne Hall in Derbyshire, for example, still show. The Princess knew intimately famous formal gardens such as Herrenhausen in Hanover and Charlottenburgh near Berlin (her brother became the first King in Prussia in 1701 and named it after his wife).

Princess Caroline began to garden at Richmond Lodge. She discussed new fashions with Alexander Pope, whose

BELOW An archetypal English scene: village cricket on the village green. These houses on Kew Green enjoy the river Thames flowing at the bottom of their gardens.

RIGHT *An Exact Plans of the Royal Palace Gardens and Park at Richmond with Sion House etc on the opposite side the River Thames. Survey'd and Publish'd by John Rocque Chorographer to his Royal Highness The Prince of Wales.* This last version was made in 1754.

OPPOSITE This sketch-plan by Lancelot 'Capability' Brown is dated 10 December 1764. West Sheen village is swept away along with the formal gardens of Richmond Lodge, field boundaries and buildings.

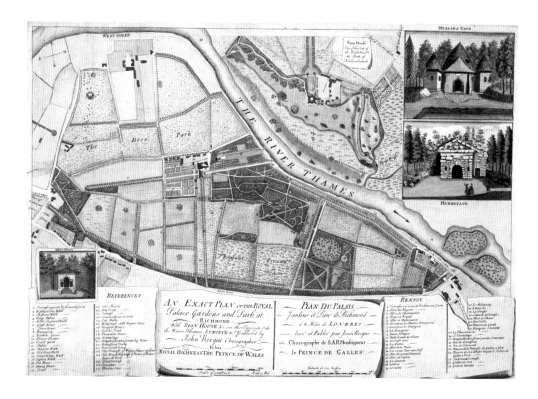

little estate upriver at nearby Twickenham became famous through his writings, and professionals such as Charles Bridgeman and William Kent were soon involved in extending the grounds both in extent and concept. By the time of George I's death and the accession of the Waleses as King George II and Queen Caroline, the Richmond Lodge estate encompassed towards 400 acres in an irregular triangle from its Deer Park base to the apex at Kew Green. The western boundary was the tidal River Thames and its famous raised terrace walk with views across to the Duke of Northumberland's Syon House. Love Lane, a public road from Richmond to Kew, was on the east.

The early decades of the eighteenth century saw garden design in England in a state of fascinating flux. Continental influences from France and Holland (and these in turn from Renaissance Italy) with their mathematical formality began to be criticised, not merely through changing fashion (and because they were foreign and frightfully expensive) but through literary, philosophical and even political thought. What develops is a peculiarly English aesthetic. 'I cannot but fancy,' wrote Joseph Addison in *The Spectator* in August 1712, 'that an orchard in flower is not infinitely more agreeable than all the little labyrinths of the most finished parterre.' And later, 'Why may not a whole estate be thrown into a kind of garden by frequent plantations,' where 'a man might make a pretty landscape of his own possessions.' These and Pope's early essays led towards what developed into the English landscape garden and arose in parallel with the agricultural revolution. Landowners' interests in the aesthetics of their properties were wonderfully supported by the economic advantages of 'improvement', a key concept of the time.

As the century progressed the idealisation of nature became even more pronounced and many estates changed utterly – especially where Lancelot 'Capability' Brown was employed – from formality to ostensibly unadorned countryside. Much of Britain's landscape today is the result of that movement. Canals were turned into serpentine rivers, walls and hedges replaced by ha-has (the sunken fences which avoid any interruption to the view, and for which Bridgeman is usually now given the credit of inventing), trees were planted in clumps rather than blocks or avenues so that, in effect, garden moved into landscape without apparent divide. All these changes flowed through Kew as inexorably as the Thames flowed by its side.

Queen Caroline's estate began at Richmond Lodge and ended at Kew Green, where she had bought or leased several houses in 1728. The estate reflected the early stages of the landscape movement. John Rocque's splendid *Plan of Richmond Gardens* (1734) show the façades of the royal houses, Bridgeman's landscapes and several of the garden buildings designed by William Kent. Of these, the Hermitage, the classical Queen's Pavilion and the particularly dotty Merlin's Cave no longer survive. The latter contained a tableau of life-sized wax figures, including Merlin himself sitting at a table with four historical figures all illuminated by light from lunettes in the beehive-shaped thatched roofs above. It looked a bit like an African kraal – perhaps the most bizarre in the whole canon of country house garden follies. The King described it as 'childish silly stuff' but that verdict seems not to have much worried the Queen who continued to play at garden making. It was her own

property, after all, which she intended to be her dower house should she survive the King.

John Roque's 1734 map contains the first depiction of the White House, country home of the next generation of royals. It stood close to Kew Green just outside the northern apex of the Queen's Richmond Lodge estate. To everyone's surprise, considering the open warfare between him and his parents, Frederick, Prince of Wales leased the existing house in 1731 and soon brought in William Kent, still busily building exotica next door, to improve it. Kent produced a quietly elegant Palladian house with fine interiors, its central pedimented block flanked by lower wings. All the principal rooms faced south across a wide lawn embellished with four classical statues. Two blocks of trees framed the view to simple gardens and open fields beyond.

In 1736 Frederick married Princess Augusta of Saxe-Gotha and while, as heirs to the throne, the Waleses lived a formal court life mainly at Carlton House (just down the Mall from what is now Buckingham Palace), the

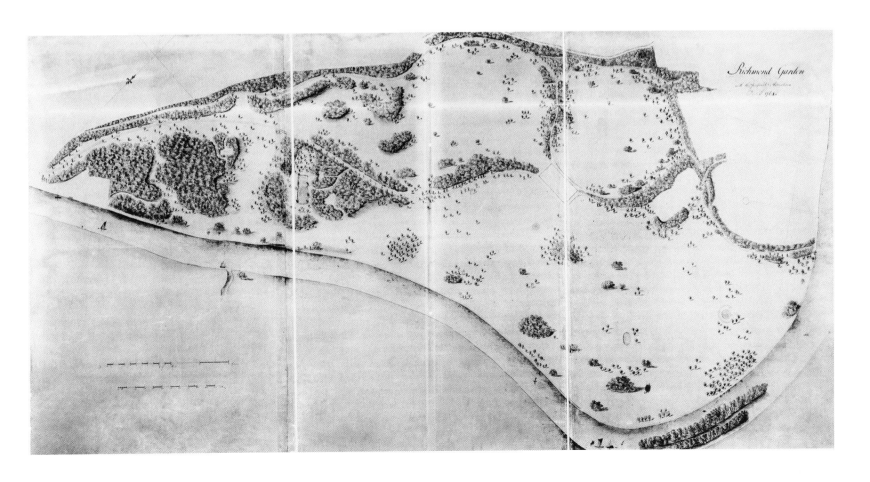

The White House, so-named because of its white stucco façades, was designed for Frederick Prince of Wales by William Kent. It was ready for use as a country retreat in 1736.

White House remained a much-loved country retreat. It became the base for the next phase in the evolution of the royal gardens at Kew in which, for the first time, the word 'botanic' is used.

Queen Caroline died in 1737 and King George, despite having ridiculed his late wife's gardening activities, continued to visit Richmond Lodge in the summer months for the next twenty years. Even the derided follies were maintained, although the recorded building of walls 1,000 feet in length and 12 feet high in 1749 and a heated glasshouse for forcing strawberries three years later indicates the change in emphasis. However, as 'place-making' in the contemporary term ceased there, across Love Lane the landscape bug, from which once caught there is no cure, struck the Prince of Wales.

In those same three years Frederick took a further 75 acres of farmland into the White House gardens. Much tree and shrub planting took place and extensive plans made for an expanse of water and for mounts and temples. Statuary was ordered from Italy. The Prince's personal involvement in the gardens (and insistence on his family and courtiers actually helping in the grounds – it is a serious hazard still to country-house guests today) seems to have led to his death at the early age of forty-four. At the beginning of March 1751 he was soaked in a sudden storm while supervising some works. He developed pleurisy and died a fortnight later aided, no doubt, by his doctors' enthusiastic bleeding and cupping and perhaps by an existing abscess in his chest.

Though Frederick had been derided by many at court who sided sycophantically with his parents in their antipathy, he was in no way the nonentity they claimed. His enthusiasm for science, especially astronomy and the arts – he was a more than competent cellist – attest to wide-ranging tastes.

His death was especially lamented by the gardening fraternity on both sides of the Atlantic. Peter Collinson, whose plant collection at Mill Hill in North London was famous, wrote to John Bartram in Virginia 'The death of our late excellent Prince of Wales has cast a great damp over all the nation. Gardening and planting have lost their best friend and encourager; for the Prince had delighted in that rational amusement a long while: but lately he had a laudable and princely ambition to excel all others.' Bartram is credited with introducing over 200 species new to British gardens and held the title of King's Botanist in America. Another of his correspondents at this time, Dr John Mitchell, clearly had doubts about 'that rational amusement', writing that: 'The Duke of Richmond and the Prince of Wales are suspected both to have lost their lives to it, by being out in their gardens, to see the work forwarded, in very bad weather. Planting and botany in England', he declared, 'will hardly be repaired ...'

Princess Augusta, the Dowager Princess of Wales as she became on her husband's death, had shared his passion for gardening. The following year, in June 1752, she set her head gardener on completing, 'that part of the garden at Kew that is not yet finished, in the manner proposed by the Plan ...'. Although she maintained Carlton House and Leicester House as London residences, Princess Augusta spent much of her widowhood at Kew improving and extending her country estate.

By the year of his death the first of Frederick's projects had been completed. The House of Confucius was the first of a couple of dozen buildings that enlivened (critics suggest 'littered' as a more suitable word) the landscape and it was soon followed by the Chinese Arch. That neither survives cannot hide the fact that they were amongst the very earliest essays in garden chinoiserie and that the Prince's building tastes were in the forefront of current thought and fashion.

It is difficult for us today, when gardening is considered the most egalitarian of leisure activities, to realise how its progress in the eighteenth century went hand in hand, not only with practical and aesthetic concerns, but also with consideration of how these might demonstrate an owner's philosophy and even his politics. Thus the Prince of Wales's espousal, though doubtless superficial, of Confucian thought, indicates how he might have attempted to rule had he acceded to the throne. The elegant octagonal House of Confucius, with its latticed window and railings, its pagoda roof and golden lamps hanging from the eaves, would evoke to the cognoscenti thoughts of Confucius' requirement that the ethical man offers service to the state and that gardens provide suitable rest, reward and relaxation from those worthy efforts.

Plans were also prepared for a 'Grecian Pavilion' to be built on a mount and surrounded by statues of philosophers, poets, and scientists. Here, visions of other golden ages would alert the sensitive and cultivated mind as they beheld Frederick's version of Mount Parnasssus. Lord Cobham's temples of Ancient Virtue, Modern Virtue (built as a ruin as a heavy hint) and British Worthies at Stowe in Buckinghamshire in the 1730s had set the pattern for this sort of polemical garden making. One's choice of heroes proclaimed one's allegiance.

These early buildings in the White House landscape were designed by Joseph Goupy, an otherwise unremarkable figure whom the Prince employed as drawing master, art adviser and 'cabinet painter'. They point the way to the next stage of development.

In 1747 a chance encounter at the Egham races led to the Prince meeting the thirty-four-year-old Earl of Bute. The association that followed had immense consequences for Kew, and indeed, the history of the country. At a time when much political power still flowed directly from the Crown, it was inevitable that the household of the heir-apparent would develop into a sort of shadow court. His friends, advisers and general hangers-on reflect and encourage his views, usually with a view to personal preferment should he accede to the monarchy. It is an uneasy world of patronage, preferment and dangerous dependence.

In this particular situation, with the extraordinary antipathy between the Prince and his parents, Frederick's circle became the political opposition with Lord Bute gradually assuming its leadership. In 1750 Frederick appointed him a Lord of the Bedchamber. After the Prince died (an event the Queen is recorded as saying she had wished for a hundred times a day), Bute maintained a key position as adviser and confidant to the widowed Princess. He also became almost a surrogate father to her eldest son, the new Prince of Wales and future George III. Over the next dozen years Bute the politician became more and more central to affairs of state. Though his only official positions were

within the royal households – he had neither a seat in Parliament nor a place in the Cabinet – in 1762 he became Prime Minister, albeit for a short time. Bute not only held a heavy influence over George III but as Prime Minister was responsible for making his intentions public. The King's reputation for competence suffered and Bute became deeply unpopular throughout the country. In London he was incessantly mobbed in the streets and lampooned in the press. For while, it is said, 'he was admirably qualified to manage the petty details of a little court he was utterly unfit to direct the destiny of a great nation'.

Bute the controversial public figure seems worlds away from the cultivated man who was instrumental in moving Princess Augusta's estate from a typical mid-eighteenth century landscape-with-buildings into the beginnings of a highly significant botanic garden. It had been the shared passion for plants and gardens that cemented the Waleses' friendship with Bute. His botanical interests and knowledge went deeper and far beyond that of a mere dilettante. He studied on the continent, in particular at Leiden with its famous botanic garden, before retiring with a young wife to his family estate on the Isle of Bute, at the entrance to the Firth of Clyde. There he planted extensively and continued his botanical studies, maintaining correspondence with other keen plantsmen. But London, polite society and possible advancement called and he and his family returned south, all hopes quickly being fulfilled. Plants and planting maintained their importance throughout the maelstrom years of political office up to the end of his life. Fine gardens were developed at Caenwood (now Kenwood) in Hampstead, Luton Hoo in Bedfordshire and Highcliffe on the Hampshire coast. It was this almost renaissance-man combination of personal knowledge and extensive connections (as well as charm and patrician good looks) that made him so invaluable at Kew to Princess Augusta and her eldest son.

LEFT Augusta, Princess of Wales, in an oil portrait (1754) by Jean-Etienne Liotard.

It seems to have been Lord Bute who introduced William Chambers to the Kew set and, in doing so, sparked off the next major phase in the development of Princess Augusta's garden. Born of Scots parents in Gottenberg, Chambers had voyaged with the Swedish East India Company during the 1740s to India and twice to China. He left the Company and, determined that architecture was a more suitable career, studied for five years in Paris and Rome before launching himself upon London in 1755. Within two years he had produced books based upon his travels, one of classical designs, the other entitled, *Designs of Chinese Buildings, Furniture, Dresses, Machines and Utensils*. It was dedicated to the Prince of Wales to whom he was soon engaged as a tutor. Chambers recorded:

> The Prince employs me three mornings a week to teach him architecture, the building [and] other decorations at Kew fill up the remaining time. The Princess has the rest of the week which is scarcely sufficient as she is for ever adding new embellishments at Kew [in] all [of] which I direct the execution (and) measure the work.

Chambers had arrived. The 'new embellishments' were illustrated in *Plans of the Gardens and Buildings at Kew* published in 1763.

Although some buildings were still unfinished at that date, others were subsequently moved and perhaps a couple were designed but never built, this year marks something of a culmination of Princess Augusta's garden. The drawn ground-plan can be seen as having attained Prince Frederick's 'laudable and princely ambition to excel all others' as Collinson had predicted a dozen years before. Though by no means large in acreage, Kew had more buildings than even Stowe and contained virtually every element admired in a mid-eighteenth-century country estate, and this only seven miles from central London. The 1763 plan clearly shows how the gardens were used and enjoyed.

The White House sits with its ancillary buildings in the extreme north-west corner, separated from the road only by a carriage circle. Its south-facing rooms give immediately on to the 40-acre Great Lawn. Beyond, the Lake with its island stretches right across the view. Groups of trees screen, point towards or carefully half-hide the garden buildings. A boundary walk moving in and out of the trees introduces what are, in effect, a series of stage-set tableaux to amuse, divert, instruct and entertain the beholder. The use of the term 'folly' for such buildings offers only one aspect of their role: though often quickly built of wood and stucco disguised as stone and not necessarily expected to last, most were essays in serious architectural languages which educated people could recognise and relate to – especially the orders and features of the classical worlds of Greece and Rome – but also could learn from. Such a promenade could provoke

thoughts of mortality in gothic chapels, visions of distant lands and exotic cultures in Chinese temples and make-believe Indian mosques. Thus the stations of sensibility could be observed as they walked around in an often programmed sequence.

Like Merlin's Cave and other buildings that William Kent had designed for Queen Caroline in the gardens of Richmond Lodge, most of Chambers's buildings failed to survive the ravages of time and changes of fashion. But enough still remain today, two hundred and fifty years later, to outline the main vistas of Princess Augusta's garden and evoke this golden age of garden-making. To the east, the eight-columned Temple of Aeolus still stands on its mound. The Ruined Arch remains, beyond the current Palm House Pond (part of Frederick's lake). Its

OPPOSITE ABOVE Merino sheep reintroduced to Kew after more than 200 years. Sir Joseph Banks obtained the first such animals for King George in the 1790s.

OPPOSITE BELOW An early-nineteenth-century view of the grounds at Kew showing grazing flocks. These sheep ensured close-cropped grass, manuring it as they fed, and provided the elegant *ferme ornèe* ambience required. They were also of economic value.

BELOW The Lake, originally created by Sir William Hooker in the late 1840s, with four islands planted for their autumn colour to reflect with effect in the water. These also function as important nature conservation areas.

None of the sequence of garden buildings built by William Chambers for Princess Augusta have survived in their original mid-eighteenth-century state. The Temple of Aeolus (right) was rebuilt in stone in 1845 while the Temple of Victory and Theatre of Augusta (below) have both been demolished. The Ruined Arch is shown (opposite, above) in its 1759 state, with blind side arches. These were opened a hundred years later but the monumental masonry of the main arch still impresses (opposite, below).

crumbling pediments recall 'the grandeur that was Rome' – which Chambers had witnessed for himself while studying Rome's monumental remains. Richard Wilson's painting of the arch soon after it was built, simply entitled *Ruin* was shown at the Royal Academy and was so successfully evocative of the warm south that for a long time it was believed to be a view in the gardens of the Villa Borghese. Newly introduced Lombardy poplars appear to take the place of Italian cypresses.

As well as fulfilling its ornamental role the Ruined Arch carried a track used for taking cattle from Kew Road (beyond the boundary wall) to graze the pastures that continued to be used south of the Lake. Sheep also grazed the Great Lawn. This is an example of *ferme ornée* – an emphasis on both the aesthetics of idealised countryside and its practical economy, which together made a highly satisfactory concept for that age of improvement and enlightenment.

In 1762 Horace Walpole wrote to a friend, 'the Pagoda at Kew begins to rise above the trees and soon you will see it from Yorkshire'. The Pagoda, 163 feet high, was intended as the cumulative eye-catcher of the longest

vista on the estate. It remains a potent image of those years at Kew when Chambers and others worked flat out to fulfil Princess Augusta's apparently insatiable taste for garden buildings. Contemporary views seem to exaggerate its height, as it is seen towering above the trees – a little artistic license never hurts. But it should be realised that this was a century before the giant redwoods and Douglas firs from North America had begun to show their potential in Britain, so the pagoda was indeed vastly higher than anything around. Hung with enamelled dragons and flanked by Chambers's mock-Moorish Alhambra and Domed Mosque with minarets, a trio of gaily gilded and painted amusements was formed at the farthest point of the belt walk, and could be visited on foot or by carriage. Today the 'Kew Explorer' visitor train is understandably popular to reach so distant a spot.

Returning to the White House along the Love Lane boundary, the walk met several more buildings. There are views across the fields to the lake, where a Palladian bridge leads on to the island, and from there, looking across the Great Lawn, another classical building can be glimpsed through the trees: Chambers's Orangery. With its stucco and elegant pediments, the Orangery effectively complemented the façade of the nearby White House. It returned the visitor from the distant exoticism of Pagoda and Mosque to the reason of the classical world and of home.

The estate plan shows that the broader landscape was complete by the early 1760s. The carefully contrived

BELOW William Marlow's illustration for Chambers' *Plans . . . of the Gardens . . . at Kew* (1763).

RIGHT Even today, though shorn of its gilded dragons and bells, the Pagoda still impresses by its height as it towers above surrounding trees.

views from the house, the belt walk linking the garden features, the glimpses of this temple from that artfully placed seat – all provided the expected outdoor pleasures of a fashionable mid-eighteenth-century country house. Only maturity of newly planted trees was required. But the Princess's and Lord Bute's passion for growing exotic plants could not be indulged there. Thus the estate plan shows a very different series of garden spaces to the south-east of the Orangery.

Backed by the roofs of the houses on the south side of Kew Green and screened from the Great Lawn by trees lay a garden that was a world away from the naturalistic landscape of fashion. Overlooked by the Great Stove, a Chambers-designed hot-house over 100 feet long built in 1761, lay a grid of narrow beds. These formed Princess Augusta's Physic Garden. It was formally designated in 1759, the date now taken as the foundation of the Royal Botanic Gardens. William Aiton, who had trained under Philip Miller at the Apothecaries' famous physic garden at Chelsea, was appointed Head Gardener, in essence Kew's first Curator.

After more than a decade of frantic activity on the White House estate, extensive landscape gardening began again at the Richmond Lodge Estate. In October 1760 King George II died and his grandson succeeded to the throne as George III. Only twenty-two years old, he was still heavily influenced by his mother, Princess Augusta, and by his tutor and 'dearest friend' the Earl of Bute, whom he at once appointed a Privy Councillor. A year later the young King married the seventeen-year-old Princess Sophie Charlotte of Mecklenburg-Strelitz; Bute had arranged the match and Lord Harcourt, another of George's tutors, was sent to Germany to wed the Princess by proxy and bring her to London. In spite of the

Though never since it was built a satisfactory growing space for plants, William Chambers's Orangery makes a magnificent statement for neo-classical architecture. Here is one of four pediments with their dentil cornices and Royal Coats of Arms. It is dated 1761 though the Gardens' records state it was begun four years earlier.

obviously dynastic background to the union and though Charlotte was not a beauty, she was 'amiable' and no whiff of scandal ever sullied a happy marriage. Marred only by the King's periods of illness, it lasted fifty-eight years. Their preference for a relatively simple domestic life and the King's interest in architecture, garden-making and agriculture (Farmer George became a title of some approbation) led to their use of Richmond Lodge. While his mother's establishment remained at the White House, from 1764 Richmond Lodge became a summer home for the growing royal family; the future George IV (Prinny) born 1762, was the first of fifteen children.

Across the river, the Duke of Northumberland's Syon House stood impressively in the expanse of its apparently limitless landscape. Lancelot 'Capability' Brown had been called in from 1760 and with Robert Adam working on the great house, Syon became transformed in the latest patrician fashion. Old enclosed gardens were opened up, walls were taken down and soon there was 'a fine lawn extending from Isleworth to Brentford'. There were ha-has, gravel walks and re-ordering of levels so that views of the Thames could be enjoyed from the house, framed in clumps of young trees.

Queen Caroline's Bridgemanic garden, with its straight canal and avenues, convoluted woodland rides and formal terrace walk separating the grounds from the river, must have suddenly seemed dreadfully old hat. 'Capability' Brown's landscape practice had, by this time, utterly changed the prospects of many great houses from Chatsworth and Harewood in the north to Petworth and Longleat in the south. It continued for another twenty years to transform half of Britain. In 1763 Brown had begun work – which went on for ten years – on Lord Bute's Luton Hoo, and Bute's influence may have helped Brown to royal favour. A year later he was appointed Master Gardener at Hampton Court and also Gardener at St James's. Soon after he was being consulted on Richmond.

Over the years Brown's reputation has vacillated with swings of the pendulum of taste. Although most contemporary commentators praised his work, there were some early criticisms that his serpentine lakes, clumps of trees and swelling landforms were too formulaic; others deplored his sweeping away the gardens of earlier times, their avenues and elaborate waterworks. However, very few changes were made at Hampton Court, 'out of respect,' he said, 'for himself and his profession,' and today we still see the elaborate Dutch-style gardens of William and Mary, whose maintenance he oversaw but did not redesign.

For the King, however, Richmond Lodge was more than a convenient inheritance, it was a chosen family retreat and he was determined to become a modern place-maker there. Brown produced the commissioned plans and the next decade saw the Thames flow between grassy banks and idyllic woodland scenes on both its sides. The still existing ha-ha between the towpath and the gardens provided privacy without obstructing the views. Merlin's cave and most of Queen Caroline's other buildings were soon removed. At the time only the loss of the raised river

walk was at all deplored. And Brown's work, with its gentle landscaping was, as can now be appreciated, an admirable preparation for the botanical collections of trees and shrubs which have taken over. The effectiveness of his major essay, the Hollow Walk, designed to give contours to the otherwise flat site, survives today as the shady and protected Rhododendron Dell. The King took great interest in the work in progress, expecting Brown to be on hand to discuss developments and variations from the plan as it went forward. It is fascinating to compare what was done with the highly accomplished drawing (now in the Royal Collection) made by the King himself in about 1760 showing Syon House from the Kew side of the river. The great house is framed by bosky trees which shade a seat from which to enjoy the prospect; a wherry drifting down-river and a couple of figures add interest. And all this long before Brown was called in.

LEFT To give interest to the flat site 'Capability' Brown created a Hollow Walk which was planted with laurels. From the mid-nineteenth century it became the Rhododendron Dell.

OPPOSITE Royal Residences. The Dutch House (left) was built by Samuel Fortrey in 1631. It was leased to Queen Caroline in 1728 and used by various royals until Queen Charlotte, George III's consort, died there in 1818. Cambridge Cottage (right) was one of several houses around Kew Green in which the children of George III lived (joining their parents for breakfast in Kew Palace each day). It became home to George's son Adolphus Frederick, created Duke of Cambridge in 1801.

Brown's plan, dated 1764 (the year the royal family began their summer sojourns at Richmond Lodge), has a blank space to the south where a new palace was being considered. With that in mind the landscaping also required the removal of the entire little village – some eighteen cottages – of West Sheen, opposite Isleworth. It is to be hoped that the inhabitants were suitably re-housed. Such apparently high-handed unconcern for existing buildings if they impinged upon the planned idyllic scene was not uncommon. The King had a close exemplar in Lord Harcourt, who had dispersed the medieval village, church and all, for the landscaping of his new villa overlooking the Thames of Nuneham Park near Oxford; their Majesties visited it with high praise in the years to come.

William Chambers's architectural tutoring had produced in George III an enthusiastic student and a potential patron; and soon after his accession the King began to toy with the idea (as had his grandfather) of replacing Richmond Lodge with a real royal palace. Their Majesties' rapidly increasing family began to make it a necessity but although Chambers produced plan after plan and though foundations and parts of a

basement floor were built, lack of funds prevented progress and the King's building interest eventually turned to Windsor. Meanwhile a decision was made, on the death of Princess Augusta in 1772, to move to the White House (soon known as Kew House) back at the other end of the two estates for the annual summer residence. With Richmond Lodge being demolished soon after, Kew became the focus of both gardens.

Kew House, however, was nowhere near commodious enough to solve the problem and for some years a strange modus vivendi was arrived at by which various children lived, with their nurses and governesses, in the Dutch House (now Kew Palace) and across the road in Cambridge Cottage and other houses around the Green. They joined their parents for breakfast each day. While the apparent simplicity of the royal family's life at Kew was considered noteworthy it was, none the less, supported by a crowd of courtiers, equerries, indoor and outdoor servants all of whom had to be provided with accommodation, with the result that Kew became almost entirely a royal estate village. In the season it became highly fashionable; the public were admitted to the gardens of Richmond Lodge on Sundays and of Kew

House on Thursdays, so carriages thronged across the new Kew Bridge and boats – often bringing bands of musicians along the river – rowed up from London or down from Richmond and Twickenham. With two parallel gardens the royals could, if they wished, avoid the public on visiting days but for further seclusion Queen Charlotte had a little thatched *cottage ornée* in a clearing in the woods down towards Richmond Lodge. Occupants of Princess Augusta's aviary were relocated to what was called the New Menagerie and joined animals such as kangaroos and unusual breeds of cattle. Queen Charlotte's Cottage was used for picnics and alfresco meals, the reign's last essay in royal garden buildings at Kew.

The fashion for visiting Kew in the second half of the eighteenth century was not confined to the *bon ton* of London. Whereas, historically, young English aristocrats with their tutors took the Grand Tour of continental courts and classical sites, a sort of grand tour in reverse began to develop with the fame of the *jardin anglais* as a prime source of study and admiration. The influence of Kew was considerable, not least because of the very strong links between European royal families, members of which frequently visited. King George III of Britain was also Elector (and King from 1814) of Hanover; and he was, as Arch-Treasurer, a member of the Electoral College of the Holy Roman Empire. Not for nothing was the family name Saxe-Coburg-Gotha (changed by George V to Windsor in 1917) and his Queen, his mother and grandmother were all from German princely families. He sent his three surviving youngest sons not to Oxford or Cambridge but to the University of Göttingen, which his grandfather George II had founded in 1737. This two-way traffic also

OPPOSITE ABOVE The Thames as thoroughfare. Here a commercial wherry and a skiff make it up towards Richmond between Syon House and Richmond House.

OPPOSITE BELOW The first kangaroo in the Royal Menagerie arrived as a gift from the Governor of New South Wales in 1792. There were twenty or so when the animal collection was dispersed in 1804.

LEFT Situated by the river behind Kew Palace, the Castellated Palace was a strange romantic vision of the Barons' Wars, as if a bit of Windsor had cast off and drifted downstream.

extended to scholars, architects and gardeners whom the royals patronised.

In 1785 an Act of Parliament was passed to permit the closure of Love Lane to the public so long as the river tour-path was maintained. This provided the opportunity to amalgamate the two royal gardens although this was not actually completed until 1802; hitherto a wooden bridge was the link.

The later years of the eighteenth century were a time of decidedly erratic activities at Kew, paralleled by the increasingly erratic behaviour of the King himself. The infamous 'Madness of King George' has now been shown to be the result of an inherited metabolic illness known as porphyria and the barbaric nature of its treatment only made matters worse. However, during a blessed decade of remission from 1789 the King determined upon a series of ill-advised projects. Architecture always remained a passion. Though Kew Palace survived (to be the place of his incarceration during later periods of instability), Kew House was unaccountably demolished and a vast mock-baronial Castellated Palace built to the west overlooking the river

and Brentford. It was never lived in and was in turn torn down on the orders of George IV in 1827. With it went all likelihood of a royal court again residing at Kew.

Were that the end of the tale Kew Gardens might have survived as an extension to the Old Deer Park and, like other royal parks, today be more or less simple open space. Certainly there would be no obvious base in the landscape strewn with once fashionable follies for the establishment of a national botanic garden, internationally acclaimed.

The genesis of this is the parallel story of Princess Augusta's enthusiasm for collecting plants for their own sake at a time when the trickle of new species from abroad began to turn into a flood. It celebrates Lord Bute's deep botanical knowledge and their shared intention to make the royal collections a *non-pareil*. In those few half-hidden acres beyond the Orangery grew the seeds of today's Royal Botanic Gardens.

2

BOTANIC GARDENS
What are they for?

THE EARLIEST BOTANIC GARDENS, as we know them, were set up in some of the rich Italian city-states during the mid-sixteenth century. Pisa, Padua, Florence and Bologna all had flourishing gardens by the century's end. The promoters were university schools of medicine, beginning to build upon Arabic knowledge and Renaissance learning, as the classical texts were re-found.

Plato's pupil, Theophrastus, can be credited with the first documented botanic garden, in the fourth century BC. He used growing plants from the garden to formulate his *Enquiry into Plants*, which attempted a systematic classification of all known plants. The attempt to make sense of the multiplicity of life forms and to understand the reason for their complexity has continued through the ages, and remains one of the roles of Kew today.

In medieval Europe, where most remedies were plant-based and doctors often made up their own medicines from the basic natural materials, it was obvious that bringing together medicinal plants as reference collections would be of great value – to distinguish, for example, between deadly nightshade and woody nightshade is clearly a matter of some importance. It is not surprising, therefore, that similar botanic or physic gardens were established at centres of learning elsewhere. The universities of Montpelier in south-west France and Leiden in the Netherlands soon followed, while in England Oxford led the way in 1621. All these gardens still exist on their original sites, as does the Chelsea Physic Garden, founded as a teaching garden by the Society of Apothecaries of London in 1673. An indication of the synonymy of the titles is given on a plaque dated 1684 on

A botanic garden assembles, documents and names collections of plants from all habitats and parts of the world. Here trees, shrubs and alpine plants in the Rock Garden are backed by the serried roof-lines of the Princess of Wales Conservatory.

the gardens east wall proclaiming it to be the *Giardino Botanico Chelseiano*. The plaque also indicates the continuing validity of Latin that botanical nomenclature maintains. In the eighteenth century Chelsea became significant as a source of trained gardening staff for Kew as well as a treasure house of rare plants.

While there was a known pharmacopoeia of those plants expected to be efficacious in the treatment of specific complaints and an established code of practice in their use, much medical science was still based upon folklore. Paracelsus (*c.*1493–1541), a Swiss alchemist and physician, formulated a doctrine that became known as the Paracelsian Doctrine of Signatures. It promoted the belief that a beneficent deity had not only provided plants for man's specific medical use but had also marked each with a 'signature' which, recognised by a careful observer, would lead to their use. Certain botanical names today still relate to those times: *Pulmonaria officinalis* (lungwort) with its grey-spotted foliage; *Hepatica* has kidney-shaped leaves and so on. The fact that some such species are still in the current mainstream pharmacopoeia indicates perhaps that the doctrine was a late-medieval attempt to explain logically what had already been handed down from earlier generations of trial-and-error users. Today, various forms of alternative medicine have brought many such plants back into common use.

The doctrine suggests that all plants are grist to the medical mill; all that has to be done is to recognise the signature and a remedy is in sight. The corollary for the developing botanic and physic gardens is that potentially their reference teaching collections have no limit (other than the space and ability to grow them). This plethora of plants makes it essential that their nomenclature and arrangement in cultivation combine to assist the understanding of them. Thus botany, as the broadly scientific study of plants, develops as a discipline in its own right – supporting medicine but not necessarily dependent upon it.

There is a further strand that might be termed 'cabinets of curiosity'. Man, it would seem, is an inveterate collector and even the earliest civilisations show evidence of this trait. Exchange of gifts between potentates, tribute paid in kind, loot from war and barter from trade all contribute to the possessions of princely houses – accumulated in good times, dispersed in bad, to be collected in turn by others. In the sixteenth and seventeenth centuries especially, a huge increase in trade across an expanding world provoked interest not only in traditional treasures of gold and silver and precious stones but also in vestiges of natural phenomena. The concept of the collectable long predates the present. Ammonites and other fossils whose origins could only be guessed at, spars, crystals and fragments of unknown plants and animals were gathered into personal museums, and for the most remarkable specimens special containers were constructed out of rare woods inlaid with semi-precious stones. The cabinet of curiosity therefore is a sort of secular reliquary, though it might also contain a splinter of the True Cross as well, embedded in rock crystal and mounted in gold.

It is a short step from the inanimate to the living collection. Menageries have existed since early times and a famous Egyptian bas-relief at Thebes dating from 1470 BC shows incense trees being brought for Queen Hatshepsut from the Land of Punt (Somalia). What fascinates about the collections from the early years of our modern age is that their assemblage is now supported by scholarship both ancient and modern. The materials themselves lead naturally to this scholarship – description, naming, recording, depiction and classification. There was an explosion in interest in new wonders of the natural world. That Tulipomania in seventeenth-century Holland turned into a South Sea Bubble of gigantic proportions does not detract from the fact that the beauty and amazing diversity shown by a single plant caught the imagination of a whole country.

Within the genus *Tulipa* are around a hundred distinct species native to southern Europe and especially the Middle East. They are enormously prized in Turkey from whence they were first brough to Europe in the 1590s. Innumerable garden forms have been selected over the centuries.

Throughout Europe, what were known as 'curious gardeners' – a diverse group of aristocrats, scholars and merchants (who often were the first to receive strange plants brought in by their sea-captains) – assembled their living cabinets of curiosities, exchanging propagating material and increasingly sophisticated knowledge. Today gardening is a commonplace activity, continually discussed and promoted by the media, so it is easy to forget that just a couple of hundred years ago the needs and morphology of hitherto unknown plant species were as mysterious as the workings of the human body. Knowledge of both was avidly pursued.

In England, the London barber-surgeon John Gerard, brought out his famous *Herball* in 1597. Although it can be shown to be a plagiarised assembly of mainly continental writings and borrowed woodcuts, his knowing what to use and bring to an English-speaking audience was supported by the cultivation of over a thousand species in his own garden in Holborn. In its published list is the first English printed reference to potatoes. Another London apothecary, John Parkinson, had a plant-filled garden in Long Acre. In 1629 he published his *Paradisi in Sole Paradisus Terrestris*, its punning title (Park-in-Sun's earthly paradise) hinting at its role to describe plants grown, as he says, 'for use and for delight'. Its focus on flowers makes it the first gardening book in the modern sense. The *Paradisi* and the 1633 second edition of Gerard's *Herball* both have references to plants grown in the Lambeth Garden of the two John Tradescants, father and son. They were amongst the very earliest professional plant collectors, and were responsible for introducing species from Europe, Russia, North Africa and, especially, the early colonies in North America. *Tradescantia virginiana*, the now common spiderwort, celebrates both collector and source. They also assembled quantities of curiosities of all sorts in their 'Ark', which eventually became the foundation collection of the University of Oxford's Ashmolean Museum.

The Tradescants were employed by a number of the leading landowners in the country including the Cecils at Hatfield and Cranbourne (the loggia on the garden front at Cranbourne Manor bears a striking resemblance to that of Kew Palace), and Charles I and Henrietta Maria, the Rose and Lily Queen. With the country settling down after the Civil War and Cromwell's Protectorate, the late seventeenth century saw a flowering of country house building and associated garden making. Interrelated noble families as well as those with 'new money' built up impressive collections of exotic plants. Those of Mary, Duchess of Beaufort are particularly significant and have connections with the story of Kew.

At Badminton in Gloucestershire, the Duchess grew 'the most curious plants from all corners of the earth' and was especially successful with South African species. Beaufort House in London was just up-river from the Chelsea Physic Garden and Sir Hans Sloane was a neighbour, friend and source of rare plants. His having bought the Manor of Chelsea in 1712, which included the freehold of the Physic Garden, offered further opportunities for the Duchess and, as will be seen, for Kew. The Beaufort collections were not merely extensive assemblages but resources for scientific study by botanists of the day, who were encouraged to use both the living plants and the Duchess's herbarium of dried specimens. Its twelve volumes preserved in the Natural History Museum at South Kensington are evidence of this.

Coincidentally, the Duchess of Beaufort's brother Henry Capel had owned the property which Frederick Prince of Wales was to turn into Kew's White House. In its time it had a famous garden where the diarist John Evelyn admired the productive orchards and recorded the oranges and lemons standing out in the summer months. Kew has an extensive horticultural pedigree, long predating the royals. It was in this context that, in a similar period of widowhood to Duchess Mary's, Princess Augusta avidly pursued plant collecting in those few acres south-east of William Chambers's Orangery. Today an engraved plaque marks the northern boundary of Kew's first botanic garden.

A few magnificent trees still survive from Kew's early plantings. Held together by iron clamps, this false acacia (*Robinia pseudoacacia*) dates from the eighteenth century. Worth noting is the wide mulched area kept free of competing grass. This technique is pursued for significant specimens throughout the Gardens.

It has already been emphasised that the ability to successfully cultivate the newly discovered species marked the most significant 'curious gardeners'. While some, such as the Duchess of Beaufort, may actually have done some gardening themselves, the need for talented professionals became paramount. Sir Hans Sloane is rightly praised for presenting, in 1724, the freehold of the Chelsea Physic Garden to the Society of Apothecaries, 'in perpetuity so long as it be for ever maintained as a botanic garden'. Almost equally important was his insistence that Philip Miller be appointed Curator, during whose incumbency over the following fifty years the Physic Garden became the most important centre of botanical and horticultural endeavour in Britain. Miller, described by Linnaeus as '*Hortulanorum Princeps*', enriched Chelsea by the continuous acquisition of plants and their successful cultivation. As Peter Collinson wrote, 'He has raised the reputation of the Chelsea Physic Garden so much that it excels all the gardens of Europe for its amazing variety of plants of all orders and classes and from all climates as I survey with wonder and delight this 19th July, 1764'.

While Chelsea was the source of many new and rare plants that found their way to Kew, its other great role was in the training of young gardeners. To have served successfully under Philip Miller was an invaluable reference to obtaining preferment. How suitable therefore that with Miller's death and Chelsea's gradual decline William Aiton, one of his protégés, should take Kew's collections to even greater heights.

In the dozen years after the death of her husband in 1751, while her son was being groomed for Kingship, Princess Augusta's gardening enthusiasms rushed forward on two fronts. There was, as has been related, the completion of Frederick's planned Elysium, as a landscape of lawns, lake, woodlands and fields embellished with William Chambers's eclectic series of buildings. Such gardens take time to show their potential (indeed many great eighteenth-century English landscapes are only now at their peak of perfection) and contemporary depictions can look strangely thin. Augusta's rapidly increasing collections of exotics provided more immediate interest. With Lord Bute's continual encouragement and help new plants were introduced directly from abroad and from the increasingly effective nurseries springing up on the edge of London.

Trees and shrubs were grown in a 5-acre arboretum of irregular beds easily reached by walking from the White House and along the front of the Orangery. For frost-tender species an enormous glasshouse was planned. In the event, Chambers's Great Stove was less than half the planned size; nonetheless at 114 feet in length and 20 or so feet in height it was then the biggest hothouse in the

Sir William Chambers's Temple of Bellona, its domed interior fronted by Doric columns supporting the pediment, was built in 1760. It was moved to its present position, surrounded by the mature trees that Chambers would have coveted, in 1803.

RIGHT Madagascar periwinkle, *Catharanthus roseus*. First introduced to Chelsea Physic Garden in the eighteenth century, it was given a ten-word Latin polynomial by Philip Miller, who was yet to accept Linnaeus's binomial system.

OPPOSITE ABOVE Dr John Hill, a protégé of Lord Bute, produced Kew's first catalogue of plants in 1768 and added to it the following year; it lists 3,400 species, using Linnaeus's binomials. The Latin text of the introduction and, of course, the plants it made available throughout the cultivated world, established Princess Augusta's collection as one of the most extensive of its time.

OPPOSITE BELOW It is essential that plants in botanic gardens are correctly named and that careful records are kept. At Kew labels show the relevant plant's name (its genus, here *Tulipa* and its specific epithet, *ingens*). Supporting information offers its family, *Liliaceae*, accession number and country of origin.

country. Today it might be compared with the Princess of Wales Conservatory as a 'state-of-the-art' machine for growing plants.

The art of providing good conditions for growing tropical and subtropical plants in cold countries was still at a pretty primitive stage. Hot water pipes had not yet been invented so the Great Stove used heat from simple furnaces behind the building which was led along under-floor flues and within the hollow back wall (elsewhere open stoves had been shown to produce impossibly toxic smoke and fumes). Beds of ground oak-bark mixed with sawdust also produced heat from fermentation. Potted plants were plunged into this mixture up to their rims. Regulation of such erratic methods, the difficulty of providing air circulation and ventilation without loss of valuable heat and the low light conditions in buildings with small panes of glass combined with the lack of knowledge of new plants' needs to make effective cultivation extremely difficult. Yet, as the century progressed it became an art and a science of the first order and the ability of successive head gardeners to lead and supervise the necessary staff was vital to success.

In 1759, William Aiton began at Kew and in 1763 he appears in Princess Augusta's accounts being paid for 'cultivating and keeping in order our Physick Garden'. Aiton becomes a highly significant name in the progress of Kew. A Scots gardener from Lanarkshire, like so many he came south for employment ('Sir,' said Dr Johnson, 'the finest prospect a Scotchman ever sees is the high road to London') and was taken on by Philip Miller at the Chelsea Physic Garden. It was the ideal preparation for the royal physic garden which it so closely resembled: 4 acres of ground, its beds formally laid out and spreading south from a fine stove house with ancillary frames and nursery space to hand.

One of the definitions given to a botanic garden, not entirely ironically, is 'a place where a wide range of plants are collected and grown and where they are all labelled, mostly correctly'. It is indeed a vital role, as valid at Kew now as in Princess Augusta's time, and it can still be a cause for dissension and debate. As T.S. Eliot might have asserted: the naming of *plants* is a serious matter.

In the Physic and Exotic Garden herbaceous plants were grown in long rows, but not for aesthetic effect – the most ornamental were repeated in the separate Flower Garden near the menagerie. Each genus was labelled by name and their species by numbered tags which corresponded to a carefully maintained written record, all according to Linnaeus's new binomial system of classification.

Linnaeus, the Swedish 'Father of Botany', published *Species Plantarum* in 1753. Today, it is still accepted internationally as the baseline for all botanical nomenclature. He insisted upon a two-word, Latinised name for each plant which, suitably published with a Latin description, belonged to it and it alone. There were contemporary critics – Philip Miller refused to use this binomial method in the early editions of his great *Gardener's Dictionary* but accepted its sense and economy later. We might compare with relief Miller's first name for the hitherto unknown Madagascar periwinkle (used today as a relief for Hodgkin's disease as well as an ornamental) *Vinca foliis oblongis integerrimis tubo flori longissimo caule ramoso fruticoso* with Linnaeus's version until recently: *Vinca rosea*. It is now called *Catharanthus roseus*.

Thus, the genesis of Kew's botanic garden was created in the most momentous decade of systematic botany. The first catalogue of the garden was published in 1768 by Sir

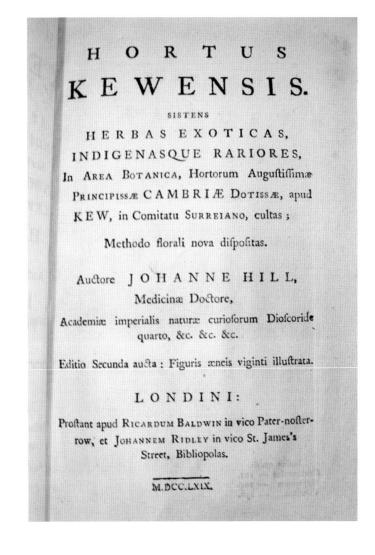

John Hill (like Chambers's the knighthood was a Swedish order given royal acceptance in Britain by George III). This *Hortus Kewensis* – a name conserved for subsequent editions – listed 3,400 plant species. That prodigious number hints at acceleration of the royal collections. As their fame grew so they attracted donations of plants from all sides. Though the aging Princess Augusta seldom visited Kew and Lord Bute's fall from political power and subsequently from the court reduced his involvement (his last meeting with the King was in 1766), the gardens under Aiton seemed to maintain their own momentum. It is comforting to know that Bute's 'wilderness years' were spent gardening on an even more princely scale at his own 4,000 acre estate of Luton Hoo in Bedfordshire and then later in coastal Hampshire, where his conservatory was twice as long as that of the King's at Kew.

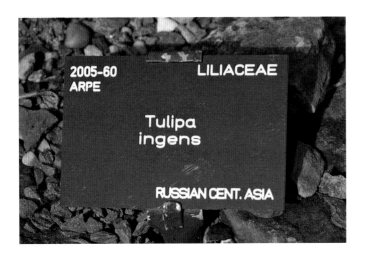

3

VISIT IT
A Perambulation of Kew

I T IS PERFECTLY POSSIBLE TO ENTER KEW by any of the four gates and spend a happy hour or even a day gently strolling in any or every direction and enjoy oneself enormously. Passing through the high wall that runs along Kew road the visitor is taken into another world. Every day of the year offers something different; there are always plants in flower. Even in the depths of winter the glow of witch hazels by the Temple of Aeolus or a sudden warm wash of scent from wintersweet by the Order Beds mark the moving seasons. In January the first snowdrops (though it will be possible to find *Galanthus reginae-olgae* out in October if you know where to look) join the precocious pansies and polyanthuses in the Palm House parterre and encourage us to believe that spring will soon come. Of course, if it's really unforgiving outside, refuge can always be taken in the restaurants or with the under-glass collections.

To go into any of the great glasshouses on such a day can be an unnerving and disorienting experience. There is that same sudden waft of humid and almost textural air that greets anyone descending from a plane at the start of a tropical holiday. Open the Palm House door and spectacles steam up and at once the hats, coats and gloves so necessary a minute ago are boring impedimenta that need to be thrown off. Where there might have been the crunch of ice outside, here is the rush of waterfalls adding to the unlikeliness of it all.

For Londoners, Kew is the quickest way to the tropics; for visitors from the warm south themselves it can combine nostalgia with a real sense of home-sickness: so near and yet so far.

Parkland with trees close to the Temperate House. Species have been chosen both to extend the Gardens' collections and to demonstrate the diversity of different genera. They are also sited to build an avenue or to point a vista for a century or more to come.

The Temple of Bellona in an increasingly rare snowy situation. Each season provides it particular pleasures: soon after it will be awash with myriad Dutch crocuses, white, purple and striped, then the trees will come into leaf.

As the seasons move forward so do the plants, and it is almost possible to dispense with the conventional calendar. Instead, it becomes chionodoxa-time, crocus-time, fritillaria-time, summertime. The outside collections become as evocative of their homes as are the winter tropicals – the Mediterranean plants around King William's Temple, the Bamboo Garden hiding the Japanese Minka House, the shuddering leaf-shadows in the Eucalyptus Grove where a whiff of essential gum-oil is emphasised by the screams of a flock of feral parakeets in the branches above – here the senses combine to give an authentic hint of 'down under', although confusingly this is also guinea fowl territory. Impression after impression in a series of real 'virtual realities' can make the Kew experience strangely confusing to anyone wishing to see beyond the immediate or to ask why this multiplicity of marvels should be here.

Botanic gardens can be read in several ways. Indeed the best description, 'a cultural institution in which research, education and public amenity are based upon the world of plants' emphasises the fact. By definition there are plant collections grouped or arranged to tell a particular story or show particular relationships. A herb garden, for example, may demonstrate the range of plants used in folk medicine or those that today provide alkaloids important in cancer cures; it may grow culinary herbs from a number of distinct cuisines or species with essential oils distilled by perfumeries. Every grouping of plants can be seen, enjoyed and studied in a number of ways, casually or in depth. Fortunately, guidebooks, interpretive plaques and, of vital importance, plant labels combine to illuminate the situation.

The Living Collections are but the tip of a vast iceberg. They support and visually demonstrate much of the scientific research taking place in the laboratories and in the Herbarium (this is discussed in detail in Chapter 8). Little of this can be seen by the general visitor who comes for a day out in beautiful surroundings but it is vital that its existence is visible to a non-specialist audience wherever possible. All museological institutions contain a dichotomy relating to their purpose: does Kew or the British Museum or the National Gallery exist to show plants, historical artifacts or paintings to a casually interested public, or to provide essential research material for their internationally celebrated curators? All museums collect and exhibit treasures as a demonstration of global cultures. Inevitably many existing holdings are the spoils of past imperialism – in Britain the Elgin Marbles and Benin Bronzes come to mind – so politically correct twenty-first century attitudes to history can threaten the museums' cultural validity, their curatorial autonomy and even their existence. Governmental funding to any cultural institution, be it a gallery or an opera company, is always both risky and at risk – and never more so than when it appears unable to balance carefully the popular with the academic.

A botanic garden is just as vulnerable in changing times but it does have certain advantages over traditional galleries and museums. It shows living plants in garden situations to which all sectors of society can easily relate. As well as aesthetic pleasure plants provide food, timber, medicines, fibres and indeed ultimately everything upon which human life depends, and with effective educational programmes and good interpretation this can be made clear. But its collections have to be not merely curated but cultivated; in times of financial hardship the gates cannot be closed, the blinds drawn, and belts simply tightened. When things improve plants cannot be just dusted down; by now they are dead. Zoos are today in a similar situation, but their problems are compounded by the increasing doubt of keeping sentient creatures in captivity: how fortunate that Kew's royal menageries are in the distant past. Such ethical concerns rightly lay at the very foundation or our culture. They need not, indeed must not, spoil our visit to Kew or any other museological institution. But it is wise to admit that the dilemma exists and that questions are continually asked and addressed: what is it for? Who is it for? In the nineteenth century, as Kew moved away from being entirely a royal appurtenance the debate became very bitter.

In order to understand Kew and to gradually absorb its heritage and its developing roles, it makes sense to take a historical approach and let it unfold, page by page, ahead of one's steps. This is not the method for a short

A Kew Calendar
Witch hazel January to fallen leaf
December via snowdrops,
hellebores, crocuses and cherry-
blossom. Unfurling fern fronds lead
to high-summer annuals and
sunflowers. Conker leaves turn as
the nuts drop while crataegus fruits
ripen with the turning year.

afternoon trip – that will cherry-pick the highlights – but it is well worth the effort and on a languorous summer day there is no shame in hitching the occasional lift from the Explorer train to help one along.

As in its royal heyday, when the two estates were still separated by Love Lane, the concentration of collections outdoors and under glass is still in the north-east corner close to Kew Green. The site of Princess Augusta's botanic garden remains a focal point although it is almost totally overlaid with subsequent works, reflecting the complicated needs of a twenty-first-century scientific institution.

Better then, is to take narrow Ferry Lane off the other side of Kew Green to get into Kew Gardens at the Brentford Gate (best of all is to come up to it by boat from Westminster Pier, if time and tide permit). The rosy old Dutch gables of Kew Palace through the trees give a hint of country, so different from the tower blocks of Brentford across the river, blessedly half-screened by a couple of bosky islands ('eyots' in Thames-speak). This is the start of an anti-clockwise progression.

From the Brentford Gate the path southward offers glimpses of the river through great English oak trees that may have been planted around the time of 'Capability' Brown's landscaping here in the 1760s. These give a logical base for a wide-ranging collection of oaks. The genus *Quercus* (the Latin name for this tree) has 500–600 distinct species strewn around the northern hemisphere, with a few stretching down into the uplands of western South America. Many make fine trees that live to a great age; they may be evergreen or deciduous. Some such as the Mediterranean Kermes oak (*Q. coccifera*) are little more than shrubs and this species could easily be mistaken for a hollybush until its acorns are noticed.

Kew Palace, a.k.a The Dutch House, Princes' House, Royal Nursery, Old Red House, Old Palace and so on, is a great survivor. It saw Kent's elegant White House in front and the bombastic Castellated Palace behind both come and go. It gave quiet repose to an ill King and a last resting-place to a dying Queen. Few such modest buildings in Britain have watched the unfolding of so much history.

BELOW Of the 500–600 species of *Quercus* (oak) strewn around the temperate world, Kew grows well over one hundred. Gold-bright unfolding leaves and glowing autumn tints offer seasonal delights.

Other distinct species here are the Armenian oak *Q. pontica*, with leaves towards a foot long and huge egg-shaped buds, and *Q. variabilis*, known commonly as the Chinese cork oak due to its thick corky bark. Obviously, with such a wide distribution extending into subtropical zones of Asia and South-America, Kew can only grow those species that are winter hardy in southern Britain: nonetheless 112 species are represented across Kew and Wakehurst Place. This sort of synoptic collection, demonstrating the diversity of species within a genus or of genera within a family (seen particularly in the Order Beds beyond the Temple of Aeolus), has been a central part of European botanic gardens since attempts were made to make sense out of the multifarious forms of plants in the sixteenth century.

But, as indicated above, a garden has to work within its climate and the conditions provided by its soil and other environmental factors. Glasshouses, of course, are an attempt to circumvent the natural climate, for gardeners inevitably wish to extend their growing possibilities. When Lancelot Brown was commissioned to 'improve' King George's Richmond Lodge Estate, he too had to

work within the possible. Often he dammed a small stream and then by hiding its bounds gave the effect of a great serpentine lake or a river. Here the tidal Thames merely had to be shown in suitably idyllic views. But the land, poor gravelly river terrace, was sadly flat. Contours were essential to enhance walks and vistas. So the Hollow Walk (now Rhododendron Dell) was made, a shallow valley whose excavated soil raised the height of its banks. What gave a shady summer walk to Queen Charlotte and her ladies now provides the same necessary conditions for later rhododendrons and other shade-loving plants – *Cornus* 'Norman Haddon' a white-flowered dogwood with dangling strawberry-fruit in autumn is especially fine.

Rhododendron is probably the largest woody plant genus with towards 800 species (and innumerable hybrids) ranging from tiny mat-forming alpines to 30-metre tall trees. In flower they are amongst the most spectacular plants that British gardens can grow and the more dramatic leaf forms are eye-catching at all times of the year. Some of the specimens growing in Rhododendron Dell today are descendents of

BELOW Dogwoods, species of *Cornus*, vary from small suckering shrubs – the type we commonly grow for their red or yellow winter bark – to considerable trees. These are the so-called flowering dogwoods, native to eastern North America as well as China and Japan. Each apparent 'flower' is in fact a cluster of tiny true flowers surrounded by conspicuous white or pink bracts.

BELOW AND OVERLEAF Kew's Rhododendron Dell began life as the Hollow Walk that 'Capability' Brown designed to give interest to the dull flat Thames-side river terrace. It was originally planted with laurels, rhododendrons being virtually unknown in the mid-eighteenth century.

OPPOSITE From tiny high-Himalayan shrublets to 100 foot-high giants of Asiatic rainforests, rhododendrons are amongst the most spectacular plants British gardens can grow. Kew's collection hugely increased when Wakehurst Place became 'Kew in the Country'. Higher rainfall and better soil are a great help.

specimens collected by Joseph Dalton Hooker (Director of Kew 1865–85) in Sikkim in the middle of the nineteenth century. Though there are a number of rhododendrons native to North America and Europe has a couple, the vast majority come from the Himalayan ranges of India eastwards to China, Tibet and Upper Burma where they flourish in the moist climate, covering, as Joseph Hooker recorded, 'the mountain slopes with a deep green mantle glowing with bells of brilliant colours'.

This oriental influence, which occurs again and again at Kew, is repeated just in from Rhododendron Dell, with the Bamboo Garden. Paths wind between huge clumps of canes, green, yellow or even black, the narrow leaves rustling in the lightest breeze like shimmering silk curtains. Bamboos are members of the grass family *Poaceae* (*Gramineae*), made especially distinctive by their woody stems. In some tropical species heights of over 100 feet can be attained (examples are doing their best to

push panes out of the Palm House roof). Hardy bamboos from temperate areas rarely reach a quarter of that, nevertheless they are amongst the most beautiful and elegant evergreens we can grow. Their depiction, with just a few strokes of a pen or brush, on Japanese and Chinese screens and on pots and bowls seems to exemplify the sparse elegance of so much oriental art.

In the centre of the Bamboo Garden now stands another example of Japanese art which, as so often with their ceramics and other daily artifacts, uses simple local materials to produce an efficient yet sophisticated product. The Minka is a traditional farmhouse of wood and mud-plaster walls under a thatched roof. These renewable materials are earthquake resistant and can be reused and recycled. Minka dwellings have become rare in Japan and the Society which presented this hundred-year-old example to Kew in 2001 is

devoted to their conservation and the ethos of such renewable construction methods. It seems very much at home in the Bamboo Garden.

Taking the diversion from Rhododendron Dell through the bamboos to the Minka House evokes eighteenth-century orientalism – the chinoiserie bridges, temples and pagoda that William Chambers confected for Frederick

BELOW Close to the Rhododendron Dell, the Bamboo Garden was first planted in a little disused gravel pit in 1891; its current form dates only from 2002 and holds over 130 species of these woody grasses.

RIGHT The thatch, wood and mud-plaster Minka House is the centrepiece of Kew's redesigned Bamboo Garden.

Prince of Wales as eye-catchers in the adjoining (and now linked) estate of the White House. That vision is wonderfully still to be found on coming out of Rhododendron Dell. Up to now the Brownian landscape of native species in careful clumps has been, though not lost, overlaid with exotic trees and brilliant flowering shrubs. But ahead is open space of great significance. Every bit of Kew is a palimpsest with its historical layers of time and taste and high fashion. This is worth dwelling on.

The Thames and the fascination that water exerts remains the constant. In earlier times it was the one efficient highway and gave the reason for the settlements that sprung up on its banks. Its beauty caused it to be lined with palaces. The early depictions from here show the Duke of Ormonde's red-brick summer-house, with Queen Caroline's river terrace and formal avenues a little further on. These are layers lost. But across the river Syon House still presides over its apparently archetypal English landscape that Brown designed and George III sketched from his side before its 'capabilities' were fully unveiled by the master. Compare the drawing with today and only the towpath is missing.

Turn around and other historical layers are evident. Far to the south is William Chambers's Pagoda, still dominating the skyline after more than 250 years. To the east stretches nineteenth-century Kew; a shimmer of the lake that Brown had considered unnecessary and, at the end of the long avenue of dark holm oaks aligned on Syon to the west, a glimpse of that most iconic of Victorian buildings, the great curvilinear Palm House.

Paths beckon in all directions and if the day is a good one the blandishments of Palm House and Temperate

House should be resisted. Keep to the landscape of the eighteenth century, especially in May when ahead is one of the most spectacular sights that Kew has to offer at any time: its bluebells. The woodland on Kew's southern boundary – separated from the Old Deer Park, its golf course and superannuated Georgian observatory beyond a ha-ha – is a remnant of the Ormonde/Richmond Lodge 'wilderness'. The few exotics – there is a monkey puzzle or two and a couple of oaks that are not the dominant English *Quercus robur* – came in later, but the 40 acres or so of woodland is a wonderfully fortuitous survival that quietly awaited its time. Now, with conservation of native plants and animals a major concern of all botanic gardens, Kew is lucky to possess a bit of ever-rarer Surrey woodland and maintains it in the traditional way. Hazel is coppiced on a 10–12 year rotation to ensure the right sun-to-shade balance that promotes understorey plants. Here English bluebell, *Hyacinthoides non-scripta*, spreads its extraordinary blue carpet every spring.

Other parts of this designated Conservation Area include a pond and an open meadow from which an annual hay crop is taken. Within the woodland modern forestry methods are not adopted; dead trees are left standing and, when they fall, are allowed to decay in their own time. Thus habitats exist for animals and plants at every level. While Kew's Sussex outpost, Wakehurst Place, is famously known as 'Kew in the Country', this cherished corner might well be called 'the Country in Kew'.

It is therefore with a sense of time standing still that in a woodland glade is found a little house – a woodcutter's cottage straight out of the Brothers Grimm or Humperdinck's *Hansel and Gretel* – entirely in accord with its setting. Weathered red brick, half-timbered and deeply thatched, Queen Charlotte's Cottage is in fact a 1770s *cottage ornée* added to and converted from the cottage once provided for the keeper of the inhabitants of the

Blue *Iris sibirica*, native yellow flag and giant leaves of *Gunnera* edge the Waterlily Pond. Above are the soft green fronds of *Taxodium*, the swamp cypress. The pond, close to the Cedar Vista, was made in 1897.

Shimmering leaf-forms from around the world. Maples from Europe and the Orient, linden, *Liquidambar*, and hornbeam. On Chile's strangely primitive monkey puzzle, the branch bearing cones looks like a vastly exaggerated club moss.

All trees flower, even conifers in their primitive way – how else would they produce seeds to reproduce? But we are apt to label only the most spectacular species as flowering trees. Few are more so than magnolias, a close relation is the tulip tree, *Liriodendron*.

Common horse chestnuts are a fine sight in April, followed and excelled by their Indian cousin *Aesculus indica*, which has more elegant foliage. *Xanthoceras sorbifolium* (from northern China), *Styrax*, *Stewartia* (named after Princess Augusta's advisor James Stuart, Earl of Bute) and cherry-blossom all embellish their seasons.

At the southern edge of the Gardens' land, separated from Richmond's Old Deer Park by a traditional ha-ha, is a wonderful remnant of native Surrey woodland where English oaks and beeches shade swathes of English bluebells. No exotics make a better show in May. Right: Queen Charlotte's Cottage was adapted from the simple accommodation provided for the Keeper of the Royal Menagerie. It was intended as a refuge from court formality in which the Royal family could take tea or even picnic.

royal menagerie. It then made a rustic retreat for the royal family. There are little kitchens and a sitting room below and at the top of a curving stair the big arched picnic room. Charmingly painted swags of convolvulus climb the walls and are said to have been executed by Princess Elizabeth (George III's third daughter). The whole exudes an air of late-eighteenth-century elegance, of mock rusticity and of a temporary refuge from court formality. Queen Charlotte's Cottage was seldom visited by any member of the royal family, although it remained private and inviolable after George III's death. It was not until 1898 that Queen Victoria agreed that the cottage in its 37 acres of woodland should be incorporated in Kew Gardens, so long as the area was not developed. This proviso has been honoured.

As the native woodland thins to the east great conifers start to dominate the scene. This is the third pinetum to have been developed at Kew. Originally, there had been the few acres for deciduous and evergreen trees in Princess Augusta's botanic garden. When that space become entirely inadequate and further land was transferred from the White House pleasure grounds, conifers became concentrated around the current Waterlily House. After becoming Director Joseph

Dalton Hooker rationalised the woody plant collections, deciding upon the southern end of the gardens for new coniferous plantings. A number of the avenues that radiate out from the Pagoda were created at that time. The Cedar Vista, which dates from 1871, is one such. It is this avenue that gives the first glimpse of the Pagoda from the riverbank; and, once halfway along it, the building becomes truly impressive. It may no longer glow with brilliant colours, as the eighty golden dragons that crouched on the eaves have long gone (despite abortive plans for their restoration appearing over the years), but William Chambers's Chinese fantasy never ceases to surprise. It is in fact a ten-storey octagon 163 feet in height. Gently tapering, each storey is reduced by one foot in diameter and one foot in height with fretted 'Chinese Chippendale' balconies at each level. From the top of the internal spiral staircase is a 360-degree panoramic view of London, and the sinuous meanderings of the Thames and the Surrey Hills appear more spectacular than anything that can be glimpsed one-sidedly from the port-holes of a plane coming in to Heathrow Airport. They seem hardly higher.

BELOW AND RIGHT An arboretum is defined as a place for 'exhibiting trees for scientific interest and educational value'. At Kew this an overarching theme throughout the grounds. Rides run through them, glades appear and about two-thirds of the area – towards 81 hectares (200 acres) – is planted with trees.

OVERLEAF The iconic Pagoda towers above mature cedars and dwarfs visitors. This is the most enduring monument to the eighteenth-century taste for chinoiserie.

As it was being built there were doubts over whether the Pagoda could possibly stand for long but, unlike the lathe and plaster construction of some of the other garden follies, the Pagoda's brickwork has survived not only the natural elements for towards 250 years but also the blast from a strike of German bombs that fell nearby early in the Second World War.

It will be recalled that originally the Pagoda was flanked by two more of William Chambers's essays in exoticism, the Mosque and the Alhambra. They failed to survive but, perhaps to emphasise the orientalism of this corner of the gardens, the site of the Mosque was chosen in 1911 as the setting for an unlikely gift, the Japanese Gateway of the Imperial Messenger (Chokushi-Mon). This is a replica, four-fifths the original's size, of the Karamon of Nishi Honganji in Kyoto, brought to London for the 1910 Japano-British Exhibition and rebuilt here. For years the Chokushi-Mon stood inconsequentially in its foreign woodland, a bit of Japanese faux-sixteenth-century rococo at sea in its Surrey setting, like a geisha in Godalming. But a restoration in the 1990s, when it was re-roofed with authentic copper tiles, also put it into a traditional Japanese garden setting with symbolic rocks, water, stone troughs, lanterns and suitable indigenous plants. Japanese gardens are not unusual in North American botanic gardens – indeed they have become something of a cliché there – but in Britain the genre is less often seen for there is always a certain cultural incongruity. Kew's long heritage of the exotic and the comforting

William Chambers's Pagoda, 163 feet in height, appears suddenly and surprisingly from so many points at Kew. At close quarters it is equally impressive and the 360-degree view from the top seems to encompass most of London and half of Surrey.

OVERLEAF Almost a quarter of Kew. Looking north from the Pagoda the Cedar Avenue is to the left and the Palm House Vista on the right. The Temperate House and Evolution House lie amongst the Arboretum collections.

loom of the Pagoda seem to help ease this. A haiku by Kyoshi Takahama, carved onto a block of granite, translates as:

Even sparrows
Freed from all fear of Man
England in Spring

The Pagoda, it will be recalled, was built at the far, southern end of the royal *ferme ornée*, a focal point and culmination, with the Mosque and Alhambra, of the royal circuit walk. Looking back towards the White House, across fields with cattle and sheep or sown with corn, the scene was typical of the agrarian southern England of great estates and its labouring population as idealised by Goldsmith and Gray, Constable and Varley. Those eighteenth-century buildings that remain today – the Ruined Arch by Kew Road and the Temples of Bellona and Aeolus – are now ahead but less as considered elements in a progression of carefully contrived scenes. Today they stand as vestiges of the past lost in another world, the world of plant collections assembled for scientific study.

The view northward hints at the daunting complexity of trying to demonstrate the riches of this planet's plants in a cool temperate country. Labelled trees and shrubs are all around. The lantern roofs of the Temperate House, the smooth curves of the Palm House, and the tip of the Campanile can all be seen. This is Kew as 'Ark', a central theme of botanic gardens today and of this book.

But the perambulation continues and we are a long way from where we began. Fortunately, the nearest building just off the Pagoda Vista is the Pavilion Restaurant, a splendid summer stop though winter walkers should be warned that it might not be open. The Pavilion, a Ministry of Works-designed essay of 1920, is described by Nikolaus Pevsner with his Bauhaus sensibility as 'a nice, straightforward piece of building'. Kew's historian, Ray Desmond, suggests 'stark,

LEFT Two aspects of the 'Georgeous East' at Kew. The Pagoda and the Chokushi-Mon presiding over its traditional Japanese garden of raked sand, rocks and carefully coifed plantings.

RIGHT Even sparrows
Freed from all fear of Man
England in Spring.

ABOVE The Pavilion, Kew's original café, dates from 1920 and is still in vital operation, selling refreshments to be enjoyed under the spreading vines. No opportunity or space is overlooked for holding a suitable botanical collection.

functional . . . with no architectural pretensions whatsoever'. It replaced Kew's first refreshment café, a Bagshot Sands bungalow opened in 1888, which was burnt down by a party of angry ladies in support of women's suffrage in 1913. The food picks up Pevsner's adjectives and can be taken inside or out – although al fresco salads can be accidentally garnished with falling fruit from the collection of *Vitis* species and their relatives grown on the surrounding pergolas. Kingfisher-blue berries of *Ampelopsis brevipedunculata* are spectacular but only marginally edible.

If exhaustion has set in or time run out it could make sense to walk back a couple of hundred yards to Lion Gate, at the Gardens' southern corner, and pick up a bus travelling via Kew Road to the Green. From upstairs is the view right along and over the high eastern boundary wall that pedestrians are only briefly afforded. Inside the wall, however, just beyond the Pavilion, is a trio of Kew's strangest buildings which should not be missed.

The route leads under the Ruined Arch, with its tumbled stones and carefully contrived classical remnants which provided both an eye catcher in Princess Augusta's landscape and a cattle track over the top from Kew Road into her fields. The incongruity therefore of the adjacent Temperate House Lodge and its neighbour the Marianne North Gallery from the eighteenth-century Arch is extraordinary; a leap both in time and culture.

The Lodge was intended to guard a new grand public entrance to the Gardens, close to an expected new railway station that would bring in the populace of London. Great gates were erected but never formally used because the route of the railway was changed and the station built elsewhere. But the Lodge, designed by

William Eden Nesfield, stands as an early example of 'Queen Anne Revival', the style Norman Shaw made so fashionable in Bedford Park thirty years later. Pevsner, as always, is invaluable, 'a tiny and very circumstantial lodge . . . all roof and chimney . . .'. Virtually next door is the Marianne North Gallery, built to display over 800 paintings of plants that the indefatigable Miss North made travelling the world in the 1870s. On her return Kew was offered not only the paintings but a gallery in which to house them. Although, apparently, she asked James Fergusson, her chosen architect, for something with Indian overtones (and indeed the veranda offers a slight suggestion), in fact it is almost as classical as the Ruined Arch nearby.

BELOW Rome comes to Kew. All the bits of classical remains that grand tourists of the eighteenth century remembered from their visits in the Eternal City are combined by William Chambers in the Ruined Arch.

With is pedimented façade, dentils and all, and its clerestory windows lighting Miss North's lifework wonderfully, it more resembles a Florentine renaissance church – Santa Marianne dei Fiori, perhaps. It was opened in 1882. The paintings inside have had a bad press over the years; chocolate-boxy has been a kind description. Now we are far enough away in time not to need censoriousness – it may indeed be a box but one of unadulterated delights. The 832 oil paintings depict over 900 species of plants, and are hung in geographical groupings above samples of different timbers. Door frames, where the pictures cannot be hung, are embellished with climbers and scramblers on a gilt ground. Not an inch is wasted: clearly Miss North had fun and posterity is rewarded.

Ahead across the lawn looms the huge bulk of the Temperate House. Covering towards one and a half acres of ground – twice that of the much more elegant Palm House – it comprises a central block with two wings linked by octagons. Pairs of sentinel *Trachycarpus fortunei*,

The Marianne North Gallery holds the life-work of that intrepid Victorian artist and traveller who presented Kew with both the pictures and the building to exhibit them. Hundreds of plants from all over the world are shown in their native habitats. With the new adjoining Shirley Sherwood Gallery this part of Kew is now an international centre for botanical art.

The work of Marianne North – tree ferns and cycads, water lilies, scarlet-seeded *Macrozamia spiralis* and the trumpets of *Brugmansia*.

the only palm reliably hardy in Britain, flank its monumental doors. Although it can boast being one of the biggest glasshouses in the world – 60 feet high and 550 feet from end to end – the Temperate House is very much a Victorian conservatory kit writ large and typically embellished with urns, fretwork grills at ridge and eaves and heavy appliqué swags all around. Designed by Decimus Burton, its construction was bedevilled by Treasury parsimony trickling funds over time; begun in 1861, the whole was not finally completely until thirty-eight years later.

Its concern, as the name makes clear, is to grow plants that are not quite hardy enough for unprotected outdoor cultivation in south-east England. This is a vast component of the world's flora and includes species from Australia and the North Island of New Zealand, Mexico, and warm-temperate Asia and South America.

Particular collections include, in the north wing, tender *Vireya* rhododendrons from the mountains of

The central block and octagons of the Temperate House framed by Atlantic cedars. With its two wings, just hinted at in this view, it is one of the biggest glasshouses in the world covering over half a hectare (1.5 acres) of ground.

Java and the Philippines while the south octagon is devoted to one of the most remarkable floristic regions of all, the Fynbos of Southern Africa. There, in an area only half the size of the United Kingdom, grow some 9,000 species of plants, 70 per cent of them entirely endemic to the region. It is something of a triumph, even at Kew, to get proteas to flower and silver trees (*Leucadendron*) to flourish in the low winter light conditions of England's high latitude.

Almost every plant here tells a story; with economic crops from tea to quinine as well as botanical curiosities on display. Such is the pressure of space, even here, that each has to justify itself fully. Some are indivisible parts of Kew. The Australian genus *Banksia* – the name coined by Linnaeus himself – celebrates Sir Joseph Banks, without whom Kew would not exist as a national institution. *Strelitzia reginae*, a name that makes clear not only who (Charlotte of Mecklenburg-Strelitz) but also what (Queen), commemorates the consort of George III who spent so much of her life here. This is the bird of paradise flower, grown at Kew since its first introduction in 1773 from South Africa.

Even more singular, literally so, is *Encephalartos woodii*, one of the evolutionarily primitive palm-like cycads. This specimen was presented to Kew in 1899 by the Natal Botanic Garden and has been cherished ever since. It appears to be extinct in the wild and thus is reasonably claimed to be the rarest plant at Kew. Reintroduction to its native habitat, as has been done with other endangered species, is impossible. As a lone male (cycads are dioecious with separate male and female plants) seed production cannot occur; it is like an old rogue elephant that has lost its herd. It has, however, been successfully propagated from cuttings, and around 500 'clones' now grow in botanic gardens around the world.

When the Temperate House is floodlit at night for special occasions, urns on the parapet appear in silhouette against the shimmering plant forms inside. Concerts and receptions are held here.

LEFT The diversity of species grown in the Temperate House is extraordinary. Here, the spear lily (*Doryanthes*) from New South Wales where it was first seen at Botany Bay (top left) a fruiting cycad; (top right); and a spectacular protea from South Africa (bottom left). The bird of paradise flower (bottom right) is pollinated by birds, pollen being picked up by their feet and transferred to the receptive surfaces as they search for nectar.

RIGHT Few glasshouses in the world are big enough to enable coconut palms to reach maturity and fruit successfully.

LEFT In 1952 this then highly unusual aluminium structure was erected as the Australian House. It is now called the Evolution House and demonstrates the development of plants since earliest times.

RIGHT This little building, designed as the Temple of Military Fame by Sir Jeffry Wyatville, was being finished as William IV died and was therefore renamed in his honour. Its classical façade now appropriately overlooks a collection of plants such as these olive trees from the classical world of the Mediterranean littoral.

In the centre block evergreen trees tower to the roof, often draped with scramblers and twiners as they would be in the wild. Climbing the forty-five steps of the spiral staircase takes in the canopy. Suddenly all is light and sky. Inside are the vast fronds of *Jubaea chilensis*, the Chilean wine palm and rat-tail branches of Norfolk Island pine; outside the tops of mature hardy trees and Kew's landmarks – the Pagoda to the south, the Palm House and the Campanile to the north. It is a splendid orientation spot.

A further conservatory just outside the Temperate House's west porch contains one of Kew's most consciously didactic displays. The Evolution House, as the name suggests, is less a plant collection than a simulated walk through time to demonstrate the evolution of life on Earth. Three major geological eras are emphasised, the Silurian, the Carboniferous, and the Cretaceous. Primeval mud bubbles, mists swirl and water rushes; it is all splendidly evocative. Relic plant forms still existing – club mosses, horsetails, ferns and cycads – grow with fossils of their long-lost relatives. The timescale of course is immense; 600 million years have elapsed since the first true plants appeared in the primal seas and it is perhaps rash to relate this to our own transitoriness. But with

global warming and associated climate change being of such importance it is interesting to note that this glasshouse was erected in 1952 as the Australian House, especially to showcase Australian plants. Many of those plants are now flourishing outside in a fashion that would have been considered impossible fifty years ago. The protected bays between the Temperate House buttresses have traditionally held tender plants but now Banksias and other Southern hemisphere shrubs and tree ferns succeed (though the latter are still wrapped up for the winter). Outside the south door several palms and even *Jubaea* are being tried. The Eucalyptus Grove over by the White Peaks Restaurant has already been mentioned and Londoners are becoming positively blasé about the showers of yellow mimosa (*Acacia dealbata* is also from Australia and Tasmania) in their February parks almost as fine as along the Promenade des Anglais in Cannes. Changes such as these provide visual proof of the effects of global warming on our climate.

Taking the eye on leaving the north door of the Temperate House is King William's Temple sitting stolidly on its mound above the Mediterranean Garden. With narrowed eyes it is just possible, through the olives and *Chamaerops* palms planted around, to evoke the

The garden buildings Sir William Chambers designed for Princess Augusta also celebrate the classical world: the domed and Doric-pillared Temple of Aeolus (above) is suitably open to all the winds that blow; the Temple of Bellona (right) also uses the simple Doric mode; while the Temple of Arethusa (left) moves on to the curling Ionic volutes on its pillars and pilasters.

Doric Hephaisteion in the Agora of Athens. This version was designed by Sir Jeffry Wyatville and built in 1837, the year of William IV's death. Ahead can be found three of Sir William Chambers's charming little Graeco-Roman follies. The circular Temple of Aeolus still elegantly adorns its mound across the Palm House Pond, though not in its original position; the domed and porticoed Temple of Bellona overlooks a suitably sylvan glade (where in a frost-free March the Himalayan tree magnolias are spectacular). Also displaced is the Temple of Arethusa which Wilfred Blunt cursorily dismisses as an 'Athenian bus stop shelter'. Between these two is Victoria Gate (the nearest to the Tube) and the Plaza with its extensive garden shop and café.

And then to Kew's great set piece: the Palm House. It is as difficult to describe with any originality, 'one of the boldest pieces of nineteenth-century functionalism in existence', as it is to find the right spot from which to first admire it. Ideally one should be blindfolded (or walk backwards as when leaving royalty) and only turn from the steps of Museum No. 1 and see it *at a gasp*. The temptation to look earlier will be like Orpheus stealing a glimpse of Eurydice but in this case the object of veneration will certainly not disappear. For there across the lake, seen through the rainbow curtain of spray from its central fountain, is this ultimate iconic building. Commentators have run the gamut of clichés; metaphors and similes tumble over each other. It is like a 'stupendous swan poised on the surface of the water'; with its reflection it becomes a 'dirigible', an 'insubstantial bubble'; it is like a 'vast grounded whale', 'an upturned Titanic' . . . and so on. In fact, with its serried white curved ribs and glistening glass the marine images do help both in description and in reference to its means of construction.

ABOVE The Campanile, over 100 feet high, though disguised as a monumental Italian bell-tower, had two important utilitarian roles. It doubled not entirely effectively as a chimney for smoke from the Palm House's furnaces and a reservoir to give a head of water to spray its tallest trees.

LEFT As an eye-catcher, seen through the trees at daffodil time, the Campanile is almost as valuable as the more generally admired Pagoda.

Begun in 1844 and taking four years to complete it was long credited entirely to Decimus Burton but is now ascribed jointly to Burton and Richard Turner, a noted iron-master from Dublin. Turner had already designed and built an elegant (and recently restored) curvilinear glasshouse range in 1843 at Glasnevin, Ireland's National Botanic Garden. It is this mode, certainly not the Italianate of Kew's 1846 Main Gates and Campanile, nor the Triple Screen at Hyde Park Corner, that is Burton's more typical signature and which marks the mastery of the Palm House. Measuring 362 feet long, 100 feet wide and 63 feet high, it stands proudly above its terrace guarded by the row of heraldic Queen's Beasts which carry in their claws the coats of arms of a thousand years of British sovereigns. This is nothing less than an epitome of tropical rainforest with its trees, shrubs, lianas, epiphytes and forest floor plants – an

The Palm House in winter guarded by the Queen's Beasts carrying the arms of the Sovereign (left). It faces Kew's first Museum also designed by Decimus Burton and built in 1856 (below right). The splendid bronze fountain (top right) shows Hercules wrestling with a giant snake – just one of his labours – and has twenty jets. It originally stood on the East Terrace at Windsor Castle and came to Kew in 1963.

OVERLEAF The pride of Kew and epitome of glasshouses across the botanic garden world. Designed by Decimus Burton and William Turner, The Palm House was completed in 1848. To the right is the Waterlily House.

entire ecosystem under glass. Brought together from around the equatorial world are palms such as coconut and oil palm and other tropical economic staples including rubber, pepper (a climber) and sugar cane (a grass). Exploitation of such species in their native habitats and their subsequent monoculture in other parts of the world has irrevocably changed the history and the economy of many tropical countries – a story with which Kew has been intimately involved over the last two centuries.

As with the Temperate House, spiral stairs lead to a gallery. Here is the forest canopy, where giant bamboo reaches the roof only too quickly and has to be continually cut back while over-vigorous palms must be entirely replaced as removal of their growing point spells death to the whole plant. Views along the wings emphasise the delicacy of the ironwork, the restrained decorative scrolls and Richard Turner's sunflower motifs. The gallery is the ideal place not only to see the concentration of other gardens and glasshouses ahead and still to be visited but also to understand the difficulties which were experienced in creating a coherent design for the landscape as a whole in the nineteenth century. It is perhaps still not fully resolved.

When 'Capability' Brown was landscaping in the 1760s he had freedom to develop the land as he saw fit – both he and King George agreed the desired outcome was a English idyll. In the 1840s the situation was very different. Kew Gardens were now under the aegis of a government department; and politicians, civil servants, the public and the horticultural media (surprisingly vocal) all had their conflicting views of what a national botanic garden should be. So did the Director, Sir William Hooker, who was determined to develop a scientific botanic garden and not merely preside over a pretty park. Once it had been agreed that a palm house should be built questions arose as to its position.

Elegant anthemions and stylised sunflowers cast in iron embellish the Palm House spiral staircases while palms and giant bamboos reach to the sky unaided.

ABOVE From the west porch of the Palm House radiating vistas stretch out beyond the Rose Garden enclosed by its semicircular holly hedge. Clipped hollies flank the walk and lines of lavender lead the eye into the distance.

OPPOSITE The vast boiler house that once heated great the Palm House above is now home to the Marine Display. Concerned particularly with importance of algae to the world's ecology, it is enlivened by an array of undersea life.

Decimus Burton insisted it should stand by the remnant of Princess Augusta's lake; John Smith, the Curator, said the subterranean boiler houses would flood. Burton prevailed and Smith was right.

The apparently inconsequential position of the Palm House, which seems so obvious from a birds-eye view of the gardens, is fortunately disguised by the scale of the building and the great terrace promenade on which it stands. The north–south orientation chosen responds both to the lake and to the importance of equal illumination along its sides.

Once the site had been chosen it was imperative to integrate the dramatic building into the landscape. This coincided with new plans for the organisation of the woody plant collection. W.A. Nesfield (the more famous father of the Temperate House Lodge architect) was brought in to design the new arboretum, with the Director's close involvement, and then, with Burton and Turner, the setting of the Palm House. In essence Nesfield's grand concept survives: the parterre of geometrical beds ablaze with seasonal bedding above the embellished

Palm House Pond and, on the opposite, west side, the Rose Garden within its embracing semi-circular hedge. Gaps permit a classic Versailles-like *patte d'oie*, three formal vistas stretching into the distance. They are closed respectively by the Pagoda, Syon House across the river and originally by a great cedar of Lebanon to the north, the whole demonstrating graphically the pendulum-swing of garden taste and fashion from the Georgians' eighteenth-century informality. It adds another stratum to Kew's evolutionary progress.

A further layer lies below. The boiler rooms under the Palm House floor that caused so much anguish in the early years (having been replaced by modern heating systems located in the shaft yard by the Campanile) are now home to collections of plant forms that would have been inconceivable to the Victorians. The Marine Display aims to show the vital ecological importance of algae – plants that in their simplest unicellular forms initiated life on this planet and continue, through the huge diversity of seaweeds, to make it possible. The display contains four recreations of important marine habitats; coral reefs and mangrove swamps from the tropics contrast with native salt marches and rocky shores. Interpretive panels tell the story but are apt to lose out against the unfair fascination of the fish.

While the Palm House was built especially for a specific group of plants, albeit a huge one (there are some 2,000 species of palms), just outside the north door is a building put up to grow just one. *Victoria amazonica* (*Victoria regia* as was) resonates with nineteenth-century horticultural chuzpah, a must-grow for the rich. A giant water lily with leaves up to 6 feet across from equatorial Brazil, appropriately introduced around the time of Queen Victoria's accession to the throne, it was the ultimate test. Joseph Paxton succeeded in flowering it first for the Duke of

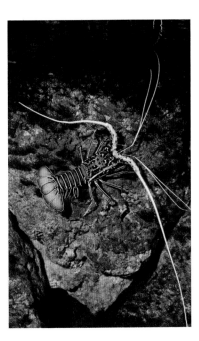

Devonshire at Chatsworth. It needed space, several feet of water and a growing temperature of 85–90° Fahrenheit. Not surprisingly, it is usual today to compromise with a little less of everything by substituting its only close cousin, the less taxing *V. cruziana*.

William Turner was brought back in 1852 to supply the ironwork for what was then the widest glasshouse span in the world. Although the Waterlily House changed its role for some years to growing tropical economic plants, it is now once more holding Queen Victoria's giant water lily, surrounded by lush exotics and draped with loofahs and other gourds. *Victoria* itself is grown as

ABOVE *Victoria cruziana*, a slightly smaller and less exacting plant than its cousin. Flowers are something of a two-day wonder gradually changing from white to pink.

RIGHT Like vast tin trays, their ribbed undersides formidably armed, leaves of *Victoria amazonica* float in the Waterlily House which was built especially for it. Above hang baskets of *Nepenthe* in whose hanging pitchers drowned insects decompose for natural nutrition.

an annual, cosseted and as grossly fed as any Strasbourg goose to bring on the vast leaves (the underside ribs of which inspired Paxton in his Crystal Palace designs) and, by the end of summer, the slightly anticlimatic flowers. A display of harvested gourds and pumpkins often takes over in the autumn.

Kew's increasing intention in the late-nineteenth and early-twentieth centuries, as a national botanic garden not only for Britain but also for a great network of colonies and dependencies, was to display the riches of all floristic regions of the world. Gradually a conglomeration of buildings were developed for this, close to where Sir William Chambers had built the Great Stove for Princess Augusta. Fern houses, cactus and succulent houses, orchid houses, houses for decorative conservatory plants and so on, each addition being a pragmatic answer to the need for this collection or that. But in the 1970s a decision was made to sweep away what had by then become a couple of dozen interlinked glasshouses. They were to be replaced, not by an iconic structure in the grand imperial mode but with a concentrated space in which plants from a range of worldwide climatic zones could be grown and which, by necessity, would need to be covered and heated. Economy, effectiveness and environmental sensitivity were key concepts of the design.

South of the Princess of Wales Conservatory the few cacti and subtropical succulents that can accept a London winter give an indication of the extraordinary diversity of water-conserving life-forms within. Great fleshy agaves, lancet-sharp tipped, contrast with the giant pincushions of *Cereus* redolent of Mexican deserts.

OVERLEAF A panorama that shows, from recently-built Davies Alpine House to Princess of Wales Conservatory, from curvilinear Palm House to biscuit-box Temperate House, how problems have been differently addressed over 150 years.

ABOVE AND RIGHT Only a glass screen and a pair of swing doors separates desert from rainforest, organ-pipe-like cacti from tree-ferns and the sconces of staghorn ferns (*Platycerium*).

The hugely effective result – the Princess of Wales Conservatory – won a Europa Nostra Award for Conservation in 1989. It combines state-of-the-art computerised technology for heating, ventilation and watering with horticultural expertise to enable the flora of dry and wet tropic regions – the aridity of deserts to the sauna-like steaminess of equatorial rainforests – to be grown under one roof. Glass screens separate the zones. Without the need to house tall trees no great height was needed and structural supports clad in bark and moss become additional habitats for orchids, bromeliads and other epiphytic genera. From the outside virtually no walls are visible (as most of the growing space is below ground level) and the serried roof lights give the impression of a delicately balanced house of cards, covering an area greater than that of the Temperate House. The conservatory's name suitably commemorates that eighteenth-century Princess of Wales, whose original botanic garden on this site began the whole extraordinary story of Kew.

Conventional conservatories have always emphasised the divide between the chilly outdoors and the embracing warmth as the doors open, the everyday giving on to the exotic; it is one of their pleasures. But the Princess of Wales Conservatory is at pains to show plants' habitats as a continuum. At the southern entrance, which leads into the Dry Tropics Zone,

xerophytic plants, including cacti that are hardy are a part of the outdoor landscaping. Others needing just a little help are sheltered by the wide, open porch before doors give entry to the first of the fully protected plantings, behind which a painted diorama, re-interpreted from the old cactus house, takes the eye into a distant desert. Having walked through half the world a similar semi-protected area at the north end leads into the open air, and on to the last three great historic buildings.

Across the lawn, framed in fine trees, is yet another fine classical building – Sir William Chambers's splendid Orangery of 1761, measuring nearly 100 feet long. Unfortunately, architecture took precedence over the needs of its intended contents and with its solid roof light levels were not sufficient for good plant

growth, even though the citrus trees in tubs were stood outside for restorative summer holidays. In 1842 windows were inserted at both gable ends and royal coats of arms were added to celebrate the effort made, though without much success being achieved. After a century of use as a wood museum a final attempt was made; but even with artificial illumination and the determination of ebullient Director Sir George Taylor the situation was not much better. The Orangery is now an admirable restaurant, appreciated by people as it never was by plants.

Close by, towards the main gates, is another superannuated essay in classicism. The Architectural Conservatory, as it was initially called, was originally built by John Nash at Buckingham Palace but in 1836, on the orders of William IV, it was taken down and re-erected

here at Kew. It served successfully as a home for tropical aroids for over a century and was used as a temporary home for plants during the 1980s Palm House restoration. The temperatures required to sustain the plants had, by this time, damaged the fabric of the building, necessitating its complete renovation. The Nash Conservatory is now used for special events and receptions.

Finally, standing modestly back behind the Orangery, is a building from whose windows the whole saga of Kew could have been seen to unfold and within whose walls significant strands of British history were woven. The other royal palaces of Kew and Richmond have come and gone while what was just known as the Dutch House, predating them all and built by a commoner, has survived to carry the title Kew Palace. It was in this unpretentious seventeenth-century merchant's house that King George spent years of his intermittent illness, here that George IV was born, and here that Queen Charlotte died. Cut into the brick over the

LEFT A sea of *Chionodoxa*, glory of the snow, washes up to the walls of Sir William Chambers's classical Orangery. Princess Augusta's little Botanic Garden began just to the right (east) of this scene. The Orangery is a much better as a restaurant than it ever was as a plant house. This strangely Parisian scene could almost be the Jardin des Tuileries, more Marie Antoinette than Queen Charlotte.

ABOVE With a glazed roof and bigger windows this essay in temple-conservatory mode by the Main Gate was more successful, and for a century it was home to Kew's collection of tropical aroids. But high temperatures and near 100-degree humidity are conditions unconducive to the wellbeing of historic buildings and the Nash Conservatory is now used for special events.

BELOW AND RIGHT The Queen's Garden is a charming recreation of a small formal seventeenth-century garden established in the 1960s to frame the river front of Kew Palace. Five terms (classical heads or busts surmounting pillars) are set into the enclosing yew-apse – they had been carved for Prince Frederick in 1735 and first set up at Carlton House.

front door are the initials S.C.F, standing for the owners Samuel and Catherine Fortrey, and the date of its construction, 1631. Standing three stories high (plus an attic and a basement), it has just two rooms either side of a cross passage on each floor. Jolly Dutch gables and towering chimney stacks surmount the whole which has now been returned to its apparently correct (but in truth a not very fetching) terracotta-coloured wash. At the back a little pillared loggia overlooks the Queen's Garden, a charming 1960s pastiche in seventeenth-century style. Following extensive renovation, Kew Palace was reopened to the public in April 2006, shortly after the Prince of Wales hosted a family dinner in the palace to celebrate the eightieth birthday of Her Majesty

The Queen. In October 2007 Kew Palace won the annual RICS (Royal Institute of Chartered Surveyors) Building Conservation Award.

The Brentford Gate and the car park is now conveniently to hand; the perambulation, an anti-clockwise circuit, has been achieved and three centuries of Kew have been glimpsed, flashes of light glancing off this building or that, each with its story to tell. Love Lane, the old public road that once separated the two royal gardens has been crossed twice; it has been possible to wander through vestiges of countryside and farmland into sophisticated landscape and fashion-conscious gardens. The passion for plants has resulted in over two hundred years of glasshouse building, each one redolent of the abilities and ideals of its age. Throughout Kew's long history this passion has been expressed through many different strands: the aesthetic – the love of beautiful things; the acquisitive – collecting for its own sake; the investigative – the sciences that make up botany; the economic – the spreading of crop plants around the globe; the exploitative – plants as a factor in colonial expansion; and, of course, the explorative – the search for plants that opened up so much of the world. Today it is expressed through the firm focus upon the greatest needs of plants and people, as voiced by Kew's new mission statement: 'to inspire and deliver science-based plant conservation worldwide, enhancing the quality of life'.

4

A GREEN EL DORADO
Collecting for Kew

I N 1764 a significant meeting took place when the twenty-one-year-old Joseph Banks made the acquaintance of William Aiton, then in charge of Princess Augusta's physic garden. It was his first visit to the collections at Kew. Banks was a vastly rich young man; on his father's death his country estates brought him an annual income of some £6,000, with which he funded a lifetime of botanical exploration. As a boy he had lived for a time in Swan Walk overlooking the Chelsea Physic Garden, where Philip Miller is said to have encouraged his interests. Formal education at Harrow and Eton, then at Oxford, failed to provide much in the way of natural history so he arranged for a personal tutor and after leaving university – without a degree – became determined to travel. From his first voyage, as a supernumerary in a naval frigate sailing to Newfoundland, he returned with a miscellaneous collection of plants, birds, insects, rocks and even an Indian scalp – his initial cabinet of curiosities. Banks became a member of the highest scientific circles after being elected a Fellow of the Royal Society in 1766 (he went on to become President from 1778 till his death). What followed is well known, a classic story from the age of empire.

The British Government, prompted by the Royal Society, planned a voyage to the South Seas to observe a major astronomical event. Effective readings and records of the planet Venus, passing in front of the sun, would facilitate mariners' navigational skills and hence support exploration of the seas. HMS *Endeavour* was commissioned, Lieutenant James Cook was appointed Captain and the ship set off from Plymouth in August 1768 bound for Tahiti; it was from here that the best sightings were predicted a year hence. But there were subtexts that almost overwhelm the original *raison d'être*. Cook was given secret instructions to search

The Azalea Garden with its blaze of late spring colour in May.

119

out the *Terra Australis Incognita* that had haunted European voyagers and cartographers for centuries. Vague reports of a vast unknown land in the Southern Ocean were even supported by a theory that such a land mass was necessary to balance the northern continents and so keep the earth on its axis. The planned circumnavigation of the globe was also a unique opportunity for the broadest scientific investigation, and the Royal Society's proposal that there be a further role for the 'advancement of useful knowledge' was accepted. Banks was their man and he was provided with space aboard for himself, a staff of eight and two greyhounds. All the essential equipment for collecting, recording and preserving specimens, elegant microscopes and other scientific instruments, combined to make a floating laboratory. 'No people,' a correspondent reported to Linnaeus, 'ever went to sea better fitted out for the purpose of Natural History, nor more elegantly.' All was assembled at Joseph Banks's personal expense.

Throughout the voyage sea-life was trawled, birds were shot and the skins preserved, plants were collected and sketches made wherever the ship made landfall, and careful descriptions of every place and its peoples were written. Every objective of the expedition was accomplished: astronomical sightings were successful, parts of what are now New Zealand and Australia (where Botany Bay was discovered and named) were discovered, and 'useful knowledge' had undeniably been advanced.

On its return to England, a month short of three years after setting out, HMS *Endeavour* carried an extraordinary harvest of scientific treasures. There were some 3,600 dried plant specimens – nearly half of which were new to science, pickled animals and seeds preserved in wax. Some even retained their viability and a bush of New Zealand's national flower, the kowhai (*Sophora tetraptera*) propagated from that original collection still grows at the Chelsea Physic Garden. Not only were there quantities of on-the-spot drawings (for in a pre-photographic age an ability to at least sketch was considered vital for every traveller and certainly any with pretensions to art or to science) but also 269 exquisite finished plant portraits, as well as preparatory works of almost 700 other species.

These were mainly by Sidney Parkinson, a highly talented botanical artist who died (as did four more of Banks's party) during the voyage. Thirty-three members of Cook's crew also lost their lives.

Back in London, Banks was feted by society and presented at court to the King. Meanwhile, Captain Cook, somewhat overshadowed by Banks's glamour, was within months involved in planning the next South Sea voyage, this time with two ships, HMS *Resolution* and HMS *Adventure*. Banks, to his chagrin, was not accommodated and instead travelled to Iceland, on his return donating lumps of lava collected on Mount Hecla to Chelsea and Kew. More significantly, he continued to employ members of his *Endeavour* team to work on the collections. Daniel Solander, Linnaeus's star pupil, was librarian and curator at Banks's Soho Square house, which became England's centre for wide-ranging botanical studies for the next thirty years.

Banks is often described as the first Director of Kew and as having an appointment as Scientific Advisor to the King; he himself once said he had 'a kind of superintendence over the Royal Botanic Gardens'. In fact, his role was an extension of that which Lord Bute had held with Princess Augusta. But while Bute's botanical activities during his public years were something of a refuge from politics, just as the Princess's were an escape from London court life, Banks's involvement went far deeper, as did the King's. In Joseph Banks the King had a botanical adviser whom he could relate to and trust utterly. Banks was an aristocrat of independent means; he had braved discomfort and real danger in pursuit of his goals (as he noted in his *Endeavour* journal, 'the almost certainty of being Eat as you come ashore, adds not a little to terrors of ship-wreck'); and he was at the centre of the world of investigative science, with an international correspondence. He could thus converse and discuss with his Majesty on a level of friendship far deeper than even a

Sir Joseph Banks, now the doyen of the world of natural sciences, President of the Royal Society and Scientific Advisor to King George III.

Painted by Tho.s Phillips R.A.   Engraved by N. Schiavonetti

To the KING'S most excellent MAJESTY

This Print of SIR JOSEPH BANKS, BAR.t President of the

ROYAL SOCIETY, &.c with His Gracious Permission Granted is Most humbly Dedicated by HIS MAJESTY'S

most devoted dutiful and devoted Servants Thomas Phillips & Nicholas Schiavonetti

grander eighteenth-century commoner ever could. More to the point their motives also coincided. Banks believed passionately that a great botanic garden under royal patronage, demonstrating as it would the power of Britain through its worldwide involvement, should be a prime jewel in the expanding Empire's crown. The King, as a monarch of the Enlightenment, accepted this, 'striving', it has been said, 'for the good of his people as he understood it, capable of rational purposes and noble ideas'. In the fifty years that followed, the political, economic and indeed geographical map of the world was redrawn. While Britain's American Colonies were lost, India, bits of the Far East and the Antipodes were gained, and the French Revolution and the subsequent Napoleonic Wars rocked Europe. Throughout this half-century, Joseph Banks laboured to make the King's botanic garden the envy of all.

There is a temptation, in considering Kew's involvement in the extension of an expanding Empire, to see it from an entirely Anglocentric point of view, as if it were a particularly English invention. In fact, continental influences and precedents are many. It was a time when the European powers with overseas possessions (which they had fought over, each edging out another as supremacy changed) scoured them for trophies to display at home. Interestingly, Spain and Portugal (the earliest colonialists of the sixteenth-century age of discovery) seemed concerned only with the conventional treasures of conquest: gold, silver and precious stones. Plants, central to any real El Dorado, were barely considered. Though Cortes noted the amazing gardens and systematically laid out plant collections at Montezuma's capital, they were not part of the booty from his conquest of Mexico.

The next wave of exploration was by the northern Europeans, who had different traditions. Following their strong horticultural background, Dutch colonists did send plants back to their homeland, from South Africa and from the Dutch East Indies, where the Netherlands maintained a monopoly of the spice trade. The young Linnaeus, employed as the personal physician of one rich Anglo-Dutch merchant, George Clifford, produced a detailed catalogue of his plants assembled near Haarlem. The *Hortus Cliffortianus* of 1738 already indicates

Linnaeus's developing thoughts on classification and nomenclature, supported by an unrivalled collection of tropical plants grown in four great glasshouses. It was here, successfully fruiting the first banana in Europe, that Linnaeus noted, 'the native place lays the entire foundation for the cultivation of the plant', an ecological consideration that was vital in effectively growing exotic plants both under glass and out of doors.

In Paris, the early seventeenth-century Jardin du Roi became the Jardin Royal des Plantes, as interest in plant science increased and altered its emphasis. Plant collecting was vigorously pursued in the French colonies. Charles Plumier was sent to New France sending back *Rosa carolina* and bloodroot (*Sanguinaria canadensis*) amongst other introductions and on his return he published *Description des Plantes de l'Amerique* in 1693 'on the orders of the King'. The Jardin Royal had effective glasshouses from the 1730s and an arboretum from which a famous *Acer orientale*, dating from 1702, survives in today's egalitarian Jardin des Plantes.

It can be seen that Banks, having personally experienced the amazing diversity of plant life on his *Endeavour* circumnavigation, had a clear vision that the obvious way to enrich the royal garden's collection was to follow the example of Louis XIV and employ knowledgeable gardeners specifically to travel in order to study and collect the flora of chosen areas. Over the years Banks's method, in association with Aiton, was to look out for young gardeners showing intelligence and promise. They were then trained at Kew in the techniques of collecting seed, making dried specimens for herbarium sheets and recording details of the habitat of each species. All this, after being shipped to Soho Square, would be the source material for scientific study by Daniel Solander, who would name and classify the material. After Solander's death in 1782, Jonas Dryander continued the work. With increasing experience in the field, such collectors could easily identify new plants to genus level but were continually meeting species hitherto unknown.

As time went on, and especially during the King's periods of illness, Banks became positively vice-regal in his dealings with collectors. Instructions for collecting were precise, itineraries were to be rigorously adhered to and any deviations were peremptorily admonished. To those in the field such criticisms were often considered unjustified. But Banks believed in keeping people in their place; his words to William Kerr setting out for Canton in 1803 are typical. To a mere gardener, the position offered, he said, 'a prospect, in case you are diligent, attentive and frugal, of raising yourself to a better station in life than your former prospects permitted you to expect'. Nonetheless, it was all for the greater glory of His Majesty's Botanic Garden at Kew and Banks was determined it should outshine those other royal gardens in Paris and Vienna.

Francis Masson was the first of Kew's designated plant collectors. In 1772 he sailed with Cook's second expedition as far as the Cape of Good Hope, (South Africa had been a Dutch Colony from the 1650s; it was taken over by Britain in 1806). He returned after two years' travel with a mass of new plants from that prodigiously rich flora. Shrubby pelargoniums, ericas and proteas, succulents such as mesembryanthemums, crassulas and stapelias, gladioli and ixias: all were grist to his mill. Masson spent the rest of his life, thirty years, collecting in the Canary Islands and Madeira, South Africa again, the West Indies and finally in Canada, where he died. Others lost their lives while still young. David

Nelson, having been on Cook's third and final voyage, next joined the ill-fated attempt to transport breadfruit trees from Tahiti to the West Indies. At the famous mutiny Nelson was one of those cast adrift from the Bounty with Captain Bligh; the day after they reached Timor in the Dutch East Indies, after forty-one days in an open boat, he died. James Smith and George Austin were lost at sea in the wreck of HMS *Guardian en route* for Botany Bay. But still the search for botanical riches went on and their names earn certain immortality in their introductions: *Kerria, Hovea, Cunninghamia* and so on. As mentioned previously, Banks himself lives today in the genus of some fifty species of so-called Australian honeysuckles: *Banksia*, named by Linnaeus from *Endeavour* specimens.

With the increasing fame of Kew's collections and Joseph Banks's indefatigable correspondence with anyone who might be able to add to them, the botanic garden began to strain at the seams. A new glasshouse intended for Masson's South African introductions became filled with Australian species and although some woody plants from the botanic garden were moved out into the wider grounds, Kew as a whole continued to be a typical eighteenth-century designed landscape of trees and open farm and parkland.

HMS *Bounty* was rated an 'Armed Transport' ship (itself a formal designation in the age of sail – a vessel with three masts, square-rigged). She was especially adapted to transport living plants, in this case it was intended to take up to 1,000 breadfruit saplings from Tahiti to the West Indies where, it was hoped, *Artocarpus* would provide an important food.

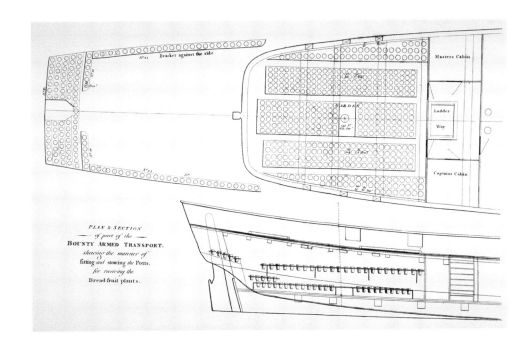

123

The King's great enthusiasm for agriculture and his belief in its centrality to the economy of the country are more generally known than his botanical interests. His nickname 'Farmer George' was indeed earned – he wrote papers, published under the name of his Windsor shepherd Ralph Robinson, for Arthur Young's *Annals of Agriculture*. At Kew, between the White House and the Pagoda, fields of corn and turnips grew and cows and merino sheep grazed the grass. These latter had been smuggled from Spain through Banks's connections in Portugal and some of this flock were eventually shipped to Australia, beginning that country's wool economy.

In 1819, a year before his death and that of King George, Sir Joseph Banks made what was probably his last visit to Kew to see the first cones produced by a specimen of *Encephalartos altensteinii*. Francis Masson had collected this cycad, one of a small group of primitive plants resembling diminutive palms, in South Africa. It arrived at Kew in 1775 and over 230 years later it is still there. This is the oldest 'pot plant' (it grows in a box in the Palm House) in Britain, but even more venerable specimens exist in Vienna and Uppsala. During the previous half-century in which Banks had overseen the botanical collections, Kew could fully appropriate the fulsome praise of Peter Collinson for excelling: 'all the gardens of Europe for its amazing variety of plants of all orders and classes and from all climates . . .' This quote was actually a comment on Chelsea Physic Garden but, as the records make clear, it is entirely applicable to Kew during Banks's time.

William Aiton, with much taxonomic help from Solander and Dryander at Soho Square, published a three-volume catalogue of the collections in 1789, maintaining Sir John Hill's earlier catalogue title (which continues today), *Hortus Kewensis*. By this time there were 5,600 species, printed with Linnaean binomials and

Almost as old as Kew Gardens itself, this venerable cycad, *Encephalartos altensteinii*, was collected by Francis Masson in South Africa and sent to Kew in 1775. It is still growing, adding leathery leaves year by year atop its saurian trunk, which is kept up by iron props.

125

an English name, each with a short Latin description much like pre-Linnaean polynomials. Country of origin, date of introduction and the collector's name combined to make the catalogue a scientific document rather than a mere list. It indicated the parts of the world where effective collecting had so far taken place: while more than half were plants from Europe (including Britain), 700 were from South Africa, with Madeira and the Canary Islands the next most popular, and with India, the Far East and the Antipodes represented by a mere few dozen species.

Thus the impetus continued. The efforts of Kew's increasing number of collectors poured in, together with gifts from colonial governors, plantation owners, the East India Company and other botanic gardens; so many specimens were received that another edition of *Hortus Kewensis* appeared between 1810–13. The author (with much assistance from others) was William Townsend Aiton, who had become the King's Head Gardener of the Botanic Garden (and soon after of Richmond Gardens across Love Lane, too) on his father's death in 1793. By this time there were significant numbers of Australian, South America and Chinese specimens among the total of 11,000 species.

This increase reflects not only the greater range of collecting but also the increasing expertise at maintaining living plants on long sea voyages. In these days of rapid air transport, plastic bags to reduce transpiration of living plant tissue and, it must be emphasised, after two further centuries of practice, it is easy to forget just how difficult it used to be to transport plants around the world. Not surprisingly the first specimens collected from any newly explored country are coastal species, which, in the lower

latitudes, are most likely to be very susceptible to cold. Their survival in primitive plant houses on the deck of a sailing ship for possibly months on end was extremely problematical. Maintenance was often neglected and indeed the time and effort spent was resented by the crew and even the Captain. One of the contributory factors to the HMS *Bounty* mutiny was anger at the amount of water lavished upon the young breadfruit trees. They were thrown overboard as Bligh and Nelson and the loyal crew members were set adrift. Archibald Menzies, the surgeon/naturalist on Captain Vancouver's HMS *Discovery*, complained vigorously about the ship's animals getting into the plant cabin and about polluted water killing his plants. He was put under arrest for his pains. Other voyages ended in complete disaster, the ship and many of the crew lost with the plants. Even after apparently successful expeditions, when the plant cabins were examined sometimes only 'dead stumps', as Menzies once recorded, were found.

The transportation of living plants over long distances did not improve significantly until the 1830s, when Wardian Cases – small closed greenhouse-like boxes with hinged glazed lids – were introduced. Nathaniel Ward's invention (which also become an article of furniture filled with ferns and begonias and suchlike in fashionable Victorian drawing rooms) was still in use a century later.

LEFT *Artocarpus altilis*: breadfruit is related to figs and mulberry, its fruit is eaten baked, boiled and fried and can be found now in most tropical vegetable markets.

RIGHT The invention in the 1830s by a London G.P., Nathanial Bagshaw Ward, revolutionised the transport of living plants across the seas. Wardian Cases like this were still in use at Kew over a century later.

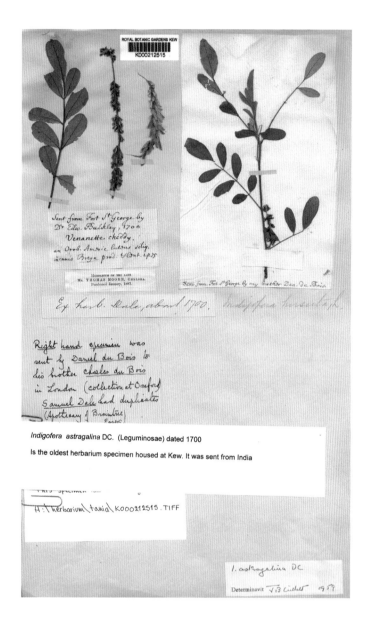

Indigofera astragalina DC. (Leguminosae) dated 1700

Is the oldest herbarium specimen housed at Kew. It was sent from India

An early sheet from Kew's Herbarium. The pressed specimen is accompanied by descriptions of its habitat, local uses, the name of its collector and date collected. Name-changes may be added subsequently as further research decrees.

diagnostic parts: stem, leaves, flowers and fruits – are dried, pressed and mounted on sheets of paper. Colour is lost, it becomes brittle with age and often looks singularly unattractive and utterly unlike the beautiful plant that it was but, as with extracting DNA from a long-dead mummy, it has the ability to provide much information that is necessary for subsequent scientific study. If the plant is new to science, the specimen is called the 'type specimen' to which, for all time, others can be compared. It is formally described, the description published and its whereabouts internationally known.

Those unfortunate collectors, therefore, whose plants suffered from the vagaries of transport, had at least this other proof of their labours: the dried and preserved materials. The *Endeavour* voyage, it will be recalled, brought few living plants back but, with some 3,600 dried specimens of which 1,400 were new to science, it was rightly considered hugely successful. The criteria for collecting were not based merely on beauty or curiosity (although both had their place). As Banks told Anton Hove prior to Hove's despatch to West Africa, he should not 'neglect those which are small and unsightly as it is just as likely that qualities useful to physic or manufacture and singularity of structure interesting to the botanist should be found in the minute and ugly'.

Good herbarium specimens were also the subject matter of subsequent pictorial representation. Sketches made in the field could be worked up into full plant portraits using the herbarium specimen as a reference. These finished portraits could then be engraved for publication. Banks was determined that Kew's collections should be made available in this way. Ironically, although he had Parkinson's wonderful work engraved on to copper plates such was the expense of printing that they languished unused in the Natural History Museum until the 1980s, when at last the *Banks'*

While Banks had been determined that Kew's living plant collections should excel those of other countries, his concern for the promulgation of botany and 'useful science' was equally strong – hence his maintenance of the Soho Square herbarium and library. It was staffed at his own expense yet made available to scholars both from home and abroad. A herbarium, the *hortus siccus*, is the resource centre and database for botanical studies of new and hitherto unknown species. Even when an expedition is successful in introducing quantities of living plants and these are successfully cultivated and propagated there is an inherent finiteness about their existence. To ensure scientific continuity typical specimens – ideally of all

Florilegium was published in a limited and hugely expensive edition.

Though many of Kew's plants had been painted during Lord Bute's years and a few drawn and published by Sir John Hill, Banks was rather miffed that the first botanically-described detailed illustrations appeared in a Parisian publication by Charles Louis L'Heritier. L'Heritier published his *Sertum Anglicum* (the full translated title is 'An English Wreath or Rare Plants that are cultivated in the gardens around London especially in the Royal Garden at Kew') in 1788. It is also significant that he had hired the young Pierre-Joseph Redouté to draw twenty-two of the thirty-five plants shown. A number of species of *Amaryllis* presage Redouté's famous *Les Liliacées*, which was painted later for the Empress Josephine at Malmaison.

Kew needed its own artist and Banks managed to catch a talented young Austrian artist Franz (Francis) Bauer. Although Bauer was considered 'Botanick Painter to His Majesty' and tutored the Queen and Princess Elizabeth from his house on Kew Green, Bauer's salary was actually paid by Banks, who also left him an annuity of £300 in his will so long as he remained to work at Kew. This he did until his death in 1840.

The late eighteenth and early nineteenth centuries can be seen as a golden age of botanical illustration. Accurate delineation of the minutest morphological details was combined with exquisite arrangement of form and colour; each painting became a perfect amalgam of art and science. It is interesting that in the twenty-first century, when photographic techniques of incredible complexity are capable of catching every apparent nuance, the traditional botanical artist is in no way superseded.

The unrivalled living plant collections, supported by an extensive herbarium and library became, in effect, a national botanic garden. But it went further than that, Banks's vision of 'Imperial Kew by Thames's glittering side' (in the words of Erasmus Darwin) at the centre of a worldwide network of colonial gardens became a fact within his lifetime. He was the ultimate gentleman amateur, spending his life and his fortune fulfilling an ideal in which he passionately believed. It combined a reverence for Kingship and the established order and for service to the crown and to country; such unalloyed patriotism seems hardly conceivable today. Yet it was not unthinking jingoism. In working for almost fifty years to develop the Royal Gardens at Kew 'into a great botanical exchange house for the empire' as he said, he never wavered in his disinterested enthusiasm for plants and for the 'useful knowledge' that their collection and study make manifest.

Over the centuries the motives that prompt the development of an empire vary. At the beginning is physical possession of a neighbour's land by conquest. It is fuelled by envy and by greed. Success encourages further conquest and throughout history, from Alexander (the Great – says it all) to Napoleon, charismatic leaders have come to power to place their own country above surrounding subject peoples, who are forced to pay taxes and tributes to their conquerors and 'protectors'. Eventually the aggressors see themselves as culturally and morally superior to their vassal states and seek to impose their values upon them.

The *Pax Romanum*, at the peak of imperial Roman power, encompassed almost all of Europe (including Britain to the Antonine Wall halfway up Scotland), much of Asia Minor and North Africa. It was, as Messrs Sellars and Yeatman in *1066 and All That* doubtless asserted, a 'Good Thing' – at least to the Romans. While subject states were expected to support themselves as well as the occupying armies and colonial bureaucracy, and although lines of communication to the ends of the Roman Empire were often stretched, they were at least continuous. They could be strengthened or even reduced if a distant province became, rather than an asset, a threat or a drain on the whole.

The later empires based upon voyages of discovery were in a very different situation. Their strength depended upon maritime power, a vigorous merchant fleet subsequently supported by a national navy. The effectiveness of colonial administrations was vital to colonial success – whether following complete conquest (as with the Spanish in South America, for example), the more mercantile system of the Dutch in the East Indies, or the complicated combination of conquest, trade and negotiated arrangements with indigenous rulers that the British evolved in India. Keeping people fed was essential for success – whether it was in the luxurious lifestyle of the plantation owners in the West Indies, or the provision of breadfruit as a cheap and easy food for slaves. This depended upon rapid development of relatively more intensive agriculture than that of the indigenous peoples.

In classical colonial times, while crops and climate might differ considerably from one end of empire to the other extremes were approached gradually and agricultural adaptations easily made. When, however, a cool-temperate, northern hemisphere power wishes to affect its tropical possessions the situation is very different. Though, as has been seen, extensive collections of exotic plants were made by enthusiasts such as the Duchess of Beaufort and Princess Augusta, seldom were they able to show their economic potential under glass – hence Linnaeus's pride at fruiting Clifford's banana and, even in the seventeenth century, some growers' success with pineapples. The increasing size of hot-houses was not only to house greater numbers of species but also to try and bring them to maturity.

Seeing a clear imperial role developing from His Majesty's Botanic Garden at Kew, Joseph Banks began to promote the idea of satellite gardens in the new colonies. They would build up their own collections of native plants of economic value, exchange plants with each other and propagate stocks of plants to be made available to settlers to support the young economy. Banks would have been aware of a particularly successful example that emerged from the Chelsea Physic Garden a few years before.

In 1733, an expedition of three ships, crewed mainly by debtors, had sailed from London to settle a section of the east coast of America. It was to be a sort of buffer state between the existing British colonies in the north and Spanish possessions in Florida. Its leader, General Oglethorpe, carried with him a plan of the ideal township they intended to set up. It would have wide streets, regular squares, and public buildings. Extraordinarily, the plan was followed and the town was named Savannah. It became the capital of the State of Georgia: today, Savannah celebrates Oglethorpe Day every February, with civic worthies and crowds of children dressed in eighteenth-century costume processing through its elegant Georgian streets and squares.

Oglethorpe carried with him a collection of various seeds from the Chelsea Physic Garden of species that Curator Philip Miller thought might help support the new colony. Upon arrival a plot of ground was designated in which to grow them (known as the Trustee's Garden). Within ten years it was said to have, 'fine nurseries of oranges, olives, white mulberries, figs, peaches and many curious herbs . . . which all thrive'. What was not specifically mentioned in that contemporary account was the most significant species of Miller's provision – cotton seeds. Their success changed the demography and history of America.

It was known, therefore, that colonies could be helped to support themselves by setting up research and acclimatisation gardens – botanic gardens in that original broad definition of the term. The Caribbean Islands were quick off the mark with St Vincent's Botanic Garden (dating from 1765) and with Trinidad, Tobago, Antigua and others coming soon after. Joseph Banks was an enthusiast of these and promoter of new foundations. It was at St Vincent that the breadfruit trees from HMS *Providence*, Captain Bligh's second and successful voyage, were landed. Soon, Kew-supported and often Kew-staffed botanic gardens also existed in Calcutta, Ceylon (Sri Lanka), Cape of Good Hope and elsewhere. Staff gathered and grew indigenous plants with economic potential, importing from other gardens and, of course, sending plants back to England for Kew's collections, to be named, studied and quite possibly sent on to yet another continent. Only Australia was a disappointment; its fascinating flora seemed singularly lacking, apart from its timbers, in species that would help support the settlers and from the first, European crop plants went with them. The staple cereals were vital and soon vineyards, orchards and olive groves became established; a new land made habitable to immigrants by ancient crops from the other side of the world.

Ripe fruits of cotton, known as 'bolls'. Cotton is one of several economic crops that have changed the world through introduction by botanic gardens.

NOTICE

IS HEREBY GIVEN,

THAT BY THE

GRACIOUS PERMISSION OF HER MAJESTY,

THE

ROYAL
PLEASURE GROUNDS
AT KEW

Will be opened to the Public on every Day in the Week from the 18th of May, until Tuesday, the 30th of September, during the present Year,—on Sundays, from 2 o'clock P.M., and on every other Day in the Week from 1 o'clock P.M.

THE ACCESS to these Grounds will be in the Kew and Richmond Road, by the "Lion" and "Unicorn" Gates respectively; and, on the River Side of the Grounds by the Gate adjoining to the Brentford Ferry; the Entrance Gates to the Botanic Gardens on Kew Green being open as heretofore.

Communications will be opened between the Botanic Gardens and the Pleasure Gardens by Gates in the Wire Fence which separates the two.

It is requested that Visitors will abstain from carrying Baskets, Parcels, or Refreshments of any kind into the Grounds. Smoking in the Botanic Gardens is strictly prohibited. No Dogs admitted.

By Order of the Right Honourable the First Commissioner of Her Majesty's Works, &c.

Office of Works, April 15, 1856.

PRINTED BY HARRISON AND SONS, ST. MARTIN'S LANE.

5

VICTORIAN KEW
At the Centre of the Empire

P RINCESS VICTORIA was just one year old when her grandfather King George III died in 1820. Her 'Wicked Uncles' in the form of profligate George IV and old salt William IV (and the Dukes of Cumberland and Cambridge) loomed in the background of a childhood spent mainly at Kensington Palace. It is unfortunate she had no early happy memories of Kew which might well have smoothed its way. She was not initially an obvious successor to the throne of Great Britain and Ireland and its 'Possessions beyond the Seas' nor, as she became in 1877, Empress of India. Yet her name is synonymous with Britain's period of imperial greatness and with the architecture, art and attitudes of her time. 'Victorian' is an adjective of extraordinary resonance and Kew, with its intimate connections with royalty, government and the expanding Empire became Victorian to its core.

Joseph Banks also died in 1820; had he lived he might have eased the transition after George III's death. The new King's (George IV's) tastes and connoisseurship in the arts and architecture were of the highest order, and throughout his life he created a series of astonishing houses and palaces that made and developed the Regency style. Carlton House was followed by the Brighton Pavilion, Windsor Lodge, Windsor Castle and finally Buckingham Palace.

Kew did not rank highly in his concerns. Certainly it was not seriously considered as a place of royal residence, although strangely he bought, after complicated negotiations, a couple of large houses at the end of Kew Green, the western end of which became enclosed with a pair of lodges and high iron gates. The gates, it was said, were for 'separating the royal domains from the intrusion of

Formal announcement of public admission to parts of what are now the Royal Botanic Gardens, dated 15 April 1856.

vulgar curiosity'. But only two years later, in 1827, the King ordered the demolition of his father's great white elephant, the Castellated Palace just behind on the riverbank opposite Brentford. It had never been lived in.

George IV's previous life as Prince Regent ('Prinny') had been more vital – if not positively outrageous – than his reign, and the term Regency is as evocative of an age as the term Victorian became. He died at Windsor in 1830 after only ten years on the throne, and by then something of a recluse. He was not lamented.

Better things were hoped for from his brother, Duke of Clarence, who became King William IV; at least his building interests were modest and not spread around the country. At Kew he revoked his brother's annexation of the end of Kew Green and the lodges were removed – the stone lion and unicorn, one from each roof, which as supporters of the royal coat of arms had proclaimed the royal decree, can now be seen on the two Kew Road gates which bear their names.

Presumably William had some thought of re-establishing Kew as a suitable place of royal residence as Sir Jeffry Wyatville, who had been the main architect of the dramatic rebuilding of much of Windsor Castle for George IV, produced plans for a huge south-west wing to Kew Palace. Drawings make it look like a cuckoo next to its hedge-sparrow foster-mother. It got no further than Wyatville's sketchpad. Nor, more significantly for Kew's plant collections, did his designs for a new 200-foot-long palm house to be built of wood, though the King did get as far as choosing a site for it. Wyatville had to be content with organising the transfer of one of John Nash's conservatories from Buckingham Palace (see page 115) and building what was initially called the Temple of Military Fame and now King William's Temple. The King died in 1837, before it was finished.

Thus in less than twenty years two monarchs, both acceding late in life, neither leaving legitimate heirs, lived out their short reigns. Throughout this period Kew had lacked a leader with vision and the necessary influence at court and with government to maintain the Banksian momentum – a dark age for the future national botanic garden.

OPPOSITE Lion Gate on Kew Road carries one of the two heraldic supporters of the British Crown, which King George IV ordered to be placed on new lodges on Kew Green. The unicorn is further down the road, on Unicorn Gate.

ABOVE King William's Temple was designed by Sir Jeffry Wyatville and built in 1837. It now presides over the Mediterranean Garden just to the north of Decimus Burton's Temperate House.

But, it must be emphasised, this was property of the Crown, private and presumably inviolate. The sovereign decides, the sovereign decrees. When George IV made William Townsend Aiton (Kew's Head Gardener from 1793) Director-General of all royal gardens it was inevitable that Kew would suffer neglect as he worked also at St James's Park, Buckingham Palace, Windsor and the Brighton Pavilion. The foremen at Kew took on direct management of their own particular charges, the Botanic Garden, the Pleasure Grounds, the Kitchen Garden and the Fruit and Forcing Department. There was effective maintenance but no cumulative vision. Unfortunately things did not vastly improve when William IV, said to dislike Aiton through some early perceived slight, restricted him to Kew and Buckingham Palace. And there were other royals to contend with, notably the two further sons of George III, both with houses on Kew Green from which they and their Duchesses made meddlesome sallies into the gardens.

In 1831 William gave his brother, the Duke of Cumberland, the Pleasure Grounds and the Deer Park for farming and shooting. Although it helped when he became King of Hanover on William's death and thus was often in Germany (Queen Victoria, as a woman, could not accede), it was a further ten years before he gave the land up. The Duchess of Cambridge complained that the remains of the eighteenth-century lake, her 'fishing grounds', would be lost. Later, her daughter, Princess Mary Adelaide, in a fit of horticultural fervour, involved herself in helping design Kew's bedding schemes. The Director William Hooker was not pleased. Not until the 1890s were the last parts of royal preserves – the meadow in front of Kew Palace and Queen Charlotte's Cottage and its protective woodland – brought under the public aegis of the Royal Botanic Gardens by order of Queen Victoria.

It was not, however, just the vagaries and eccentricities of the royal family that caused Kew's decline in 1820s and 1830s. Without a strong guiding hand with unimpeachable social connections (such as that of Sir Joseph Banks) to speak for it, Kew's lobby in government circles fell away. Different departments were involved but all were enjoined to reduce costs at a place no longer in the full favour of the King. Expenditure dropped by a third and it was symptomatic that the only plant collector still in the field, Allan Cunningham, was recalled from Australia in 1830.

All this was strangely at variance with the developing tenor of the age. The study of scientific botany, the improvement of horticultural techniques and the innovations in glasshouse building and heating technology fuelled by the industrial revolution, combined to promote keen interest in plants and gardening at every level of society. The (now Royal) Horticultural Society of London had been founded in 1804, the Botanic Gardens at Oxford,

Cambridge and Edinburgh were flourishing and some industrial cities set about establishing their own.

London was lagging behind: the gardens at Kew were in decline and the Apothecaries' historic Chelsea Physic Garden could not extend its role. There were moves to establish a 'National Garden' elsewhere in London, a garden where cultivated varieties of fruits, vegetables and flowers were of equal importance to botanical species. The first serious attempt had occurred in 1812 when, following a discussion of the issue at the Linnean Society, a new association produced a prospectus proposing a 'National Botanic Garden, Library and Reading Room in the Regents Park'. Rather prematurely – considering that Kew was still happily under the benevolent directorship of Banks – the association offered to take over Kew's collections. The idea did not even approach fruition but discontent in the scientific community continued for years. Both sides – those who supported a renaissance at Kew and those who deplored London's lack of a suitable National Garden – kept the debate alive in the Press. John Claudius Loudon's *Gardener's Magazine* (established in 1829) became particularly involved in the debate, with Loudon firmly in favour of a new national garden. It was an issue that just would not go away.

The accession of a new young monarch in 1837 provided an opportunity for a thorough governmental review of the costs of the royal household – an activity still regularly pursued by egalitarian politicians today. Queen Victoria's coronation took place on 28th June 1838 and already a working party under the chairmanship of John Lindley, Professor of Botany at London's University College, had been set up to look at the funding and effectiveness of all the royal gardens. In times of financial scrutiny gardens always seem to suffer the first of the cutbacks, even though by their very nature they take the longest to recover when the pendulum swing eventually occurs.

As well as Frogmore and Kew, Windsor Castle, Hampton Court, Buckingham Palace, and Kensington Palace were all to be examined. Joining Professor Lindley were John Wilson and Joseph Paxton, head gardeners respectively to the Earl of Surrey (himself Treasurer to the Royal Household) and the Duke of Devonshire. Paxton, of course, went on to an important career (including designing Crystal Palace) and a knighthood: an archetypal 'eminent Victorian'.

Within days of the group being convened they got down to work, inspecting greenhouses and gardens, accounts and records, as well as interviewing superintendents and foremen. Now over seventy years old Aiton was still ostensibly in charge of the Botanic Garden and the Pleasure Grounds at Kew as well as the gardens of Buckingham Palace. He was not happy at this unwonted exposure.

The working party completed its inquiries within a few weeks and Lindley submitted its report to the two Members of Parliament whom the Treasury had charged with setting up the team. Their approval of the recommendations reached the Treasury a fortnight later. Kew and Windsor were to continue as royal kitchen gardens supplying the London palaces; this was a simple and logical use of resources. More difficult for Parliament to swallow was the inherent acceptance that because of its superb plant collections Kew was the existing nucleus for a national botanic garden; in fact it was hard for Parliament to accept the need for a national botanic garden at all. The amazing efficiency and speed of the actual inquiry was not matched by subsequent government action and it was a further two years before Kew was safe as an intact estate with a clear mandate for the future.

What was now needed was someone of standing, of known ability within the world of plants and with the charm and charisma necessary to woo politicians, mollify resident royals and unite the existing staff. In short, someone who could fan the faint embers of Banks's fire back into a blaze. This man was Sir William Jackson Hooker, Professor of Botany at Glasgow University. Significantly, both professors Hooker and Lindley had been encouraged as bright young men by

Banks at his Soho Square home, which had functioned as a sort of botanical Socratic academy; both shared the vision of a national institution at the centre of an expanding empire. This is evident in Lindley's 1838 report and, on his appointment as Director of the Royal Botanic Gardens in 1841, Hooker's acceptance of its ethos and most of its recommendations.

William Jackson Hooker was brought up in Norfolk as an enthusiastic amateur naturalist. At the age of twenty he discovered a new species of moss; at twenty-one he became a Fellow of the Linnean Society of London and began to move in fashionable scientific circles. His expedition to Iceland in 1809 (for which Banks helped to find funding) echoed Banks's own voyage there forty years earlier. But Hooker did not have Banks's private fortune and his move to Glasgow in 1820 (again with

Sir William Jackson Hooker became the first formally designated Director of Kew in 1841. He held the post until his death at the age of eighty-one in 1865.

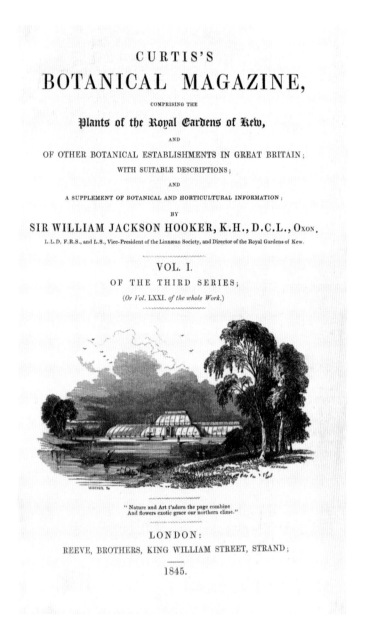

CURTIS'S
BOTANICAL MAGAZINE,

COMPRISING THE

Plants of the Royal Gardens of Kew,

AND

OF OTHER BOTANICAL ESTABLISHMENTS IN GREAT BRITAIN;

WITH SUITABLE DESCRIPTIONS;

AND

A SUPPLEMENT OF BOTANICAL AND HORTICULTURAL INFORMATION;

BY

SIR WILLIAM JACKSON HOOKER, K.H., D.C.L., Oxon.

L.L.D, F.R.S., and L.S., Vice-President of the Linnæan Society, and Director of the Royal Gardens of Kew.

VOL. I.

OF THE THIRD SERIES;

(Or Vol. LXXI. of the whole Work.)

" Nature and Art t'adorn the page combine
And flowers exotic grace our northern clime."

LONDON:
REEVE, BROTHERS, KING WILLIAM STREET, STRAND;

1845.

ABOVE The title page of *Curtis's Botanical Magazine*, which William Hooker continued to edit after his move from Glasgow to Kew.

OPPOSITE Love Lane, the public road that once separated the royal gardens of Richmond Lodge and Kew Palace is now marked by the Holly Walk.

OVERLEAF William Eden Nesfield's landscaping plans brought eighteenth century eye-catchers, such as the Pagoda, back into focus within the developing botanical collections.

Banks's assistance) was less from choice than the need to provide for his wife and family. For the next twenty years Hooker looked for a suitable job in the south – Kew soon came into his sights – yet Glasgow enabled him to pursue a productive career in addition to his university responsibilities. Treatises on ferns, floras of North America and Britain, and the editorship of periodicals including *Curtis's Botanical Magazine*, led in 1836 to a knighthood from King William IV for services to botany. When Sir William Jackson Hooker became Director in 1841 he was already fifty-six years old – in these days retirement and golf might be more in mind – and he died in 1865 at the age of eighty-one, still in post.

In just under twenty-five years Hooker promoted and oversaw the transformation of a confusing melange of royal gardens into a Kew that we would clearly recognise today. The building programme itself is daunting, as is the political lobbying behind the scenes that ensured the necessary flow of funds. By the end of his directorship the Palm House, the centre block and octagons of the Temperate House, the Waterlily House as well as a number of more transient support glasshouses were all in place for the cultivation of exotic plants. So too was Decimus Burton's fine museum by the Palm House Pond. Lengths of walls and fences that separated the original botanic garden from the Pleasure Grounds, the King of Hanover's property from the Palace lawns and so on were gradually taken down. Nesfield's landscaping of formal walks and vistas brought eighteenth-century eye-catchers such as the Pagoda back into prominence. It became possible to walk from Kew Green to the Deer Park and from Kew Road to the river without hindrance.

In 1847 the first guidebook was published – an attitudinal breakthrough of the first order. But for whom was it produced? In recounting the progress and successes of Sir William's directorship – and they were indeed dramatic – a calm and happy sense of Victorian order may seem to have prevailed. Of course it was not like that at all. Warfare between Hooker and whichever government department was currently in control of funding was never far from the surface. In the early years of his directorship problems were compounded by

the competing claims of the royals. As far as the royals were concerned, these were still private places. Government, on the other hand, needed to consider a wider public, whether this be a window-breaking mob (as when Lord Bute was advising Princess Augusta) or a newly enfranchised electorate made mobile by new railways (the first Reform Act was passed in 1832, although women had to wait almost another century before getting the vote). The clamour for regular public access to Kew would not go away.

Even during the reigns of George III and his two brothers, some limited visiting to the small botanic garden was permitted; although when the Pleasure Grounds were in the control of the King of Hanover a rather bizarre dress code was demanded which dissuaded many prospective visitors. In the 1820s visitors had to knock at a door on Kew Green and were let in on a daily basis from 1 pm, but were usually escorted by a staff member – a frightful waste of labour that had ceased by the time Hooker appeared. The replanning of the grounds and the opening of Decimus Burton's great gates on Kew Green changed all that. In 1841 9,174 visitors were recorded; by 1861 numbers had swelled to over 500,000.

Charged with the administration of a scientific institution with both academic demands and economic responsibilities to the Empire, the Director was perhaps concerned that if the gardens be fully opened to the public they would gradually develop – decline would be his interpretation – into little more than a superior public park. In today's parlance, dumbing-down would be the relevant term. The issue is indeed of relevance to botanic gardens today, as they face the challenge of obtaining essential income from the turnstile to supplement fluxuating government grants. Hooker fought manfully, giving way graciously when necessary to the demands for more flowerbeds, more colour and extended opening hours. As an entrance fee (one old penny) was not imposed until 1916, a vast increase in visitors increased costs and inevitably demanded greater public subvention. Such ongoing debate maintained public

ABOVE AND RIGHT Except when Dig for Victory war efforts demanded more utilitarian planting, the Victorian tradition of seasonal bedding on the Palm House terrace has continued unabated and with ever more innovative displays.

interest in Kew with the popular newspapers demanding greater access, the gardening press better labelling and informative educational displays, and the botanical journals advising caution. All were grist to the mill in the building of a national botanical garden. It is said there is no such thing as bad publicity.

Kew reached a pinnacle of horticultural display in 1859. With propagation becoming much more effective due to improvements in glasshouse heating, Kew was able to display 400 flower beds with an average of 100 plants apiece. A blaze of bedding – geraniums, calceolaria,

verbenas and begonias – filled the parterres around the Palm House and lined the Broad Walk. Hooker's immediate civil service superior, Lord John Manners, as well as enjoying the sight maintained 'that our thus gratifying the public is the surest way of making the estimates palatable'. In the debate on the estimates in the House of Commons in July of that year, Joseph Paxton – who had been one of Lindley's investigative committee and was now Member of Parliament for Coventry, with a knighthood – decried Kew's becoming 'a gaudy flower show'. Lord John responded that he 'was certain that where one person was interested in the botanical specimens, one hundred were attracted by the flowers'.

It remained with the Director to promote and fulfil the roles of a modern botanic garden that had been the vision of Sir Joseph Banks almost a century before and which had been reaffirmed by Lindley and Paxton. A necessary element of this was to enlarge the Living Collections, and through the 1840s and 1850s extensive tree planting built up the new arboretum and pinetum, while the old Royal Kitchen Garden became the Herbaceous Ground and by 1854 4,500 species were cultivated there. With Kew's future in safer hands donations of plant collections large and small again increased the holdings: cacti and tropical orchids were noteworthy, though success with the latter was difficult to achieve. Planned collecting abroad began again on a limited scale.

However, the acquisition and cultivation of a range of plants, however extensive, does not make a botanic

garden. Their study, through the classification and naming of new species, and the inquiry into their chemistry, genetics and possible economic value must be pursued in parallel. Botany is, of course, an accumulative science. No doubt there are eureka moments but taxonomy – the aspect of botany especially supported by the existence of botanic gardens – is built upon assembled painstakingly revealed evidence recorded in books and documented in herbarium specimens. Kew lacked these vital supports.

In Banks's time such activity went on at Soho Square where his assistants and librarians, Daniel Solander and Jonas Dryander, protégés of the great Linnaeus himself, worked on Banks's own *Endeavour* collections and all the other new plants that Banks solicited for the King from around the world. Both Solander and Dryander had been essential to the successful production of William Aiton's *Hortus Kewensis*. Robert Brown succeeded Dryander as Banks's librarian. After Banks's death in 1820, he went on to become Keeper of Botany at the British Museum. As Brown had been bequeathed a life interest in the collections, the herbarium and library went with him. He was, therefore, virtually the anointed botanical keeper of Banks's flame during the interregnum and he was in control of the taxonomic material that supported Kew's Living Collections.

Unfortunately these years gave plenty of opportunities to the anti-Kew camp – economising politicians and civil servants, as well as those with agendas to promote other sites, for example, Regents Park or the Horticultural Society's garden at Chiswick, as more obviously central locations for the capital's botanic garden. Either of those locations, it was argued, would be more conveniently close to the British Museum's botany department. But for various reasons those plans came to nothing. Hideously

One of Sir Joseph Hooker's prime tasks when he assumed the Directorship was to develop the plant collections. A new Arboretum and Pinetum were planted, extensive herbaceous plantings were made and, under glass, cacti (above) and orchids (right) were noteworthy.

increasing atmospheric pollution – notably the infamous pea-soup fogs of Dickens's novels – was not on their side; whereas Kew's situation seven miles to the west avoided the worst excesses (although the present author recalls, when a student at Kew in the mid-1950s, all the flower-buds in a house of *Calanthe* orchids having aborted by the morning after a night of virulent smog).

The battle over the Herbarium and Library Collections continued well into Hooker's directorship. In 1848 a royal commission was set up to determine the role of the British Museum itself; more space was needed for displays and exhibitions as well as to meet curatorial demands. Proposals were made that the natural history material, which covered several

disciplines, should move. Brown was vehement that this should not happen, and for all the time he remained Keeper nothing changed. Eventually the Museum's problems were resolved by the opening of grandiloquent new buildings in South Kensington in the 1880s. That the new British Museum (Natural History) – generally known simply as the Natural History Museum – included a Department of Botany to some extent reaffirmed its separation from the Living Collections at Kew, but by this time Kew had made its own arrangements for taxonomic support. Sir William Hooker himself had built up an impressive herbarium and library over his years in Glasgow and at Kew and allowed free scholarly access to it. After his death in

The first of the custom-built museums at Kew stands across the pond from the Palm House. It first housed William Hooker's own collections of 'Vegetable Products' to which were added materials from around the Empire and also a vast number of exhibits from the Crystal Palace Great Exhibition of 1851.

MUSEUM.

Interior of the Principal Room.

1865 the herbarium, together with his library, archival material and collection of plant portraits, was bought for the nation.

As Kew's accumulations of post-Banks holdings grew, sufficient space for their safe storage and study was required. In 1852 Hooker learned that he could, for a limited time, use the ground floor of Hunter House (which had belonged to the late King of Hanover) – a temporary measure that eventually became permanent. One year later its first curator was appointed. In addition to Hooker's own herbarium – probably the biggest and most valuable in the country – other collections were donated. Most noteworthy was that of George Bentham, who had been secretary of the Horticultural Society of London and later President of the Linnean Society. He was a friend and supporter of Hooker and had worked at Kew as a freelance botanist for thirty years. Over time, Hunter House become the established home of the ever-expanding Herbarium and Library, with wings and extensions being added as necessary (the latest extension will become operational in 2009).

Hooker's typically Victorian enthusiasm for collections of virtually anything that was related to or derived from plants led to what he first called a Museum of Vegetable Products and later a Museum of Economic Botany. 'Economic botany' was a phrase that underpinned much of Hooker's thinking about Kew and its imperial role. These often-bizarre objects from around the world demonstrated textiles and the fibres that produced them, dyes and dye-plants, gums, resins, basketry materials, wood and wood products. The museum was initially displayed in a converted royal fruit store and opened to the public in 1848; Queen Victoria, visiting that same year, was said to have found

it of great interest. How suitable, therefore, that a vast number of exhibits from the Great Exhibition of 1851 – one of Prince Albert's particular enthusiasms – should join Kew's collections. The collections quickly outgrew the old fruit store and plans for a custom-built museum were developed.

Decimus Burton's resulting design has come in for a lot of stick; for instance, Sir Joseph Paxton said in the House of Commons that it looked like 'a third-rate lodging house'. One hundred years later Pevsner was no kinder, calling it 'utilitarian minimum-classical'. In fact, Museum No. 1 is not that bad and seems at last to have settled more comfortably into its site; it would be a remarkable building indeed that could compete with or even complement the Palm House just across the water. What surprises us is the realisation that both buildings come from the same hand.

Successful museums appear to generate their own momentum and attract further objects as a magnet does iron filings. It was the age of international exhibitions and Kew became the repository of many of their plant-based exhibits. The Orangery, finally being accepted as an ineffective place for growing live plants, became a museum of wood and wood products in 1863. With the establishment of these museums William Hooker had effectively developed the essential scientific and museological bedrocks of a modern botanic garden: Herbarium, Library, Museum and Living Collections all mutually supportive and inter-related. Kew was living through its own renaissance.

There was a renewal of plant-collecting abroad, with varying amounts of success. Small areas of California, the West Indies, Central and South America, Hong Kong, Formosa (Taiwan) and Japan were visited. As in Banks's time, the collectors chosen were usually young Kew-trained gardeners minutely briefed by Hooker and attached as naturalists to Royal Navy hydrological and explorational voyages. As well as collecting living plants and seeds they were expected to keep journals and make careful notes about habitats and aspects of the plants that would not be apparent from the dried specimens they sent home – for example, scent and flower colours. Both ornamentals and species of economic value, sometimes only hitherto known of through the artifact or product they furnished, were to be sought. Basic equipment and a few books were provided, though inevitably any flora of the region to help identification was yet to be written; that was another reason for their presence. For the young explorer-botanist such expeditions combined excitement and frustration in equal measure: the excitement of 'far away places with strange-sounding names', and the wonders of plants of all sorts whose identity could only be guessed at; frustration of being at the mercy of the ship's timetable and itinerary and the particular difficulties of keeping plants alive. For Hooker the same emotions prevailed: excitement and huge satisfaction

when new species were added to Kew's Herbarium and Living Collections but near-apoplexy when collectors underperformed or dared to go their own way.

One collector, however, seems to have received complete approbation – the Director's own son, Joseph Dalton Hooker. That he went on to succeed his father as Kew's next Director might appear a clear case of nepotism and it is true that Hooker *père* saw his son as a natural successor and helped in any way possible to further his career; but he seems to have won his spurs legitimately.

Joseph Hooker's significant travels began in 1839 – the same year that he qualified as a doctor at Glasgow University – when he was appointed Assistant Surgeon and Botanist on HMS *Erebus*. For almost four years *Erebus* and her sister ship HMS *Terror* explored the far southern oceans and the lands bordering them. Hooker's six-volumed *Botany of the Antarctic Voyage*, the first of which was published in 1844, made his name as a taxonomic botanist.

Four years later, now on naval half-pay and working for the British Government's Geological Survey, Hooker travelled to Northern India. Sikkim lies 300–400 miles due north of Calcutta and is remote even today. In the mid-nineteenth century it was a land unmapped, virtually unexplored and botanically unknown. The terrain is extremely inhospitable, beginning with subtropical Himalayan foothills and reaching the massif Kanchenjunga, which at almost 8,600 metres high looms on the border with Nepal. Three years of mapping, sketching – in a pre-photographic age there was no other way of visually recording new worlds – and collecting plants for Kew confirmed his reputation. His *Himalayan Journals* (1854) document the work formally; while gardens great and small around the temperate world continue to demonstrate his success as a collector with a keen eye for good garden plants. Sikkim is towards the epicentre of the extraordinary concentration of Himalayan rhododendrons and Hooker's introductions encouraged later collectors – Forrest, Wilson, Ludlow and Kingdon-Ward – to scour the Sino-Himalayan region for the hundreds of species (which have contributed to the thousands of cultivars) that are grown in gardens today.

Sir Joseph Dalton Hooker (1817–1911) succeeded his father as Director of Kew in 1865. His travels and collecting in the wild, publications and training made him an obvious choice for the Directorship.

It is no exaggeration to state that the rage for woodland gardens in Britain began with Joseph Hooker.

From Joseph Banks, from Lindley's Report and from Sir William Hooker's own deeply held beliefs, Kew's *raison d'être* was never to be merely museological, still less just ornamental. To hold the best and most diverse collections of living plants, of course; to accumulate the most effective supporting herbaria and library, naturally; to build an effective compliment of scientific and horticultural staff, self-evident; but it was the use of these resources to further the economy of the country and the overseas territories that lay at the heart of it all. It was never to be one-way traffic; Kew's role as an entrepôt can hardly be overstated. In William Hooker's own words Kew became, 'the botanical headquarters of the British Empire and its dependencies'. As early as his 1844 Annual Report, Hooker asserted that

> there scarcely exists a garden or a country however remote, which has not already felt the benefit of this establishment. All our public gardens abroad – those of Ceylon, Mauritius, Sydney and Trinidad; and cultivators of the soil, Governors of our own colonies and consuls are supplied with various products of such other climes as may be deemed suitable to them.

It all helped to garner support for his vision of Kew.

While whole lists of economic plants cultivated at Kew and sent abroad could be given, there are two whose stories are almost 'stranger than fiction', and encapsulate the ethos of the place and the age. These are *Cinchona*, the source of quinine, and *Hevea brasilienis*, the commercial rubber tree. Each has affected history and changed the world, and Kew's role in the early collection and dissemination across the globe was instrumental to their success. As with the consignment of cotton seed that the Chelsea Physic Garden sent with the founding fathers of Georgia, the economy, demography and culture of whole continents were changed.

One of innumerable native Indian medicines in Peru, *Cinchona* (as the genus of trees was later named by Linnaeus) first came to the notice of the Spanish colonial authorities in the seventeenth century. Preparations made from this 'Peruvian bark' or 'Jesuits' bark', used as a preventative and treatment for the quartan ague, as malaria was known, was in use in Europe by the second half of the century. John Evelyn records seeing a plant in the stove house at Chelsea in 1685 but *Cinchona* species could only be grown to maturity in tropical and subtropical climates. Quinine's efficacy became widely known in parallel with increasing European populations in India and the Far East; the quantities of bark exported from South America were so large they endangered wild populations. Although Sir Joseph Banks had suggested *Cinchona* should be cultivated in India years before, it was left to the French and the Dutch, who managed to get the first live plants to Java in the 1850s. The East India Company, which would have gained immeasurably from a local source of quinine, remained unconvinced but after the Indian Mutiny of 1857 the new government-established India Office that took over administration of the sub-continent pursued the quest

VICTORIAN KEW: AT THE CENTRE OF THE EMPIRE

with greater vigour. It was led by Clements Markham, an India Office staff member who had travelled in Peru and spoke Spanish in addition to some of the native languages. Kew was asked to participate. Hooker recommended others to join Markham's expedition and suggested searching areas of Ecuador and Bolivia as well as Peru. Seeds were sent to Kew for germination and also directly to British India and Ceylon where plantations were soon established.

All this was very good for both Kew's reputation and that of its Director. The complicated operation had gone splendidly but the species collected proved to contain disappointingly low amounts of the vital drug. Not long after, another species, *Cinchona ledgeriana*, also native to Bolivia, was obtained by the Dutch. This species contained the highest quinine content known. The Dutch quickly established large plantations and soon led the world in quinine production: British Ceylon and Malaya followed suit.

The story of rubber is even more remarkable. It begins in the early seventeenth century, with the Spanish colonists in South America noticing a game played by natives with an extraordinary high-bouncing ball; it culminates with rubber established as a substance that impinges on every facet of modern life. Kew played a central role in developing its economic importance to the burgeoning Empire.

Travellers in tropical South America had also reported that, as well as making high-bouncing balls, the substance – an exudate from trees – could also be used to waterproof boots. Samples, typical of so many exotic natural curiosities that flooded into enlightenment Europe, were marvelled at and studied. In Britain, Joseph Priestley (who discovered and named oxygen) noted that it could rub out pencil marks on paper much better than a piece of soft bread, which was the normal method. Priestley's simple name – India rubber – has stuck: a rather demeaning name for such an important

A leading shoot of one species of *Hevea*, the source of commercial rubber.

commodity. The French *caoutchouc* from the native name meaning 'weeping tree' tells more. There were attempts to commercialise its waterproofing properties, with Charles Mackintosh's name (like Hoover, Linoleum and Barbour) becoming generic for one of the resulting products. It was, however, Nelson Goodyear in America who succeeded in creating a high-tensile material with enormous potential. The process was called 'vulcanisation' and involved heating the rubber with sulphur. The result – solid rubber tyres – were displayed at the Great Exhibition and caused great interest, resulting in rubber's first manufacturing boom.

The source of rubber, like that of quinine, was only found in the equatorial forests of Spanish and Portuguese South America, and it was harvested inefficiently by native peoples in thrall to the exploiting colonists. As demand increased so did the pressure on the native populations, both human and *Hevea brasiliensis* itself. In 1870 Clements Markham, with his cinchona experience behind him, recommended 'that it was necessary to do for the India-rubber or caoutchouc-yielding trees what had already been done with such happy results for the cinchona trees'.

The India Office, with Kew's initial advice and agreement to grow and disseminate what could be collected, funded the operation. Robert Cross, one of the cinchona team, travelled to Panama in 1875 to collect *Castilla elastica*, a related genus. In spite of becoming shipwrecked off the coast of Jamaica on the way home he returned with thousands of seeds for Kew. None germinated but sufficient plants were raised from cuttings. These were sent to Java and West Africa as well as Ceylon. Within a year he was back in South America, this time assembling *Hevea* seed in Brazil. Again, back at Kew germination rates were very poor, and it was realised that the seeds soon became rancid and lost viability – speed from collection to sowing was of the essence.

It is at this point that the story takes a 'Boy's Own' swashbuckling turn, with the entrance of Henry Wickham, a one-time coffee planter and trader in birds' skins. He had offered himself to Kew and the India Office took him on. Wickham's account escalated over the years and its more

colourful episodes were probably more swash than buckle. However, whether or not he smuggled his cases of *Hevea* seed in the face of adversarial customs officers at Para on the Amazon it is certain that he did get them on to a specially chartered steamer – whether or not a Brazilian gunboat was in the offing hardly matters. It was full steam ahead for Liverpool where a special train awaited. The 60,000 seeds were sown at Kew next day, a number successfully germinated and three months later nearly 2,000 seedlings in closed Wardian cases were transported to Ceylon. The next year, 1877, they were planted out and in 1880 some were recorded as being 30 feet high and

starting to produce seed of their own. The seed was distributed, with Kew's encouragement, not just to British territories but also to German, Dutch and Portuguese colonies. But it was from Singapore Botanic Garden – supplied by Kew with *Hevea* seedlings in 1877 – that the rubber industry really took off, encouraged by the popular demand of John Dunlop's revolutionary pneumatic tyres.

Rubber became an important cash crop in Ceylon, for a time even more so than tea. But the Far East soon became dominant. Such was the extent of planting, combined with speed of growth and improved methods of tapping the trees, that within thirty years production in

A young rubber plantation already being 'tapped' to produce latex. A wound spiralling around the *Hevea* trunk is made with a sharp implement and regularly kept open. The sticky 'sap' accumulates in cups and is regularly collected, taken to a local centre where it is heated to remove moisture and turned into rough sheets of natural rubber. The process is very similar to that used in North America to make maple sugar.

Malaya and the Dutch East Indies exceeded that of Brazil. Clearly, Markham and Wickham had earned their knighthoods. It is interesting to learn that Sir Clements Markham later became President of the Royal Geographical Society. Having been on one of the voyages that failed to find Franklin's North-West Passage he remained a proponent of high latitude exploration and later a patron of Robert Falcon Scott (of the Antarctic).

As an afterword, to emphasise how the planned transfer of plants around the world affects us all, it is salutary to note how seriously Allied operations in the Second World War were compromised by the Japanese capture of so much of the world's rubber- and cinchona-producing areas. Knock-on effects continue to reverberate. Shortage of the natural materials promoted research into man-made alternatives: synthetic rubbers are now legion (but do not replace the original) while alternatives to quinine have provoked resistant strains of the *Anopheles* mosquito carrying the malaria-causing *Plasmodium*, which the true Jesuits' bark can still effectively treat.

The romance of the lone collector – battling almost insuperable odds in the depths of a tropical jungle to search out plants and get them home – is the stuff of legend and does not need a Henry Wickham to puff it up further. Tales of true heroism and extraordinary bravery in appalling conditions can be easily read in the often dry and understated reports and journals of Kew's explorers. These are made easier to comprehend when we can see the actual plant they have laboured to find – the giant Victoria water lily in its specially constructed greenhouse for example, which is otherwise almost beyond all imagining. The other aspects of the work, collecting, pressing and drying samples of new plants, is equally important in

unravelling the mysteries of the natural world. They must be sent back to the herbarium and library where scientific comparison can lead to understanding. Gradually knowledge of an area's plant population can be assembled.

This is just what the early settlers and colonial administrators needed if the new land was to be effectively farmed and made able to support its new population. That word 'new' as a place name prefix – New England, New Hampshire, New Zealand, New York (previously New Amsterdam) – reveals the colonists' hopes and intentions. These are to be homes-from-home, without the baggage of the past, better: 'Oh brave new world, that has such people in't.' And it follows that the land is to be exploited – used has perhaps a less pejorative ring – in a vastly different way from the practices of its indigenous inhabitants. In all the countries and continents which Europeans 'discovered' from the fifteenth century, the native peoples (with the strange anomaly of Easter Island being a possibly unique exception) seemed to live on and off and within their lands lightly. Populations were relatively small, but nevertheless it is clear that, whether as hunter-gatherers or agriculturists, some sort of self-sufficiency had been built up over time. The indigenous cultures depended upon indigenous plants and animals for food, medicine, fibre and so on. This knowledge was potentially of great importance to the settlers. Beyond the classic case of cinchona, travellers tales are peppered with wounds healed and fevers cured through the ministrations of native medical practitioners – though witch doctor or medicine man is the rather apprehensive job description usually employed.

A raft of yard-wide floating leaves surround the central clusters of ephemeral flowers. Travellers' tales and even sober reports from botanists in the field could not properly describe such a prodigy-plant. *Victoria amazonica* had to be seen to be believed and special hot-houses were built to grow it.

The roles, therefore, which European botanic gardens and later their colonial satellites assumed related to these incompatible and ultimately deleterious situations of settlers versus indigenous populations in the expanding world. On the one-hand, the post-Renaissance voyages of discovery were ostensibly just that – a search for knowledge and understanding of the world. On the other hand they were for profit and power; ultimately, of course, knowledge is both of those things. The naturalists sent on such voyages were, as we have seen, instructed to collect plants of economic significance which might help to found a new ex-patriot community there or support one already established with a similar climate elsewhere – the Tahiti-West Indies breadfruit transportation is infamous. Because of their horticultural knowledge – most Kew collectors began as gardeners – they were also able to report on the potential of any potential colony for being at first self-supporting and subsequently being profitable to its sponsors. Were there native crops that could be grown in the necessary quantities for a settlement? Were there indigenous plants of industrial significance? Could they be cultivated and manufactured there? Or should they be grown there but utilised somewhere else?

These considerations have changed the world. Societies have been constructed around them, interrelated yet utterly dissimilar: cotton-growing British India and the mill-towns of Lancashire, rubber-producing Malaya and the industrial users in motor-car towns such as Dagenham or Detroit. Such examples, just two of many, would have been inconceivable to Sir Joseph Banks, although first-hand observation on the *Endeavour* voyage in the 1760s established the principle when it was noted that Australia seemed strangely lacking in useful plant-based commodities. While being entirely adequate for Aboriginal peoples whose culture had evolved in parallel with its plants and animals, there was little for a European mind-set to exploit. The land could, however, accept European agriculture, its crops

and its animals: Banks was sending them within thirty years.

Sir William Hooker's Directorship at Kew saw the effective launch of an Empire-wide survey of its floral riches in a series of floras which catalogued all known plants country-by-country. It was an enormous undertaking and not surprisingly there were problems with staff and with funding. But not least among Sir William's talents was his ability to bring people on side and to gather support from those in positions of authority whom he cultivated as friends. In this way the Colonial Office promoted a *Flora of the British West Indian Islands* and in 1861 the Governor of Madras encouraged the India Office to subsidise the preparation of what became a seven-volume flora of British India. Such a coup also gave Hooker more personal satisfaction in that the project had begun – and the first volume produced in 1872 – by his son Joseph in his Himalayan travels. Soon after that first volume went to press the East India Company was disbanded and replaced by the India Office.

When Sir William died at the age of eighty-one, still in post and full of years and honours, many British possessions had, through his efforts, a flora compiled or in progress. Geographically they ranged from parts of Canada (his own *Flora Boreali-Americana*) through to the Falkland Islands, Tasmania, New Zealand, South Africa, Hong Kong and a vast *Flora Australiensis* in seven volumes. More were planned as more of the world came under British influence. Sir William Hooker's twenty-four-year tenure had saved Kew for the nation and set it clearly in its place as a vital resource for British overseas territories. He also managed, often in the teeth of opposition, to assemble and drive the difficult troika that defines a botanic garden: science, education and public amenity.

He also never forgot how in the interregnum years before he took up the reigns, the plant collections in the Royal Botanic Gardens had declined and the Estates

fragmented without a unifying Director in post. Not surprisingly he was deeply concerned about the succession. He had always seen his son Joseph as a botanist rather than a practicing medical man and, naturally, through his friends and contacts he had helped to further Joseph's career. A Hooker dynasty at Kew was certainly in his mind. Joseph had demonstrated his commitment to taxonomy and investigative botany through his travels and the publications that followed the Antarctic and Sikkim years. Various positions presented themselves at colonial botanic gardens but in the event he was appointed Assistant Director at Kew in 1855 and ten years later succeeded his father as Director. It seems extraordinary today that neither appointment seems to have been contested. For nineteenth-century Kew the seamless succession was very satisfactory. Joseph Hooker recorded how happily he worked with his father, sharing similar hopes and ideals for Kew and its worldwide role, but he was less sanguine about actually taking up the Directorship.

Though it could have come as no surprise to him, the formal administration of running what was in essence a sub-department of government was decidedly irksome. Nor was he a natural courtier like his father, lacking the charm to smooth his way through civil service obstructions. Diplomacy in dealing with increasing vociferous public demands was also not a strong suit. Possibly as an escape from all this, Joseph Hooker quickly took personal interest in replanning and replanting areas of the gardens. With the new curator (a second John Smith, who had joined Kew from Syon in 1864) the Arboretum was completely re-designed to continue Sir William's idea of planting synoptic collections which could demonstrate current knowledge of botanical relationships. The new glades would be like walking through a living textbook. Thus acacias, cedars, thorns, sweet chestnuts and so on had avenues to themselves. To the south of the lake, which he extended and landscaped with sweeps of trees and shrubs approaching the water and then falling back (even Lancelot Brown might have approved), Kew's main collection of conifers was assembled. By the 1870s the Pinetum held over a thousand trees, many new introductions from the west coast of North America. There must have been speculation as to whether any of these young trees would eventually attain the size of their parents in their British Columbia homes. The gift and placing of the first great Douglas fir flagpole in 1861, 159 feet high, suggested the trees' potential. Kew's last flagpole, in place from 1958 to 2007, originally stood 225 feet high: the tallest wooden flagpole in the world.

LEFT Both Sir William Hooker and his son Sir Joseph, Directors of Kew for over forty years, are commemorated by Wedgwood plaques in St Anne's on the Green.

BELOW Sir Joseph Hooker's Lake was created in 1856; only in 2006 after 150 years was it able to be fully enjoyed. The elegant line of the Sackler Crossing was designed by John Pawson.

Views in the Pinetum at the south end of the Gardens. Until the mid-twentieth century atmospheric pollution – London's infamous smogs continued until then – made life difficult for many evergreen species and alternative sites in the country were used. Deciduous larches succeeded happily (right).

OVERLEAF Autumn by the Lake, which Joseph Hooker extended and landscaped in the late 1860s. Sweet chestnut can always be recognised even when the leaves are fallen by its typical spiralling bark.

ABOVE A primary school class picnics in the Rose Garden at the start of Syon Vista. It is framed by mature holm oaks (*Quercus ilex*), an evergreen species from the Mediterranean.

RIGHT Swathes of wild bulbs – here *Narcissus pseudonarcissus* – enliven the slopes leading to the Temple of Aeolus. Kew's phenological records show it flowers a month earlier than fifty years ago.

During the 1870s some of Nesfield's more convoluted parterres around the Palm House were simplified or entirely laid down to grass, as was, in 1882, the Syon Vista; such an area of gravel being vastly labour intensive to maintain to perfection in a pre-herbicide age. Increased collections and donations of a wide range of species led to new developments: rock gardens, a wild garden around the Temple of Aeolus, new glasshouses for ferns, orchids, and alpines and so on. These were mainly species of botanical interest (though often very beautiful as well) chosen to demonstrate the amazing diversity of the world's – and especially the Empire's – floral riches. This was emphasised by turning the Waterlily House into an Economic Plant House containing medicinal and culinary plants.

The purpose of cultivating wild species was always primarily to provide a research tool for the Herbarium and its taxonomic staff, rather than to educate and divert the visiting public. And it was for this reason that longer opening hours was vigorously resisted: as an academic botanist himself, Joseph Hooker protested that mornings should be kept clear of nursery maids and their charges from the new villas across

Kew Road, so that gardeners could get on with their work and scientists study without interruption. After a short honeymoon period Hooker spent his first decade in post fighting battles on several fronts to maintain, as he saw it, Kew's integrity as a scientific institution, acceding only with the greatest reluctance to more public access and demands for 'prettification' of the place. He had inherited the colourful parterres as a *fait accompli*; to his horror, insistence on carpet bedding followed. It was, he asserted, a slippery slope from which there would shortly be no return. Kew would be given over to recreation seekers 'whose motives are rude romping and games' and 'a swarm of filthy children and women of the lowest class' – extravagant sentiments that fuelled a fight which continued for years.

The local and national press became involved; the *Gardeners Chronicle*, the *Edinburgh Review*, The Royal Society and other learned societies all threw their hats in the ring predictably for or against morning openings depending upon their clientele. The Lords Day Observance Society, of course, demanded no opening of anything at all on Sundays. In 1877 the Kew Gardens

Public Rights Defence Association was formed with two main demands, morning opening and the replacement with railings of the boundary wall along Kew Road. Hooker responded undiplomatically by raising the wall by three feet to prevent, he said, the Gardens' labourers from climbing out to drink in the local pub. As a slight sop he decreed that Bank Holiday opening would begin at 10 am – less than half a dozen days per year.

During this period Gladstone's government, committed to reducing costs, had appointed Acton Ayrton (Member of Parliament for Tower Hamlets, an East London constituency) as First Commissioner of the Office of Works. Kew became part of his empire and the first objective in his sights was to make economies: science was to go and Hooker discredited through the gradual undermining his authority. In early 1872 Hooker wrote to George Bentham: 'My life has become utterly detestable and I do so long to throw up the Directorship . . .' Denying Ayrton's allegations of misconduct, Hooker sought to appeal directly to the Prime Minister and was granted permission to make direct contact through Gladstone's secretary, Algernon West. The Prime

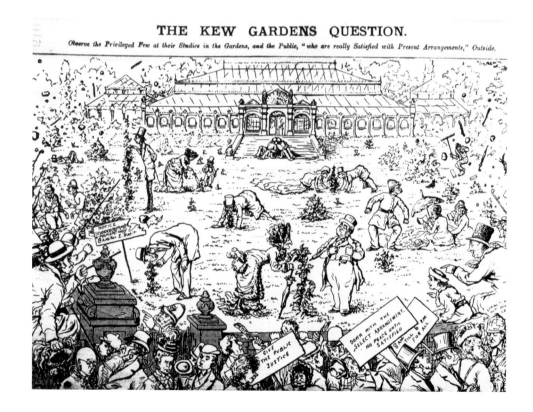

THE KEW GARDENS QUESTION.
Observe the Privileged Few at their Studies in the Gardens, and the Public, "who are really Satisfied with Present Arrangements," Outside.

A contemporary cartoon that appeared when 1870s agitation for longer public opening hours was at its height. 'Botanists' study plants in front of the Temperate House while the hoi polloi demonstrate outside on Kew Road.

Minister set up a Cabinet Committee to consider Hooker's request that his Directorial powers be restored. When it havered, Hooker gained support from the Presidents of the Linnean Society, Royal Institution and other scientific bodies as well as eminent scientists such as Darwin, Huxley and Lyell. They presented a memorial to the Prime Minister which stated, 'The resignation of Dr Hooker would we declare be a calamity to English Science, and a scandal to the English Government.'

Press comment on the memorial was almost entirely pro-Hooker but Ayrton did not give in. In a fascinating sub-plot to the 'Kew Scandal', as it became known, Ayrton received support from Richard Owen, Keeper of the Natural History departments at the British Museum, which had long been promised grand new quarters in South Kensington. Not surprisingly he was in agreement with Ayrton that money saved at Kew could sensibly be used at South Kensington, suggesting that Kew's role was more to give 'instructive pleasure to the public' and continue its activities in economic botany with the colonies. 'Proper' science should be concentrated at the Natural History Museum; Kew's herbarium could well be moved to South Kensington. And so it continued with none of the major protagonists coming out of the battle unscathed or in a particularly good light. Vested interests seem to bring out venality in the most high-minded people. Algernon West, who as Gladstone's secretary saw it all at first hand, commented that, 'Ayrton had an evil tongue, but I confess I thought him the more reasonable man of the two'.

Eventually the final report of the Royal Commission recommended that Kew and the Natural History Museum should both keep botanical collections as both had legitimate and different roles. But it was many years before the two institutions entirely buried their swords. For Kew, the end of open hostilities marked less a turning point than a confirmation of the direction envisioned by Banks and William Hooker. Hunter House on Kew Green became the official home of the Herbarium (as it still is today) and a new wing was constructed at the back. The collections were rearranged in accordance with a new system of plant classification that had been produced by George Bentham and Joseph Hooker over a twenty-year period.

One of the problems of plant nomenclature is that of synonymy. Plants can be collected and named by different people in different countries, and it may take time to discover that the same species exists in more than one guise. Even with today's international agreements and cooperation confusions can occur and new research upset existing names. In the nineteenth century, with European colonial powers busily carving up the world and trying to evaluate their possessions, difficulties were bound to occur. The first major post-Linnaeus list of the names and synonyms of all known flowering plants was compiled by the German botanist Steudel. His *Nomenclator Botanicus* came out in 1821 with a second edition following twenty years later. The whole community used it, but over time confusions accumulated. In 1880, when Hooker sought financial help in updating it, his old friend Charles Darwin offered assistance.

Hooker had classified plant species from Charles Darwin's famous *Beagle* Tierra del Fuego and Galapagos voyages and this started a life-long correspondence and friendship. Hooker was the first person Darwin took into his confidence when he wrote to him in 1844 that 'species are not immutable', later recording that Hooker was 'the one living soul from whom I have received constant sympathy'. As is well known, it was many years before Darwin could be persuaded to make public his revolutionary theory. He was halfway through the planned book in 1858 when Alfred Wallace's letter outlining similar conclusions reached him from Ternate. Darwin immediately renounced any claims to priority for his own 'outline of evolution' until Hooker reminded him that both he and Sir Charles Lyell had read his outline fourteen years earlier. Hooker proposed the simultaneous publication of both men's work. As Darwin wished to avoid any personal exposure, Hooker arranged for himself and Lyell to deliver the joint paper to the Linnean Society. It was given on 1 July 1858 – with Darwin at Down house and with Wallace in New Guinea. A furore both scientific and social ensued, with the

1817 · 1911

JOSEPH · DALTON · HOOKER
O.M., G.C.S.I., C.B., M.D., D.C.L., LL.D.
ASSOCIE ETRANGER OF THE INSTITUTE OF FRANCE
KNIGHT OF THE PRUSSIAN ORDER 'POUR LE MERITE'
SOMETIME PRESIDENT OF THE ROYAL SOCIETY.
FOR XX YEARS DIRECTOR OF THE
ROYAL BOTANIC GARDENS, KEW.
BORN AT HALESWORTH 30TH JUNE 1817
DIED AT WINDLESHAM 10TH DEC. 1911.

THE WORKS OF THE LORD ARE GREAT
SOUGHT OUT OF ALL THEM THAT HAVE PLEASURE THEREIN.

TOP The Biblical quotation on Sir Joseph Hooker's memorial plaque in St Anne's on the Green has a strange ambiguity: 'The Works of the Lord are great sought out of all them that have pleasure therein.'

ABOVE Sir Joseph Hooker's grave at St Anne's on the Green.

RIGHT The garden front of Cambridge Cottage, the Georgian house recognised by its fine Doric-pillared *porte cochère* on Kew Green. One of several houses used by members of the royal family, this only came to the Gardens on the death of the second Duke of Cambridge (King George III's nephew) in 1904.

arguments still rumbling round today. Just as Hooker had, in that instance, helped Darwin, now Darwin came to Hooker's rescue with support that not only lasted Darwin's lifetime but was continued by his family after his death.

With Darwin's financial and scientific help a revised and renamed *Nomenclator Botanicus* could go forward for use by botanists, and ultimately gardeners, worldwide. Staff were appointed but the first volume (of four) of *Index Kewensis* was not published until 1892. Hooker himself proofread the 375,000 specific names. Synonymous names, authors, and the publications where the names first appeared were also recorded for each plant. This invaluable resource has been kept current with regular supplements and today its twenty-plus volumes (with 1.6 million names) can be accessed electronically by botanists around the world.

Although rather unfashionable today, taxonomy must be seen as botany's core, its heart: plants must have names that define both their uniqueness and their relation to other species in order to be discussed at all. Only then can there be inquiries into what they consist of, how they work and why – studies that may begin as pure science can develop into practical and economic concerns.

Physiology and anatomy were being pursued more vigorously in European universities than in Britain but Kew was offered the opportunity to move into these fields, and later into chemical plant research, when Thomas Jodrell Philips-Jodrell (a private benefactor) offered to fund research facilities. The Jodrell Laboratory opened in 1877, its wide-ranging scientific programmes being encouraged by the recently appointed Assistant Director, William Thistleton-Dyer, whose academic background included professorships at the Cirencester Agricultural College and Dublin's Royal College of Science.

The year 1877 also saw two significant events in the Director's private life. Joseph Hooker's investiture as a Knight Commander of the Order of the Star of India marked his achievements within Kew but especially, as a memorandum to the Office of Works presented in 1881 records, Kew's activities abroad. Kew 'literally carries on all economic and scientific botanical work of the Empire under the direction of the various departments of the State'. Also in 1877, Thistleton-Dyer became Sir Joseph's son-in-law by marrying his daughter Harriet. The Hooker dynasty, albeit at one remove, looked likely to continue.

Sir Joseph had always hated administration duties and was clearly relieved when his Assistant Director gradually relieved him from its formal tedium, enabling him to concentrate on his scientific work. He retired in 1885 at the age of sixty-nine and for another twenty-six years worked meticulously on the floras of India and Ceylon: he was appointed to the Order of Merit (a signal honour in the gift of the Sovereign restricted to twenty-four members) in 1907. With Sir Joseph Hooker's death in his ninety-fifth year the Linnean Society was said to have lost the most renowned of all its Fellows and one of the most remarkable men who ever devoted his life to the advancement of science. Westminster Abbey was offered as a final resting place but his family chose St Anne's on the Green.

Thistleton-Dyer was appointed Director in 1885, after ten years in the shadow of his father-in-law. Now he had twenty years ahead of him in which to impress his own vision upon the institution. It seems almost invariably the case that, however academic a new botanic garden director may be, he cannot resist rushing out into the grounds to plan new works. Landscaping is the most delicious drug whose addiction can only be assuaged by immediate immersion followed by an impatient wait for the chosen effects to mature. Thistleton-Dyer was no exception. He was a difficult, autocratic man given to issuing detailed memoranda of criticisms to the senior garden staff and picking fights with anyone – royalty, politicians, civil servants – who opposed his views. Nonetheless it can be argued that he initiated and oversaw the changes that moved Kew from a Victorian enclave still in thrall to its royal past into the twentieth century, as was emphasised when Kew was transferred from the Office of Works to the Board of Agriculture in 1903. Several acres of lawn in front of Kew Palace and the separating ha-ha had already been transferred to the Gardens and in 1898 Queen Victoria had ceded the Palace itself, along with Queen Charlotte's Cottage and the surrounding lands. On the Duke's death in 1904 Cambridge Cottage became a wood museum.

Hardy plant collections were extended into a new Rock Garden and the old one by the Ice House was replanted with ferns; large donations of plants encouraging these developments. Superannuated gravel pits and spoil heaps, always the origin of contours on Kew's flat site, were pressed into service – creating a new Bamboo Garden, a Pond for aquatics beyond the lake (itself improved) and a Sunken Garden for species roses. Much of the Arboretum was replanned and the Rhododendron Dell replanted. Around 20,000 plant species and cultivars were in cultivation in 1894, of which 3,000 were hardy trees and shrubs; towards 600 different conifers are listed two years later. Swathes of flowering shrubs were underplanted with spring bulbs in the then current Robinson manner. Vistas were opened to the south.

Progress under glass was also striking. Separate houses were built for temperate ferns, filmy ferns and nepenthes – these carnivorous pitcher plants from South East Asia were of particular interest at the time and may be seen today in the Princess of Wales Conservatory. The Temperate House was finally completed, and its North Wing opened to the public in May 1899, a suitable celebration for the close of the century (no doubt Thistleton-Dyer's knighthood in the same year offered a further fillip). A considerable help to the success of plants in the houses was the Director's ban on the use of green glass when reglazing took place. It had long been believed that green plants would naturally do better if the light they received came through a green filter. It did, of course, reduce its power – a virtue only in high summer. And with Victorian London's appalling atmosphere pollution leaving a film of soot on every surface, further shading was seldom necessary. Indeed the problem of keeping glass clean became an increasing concern that only the Clean Air Acts in the 1950s effectively dispelled.

The last two decades of the nineteenth century saw the Royal Botanic Gardens fully embrace the role envisioned by Sir Joseph Banks and the two Hookers, that of being the epicentre of botanical activity for the whole British Empire and by extension the majority of the developing world. It was almost inevitable that colonial botanic gardens and agricultural experimental stations would be led by ex-Kewites and thus a network, a pre-computer worldwide web of expertise, encouraged exchange of plants and cultivation techniques throughout British India, Ceylon, the Far East, much of sub-Saharan Africa, Australasia and the West Indies. While the United States no longer belonged to the club the same opportunities and reciprocity occurred.

In Britain, officials from the Foreign Office, the India Office and the Colonial Office naturally turned to Kew in the search for new or improved crops to strengthen economics. Joseph Chamberlain, who as Secretary of State for the Colonies 1895–1903 effectively laid the economic foundations of the British Commonwealth, was a significant supporter of Kew, stating in the House of Commons: '. . . there are several of our important colonies which owe whatever prosperity they possess to the knowledge and experience of, and the assistance given by, the authorities at Kew Gardens. Thousands of letters pass every year between [them] and the Colonies.' The Director was formally appointed botanical adviser to the Colonial Secretary in 1902. It is interesting to note that, though Thistleton-Dyer's two immediate successors continued to fill the role, it was Chamberlain's developing support for the idea of 'Imperial preference', by which British Dominions and Colonies were to become self-contained economic units, that led to the gradual decline (although by no means cessation of) their dependency upon Kew. Stirrings of independence began to emerge.

LEFT Extravagant urns, swags and classical iconography embellish the main entrance to the Temperate House. The whole building was finally finished in 1899.

6

INTO A POST-COLONIAL WORLD
Kew in the Twentieth Century

I T IS PROBABLY A MISTAKE to read the faces of historical figures as epitomes of their age but it is a temptation difficult to resist. From Holbein's Henry VIII to Lely's Restoration ladies there is something that remains and is passed down to us. Kew's gallery of worthies is equally evocative. Some, it seems, are confected to confuse posterity – Philip Mercier's jolly *Music Party* of 1733 shows Frederick, Prince of Wales and his sisters happily making music together when in fact, gossip had it, they were barely on speaking terms. Others we need not doubt, such as Allan Ramsey's portrait of Lord Bute and Reynolds' Joseph Banks as confident young men in an age of elegance, and Lancelot Brown and William Aiton seeming happy with their acclaimed expertise and position in that stratified society. The Hookers, *père et fils*, seem to evoke Victorian values of considered probity while Thistleton-Dyer, martinet, seems to dare us to laugh as he poses in the uniform he had specially run up for himself as Inspector of Kew Constabulary. It is pure Gilbert and Sullivan, without the humour. Sir David Prain, the next Director, was perhaps the last of the icons, a handsome Edwardian figure like Elgar or Lloyd George, and one can read into his career both the certainties and the disillusionments of the first two decades of the twentieth century. First there was that 'golden afternoon' when King Edward VII (*Edward Dei Gra Britt Rex Fid Def Ind Imp* – by the Grace of God, King, of the United Kingdom & Ireland, Defender of the Faith, Emperor of India) was proclaimed on copper pennies and gold sovereigns alike. Then came the cataclysm of the First World War and its aftermath.

The serried roof-lines of the Princess of Wales Conservatory with the Victorian Campanile beyond. In the foreground is a bronze by Edward Paolozzi called *A Maxima Ad Minima* – from the greatest to the least, which surely refers to the world of plants.

David Prain was an Aberdeen- and Edinburgh-trained Scots doctor (medicine and botany were still closely linked) who worked first for the Indian Medical Service and then at the Royal Botanic Garden in Calcutta, as Curator of the Herbarium and then its Director. Calcutta had one of the earliest and most significant tropical botanic gardens; it had been set up in 1787 by the East India Company, warmly supported by Banks and thus intimately connected with Kew and the imperial network. Ray Desmond provides us with a typical Thistleton-Dyer quote, from when he learnt that Prain was to succeed him at Kew: 'India has recognised its debt by supplying Kew with a director'.

Though not a revolutionary by nature, Prain can be seen to have set Kew on to its modern trajectory by responding – albeit conservatively – to the trends of the times as well as initiating new projects. He showed concern for the welfare of Kew's traditionally unsung gardening staff, whose pay and conditions were decidedly ungenerous. There is a clear intimation from Banks's time that ambitious young gardeners should consider themselves fortunate to have the opportunity to work with unrivalled plant collections under knowledgeable foremen but shouldn't get above themselves. A little formal training had begun as far back as 1859 when lectures on elementary botany, chemistry and meteorology were offered, and a reading room had already been made available, all to follow, of course, after the then six-day Monday-to-Saturday working week. But government used these opportunities as an excuse to keep wages low: by providing them it could assert that the staff received free tuition. Following protests, questions were asked in Parliament. Prain viewed the situation less confrontationally and made changes. Four rather than five years' practical experience would be required for entrance, a wider lecture programme (though, still offered very early or late in the day) would be offered, and what were virtually labourers wages were to be considered 'a subsistence allowance' – a somewhat cosmetic confection but one which enabled Prain to also consider Kew an 'Imperial School of Horticulture'. While the grandiose title was

never officially used and 'International' should be substituted for 'Imperial', Kew's important role in horticultural education can hardly be exaggerated. There is no better training in plantsmanship than being in intimate contact with extensive labelled plant collections in the company of like-minded enthusiasts and for this Kew's modern School of Horticulture remains supreme. It is worth noting, now that men and women enter the Diploma Course without thought of proportional representation or affirmative action, that the first women gardeners appeared in 1896. Inevitably, there were concerns about how these three young ladies should be dressed, in order to comply with late-Victorian ideas of decency. The public had its say and the press chimed in but, as *The Times* pointed out, in brown bloomers, jacket and waistcoat, woollen stockings, boots and peaked cap at least they were not like 'the first gardener, Eve'.

The First World War caused a tenfold increase in women gardeners as men went to fight (more than thirty who lost their lives are commemorated in the Temple of Arethusa), as well as effecting on the ground an echo of Kew's eighteenth-century Kitchen Gardens. The Palace Lawn was ploughed up for potatoes (with a crop of 27 tons in August 1918); lettuces, cabbages, carrots and so on were grown in the Broad Walk beds and an archival photograph shows a splendid crop of onions ripening across Nesfield's Palm House terrace. The urns along the Pond wall look particularly incongruous in such a utilitarian scene. Today's more restrained pattern of beds there dates from their post-war reinstatement and a return to brilliant displays of spring and summer flowers. Modern-day interest in the ornamental potential of vegetables and a huge extension of what is considered suitable for bedding schemes has meant that designs frequently include plants grown for that 1914–18 war effort. The process began all over again, only twenty years later, with another Dig for Victory campaign. It is salutary and slightly depressing to note how in times of peace and easy availability of imported food and resources the country neglects its own ability to feed and care for its people with the result that agriculture and horticulture decline. But the moment trade routes are cut farmers and gardeners are wooed like debs at a dance – a story that is only too familiar today. At the start of Second World War hostilities a Kew scientist was immediately brought on to the Government's Vegetable, Food and Drugs Committee, set up to increase home production, and the Gardens began to grow commercial quantities of drug plants.

As we saw in Chapter 5, Kew initiated social change throughout the British Empire through its promotion of economic botany; without this, the pattern of the Empire would have been very different. But whereas the extrovert nineteenth century seemed certain of its

mission to civilise the world in its own Eurocentric image, the twentieth century was less pro-active in this regard. Kew helped to alter some of the hitherto unchallenged opinions during this rapidly changing century. Empire became Commonwealth, as Joseph Chamberlain had foreseen, and self-government, even independence – initially unthought-of – took the stage. Throughout the 1920s and 1930s more specific departments of government were set up to support the traditional colonial and foreign offices in new ways. The

Vegetable plots at Kew today, created and nurtured by diploma students from the School of Horticulture.

LEFT A wonderfully evocative
archival photograph of Harry Ruck
packing a Wardian case with *Hevea
brasiliensis* for the Far East.
Although the photo was taken in
the 1950s it could well have been
any time in the last 150 years.

RIGHT By the end of the Second
World War most of the glasshouses
were in a parlous state as the T-
range abundantly shows. The
curved wall to the left is of the old
Cactus House whose painted
desert diorama has been adapted
for the current collection in the
Princess of Wales Conservatory.

Imperial Institute at South Kensington dates from 1888 and, though initially concentrating on the physical sciences, as its work increased it gradually expanded to become the focus of colonial crop production, which had formerly been the prerogative of Kew. The Gardens' role inevitably was lessened.

Nonetheless, other aspects of plant science appeared: The Imperial Bureau of Mycology, investigating diseases of economic crops throughout the Empire, became established at Kew in 1919. Later, in 1927, the Empire Marketing Board provided funds for new Kew staff to be sent as roving advisers to overseas territories. It also paid for tropical greenhouse space specifically as a quarantine station in which crop plants could be ensured free of pests and diseases before being sent to their final destinations, usually colonial research stations. Rubber, bananas, cocoa and cassava came and went, often, until the 1960s, in those old-fashioned but still highly effective Wardian cases. Such practical quarantine work,

in essence Sir Joseph Banks's entrepôt vision, continued until 1986.

Whilst worldwide social changes led to a reduction in Kew's involvement in overtly economic activities abroad, its academic work increased. From the earliest times, knowledge of a region's flora was deemed essential to understanding its potential for colonial settlement and cultivation of economic crops, as well as the possible exploitation of other endemic plants. George Bentham and the Hookers spent much of their lives compiling such floras and their development of Kew's living and herbarium collections was expressly to support that work (hence their impatience with pressure from mere flower-demanding visitors and horror that Kew ever be thought of merely as a public park). Thus, with a few further extensions to the Herbarium and more staff, the riches of South Africa (resulting in the *Flora Capensis*, completed in 1925) and much of tropical Africa were studied in depth. This sort of work is

seldom, if ever, completely finite: each publication encourages further study and further collection; knowledge is accumulative. For example, while a two-volume *Flora of West Tropical Africa* was completed in 1936, a three-volume extension came out from 1954–72 – and there is no reason to suppose that this vast region will not produce further quantities of plants hitherto unknown with further compilation needed.

Indeed it is now recognised that towards 40 per cent of the world's biota – with many species still to be classified and named – is to be found in the canopy of tropical forests. A very different ethic from that of the imperial past dominates: for exploitation read conservation. This entirely laudable and indeed essential concept can breed its own misconceptions. It's all very well, some self-styled pragmatists insist, for conservationists to call, for example, for a ban on indiscriminate logging of tropical forests, but what about economic needs of the indigenous inhabitants? And

anyway is it not their country, their land? Kew's answer and that of responsible bodies and governments worldwide revolves around the word 'sustainable'. How much of any plant resource can be used without impairing regeneration? How can a developing country assert ownership of its flora to its own economic benefit?

In some ways the Gardens were in a worse state after the Second World War than after the First – and not merely because of the odd stick of bombs which blew out a lot of glass and rocked the Pagoda. The great Victorian plant houses, as well as much of the multifarious huddle that made up the T-range (which the Princess of Wales Conservatory eventually replaced), were showing their age and problems were compounded by the inevitable neglect of the war years. No buildings are more vulnerable to decay than tropical conservatories; inside there are high temperatures, outside the vagaries of the weather and the seasons – these combine to rot wood and rust iron. Additionally,

the atmospheric pollution of London – once the fog capital of the world as someone called it – pitted stone and darkened glass. The Palm House showed the worst effects, and in 1952 it was deemed unsafe and closed to the public. For a while its very existence was threatened and many feared this unique building might go the way of Philip Hardwick's great Doric Euston Arch at Euston Station and other nineteenth-century architectural gems. Many agree that ideological planners wreaked more havoc in the 1950s and 1960s than all Hitler's bombs – they had more time and could be both more selective and comprehensive.

Fortunately it was resolved to restore, repair, and reglaze the Palm House, which was ceremonially reopened in Kew's bicentenary year of 1959. But within twenty-five years the vast structure was again found unsafe. This time, however, there was no thought that

Burton and Turner's wonderful conception should not be assured for life. The conservation mantra for historic buildings, 'as much as necessary and as little as possible', was rigorously followed and meant replacing the wrought iron glazing bars with ones made of stainless steel and new toughened glass. This radical remedy should reduce problems of maintenance over the years to come.

To celebrate the physical rebirth of the building was entirely suitable: problems solved by all the panoply of modern engineering and state-of-the-art materials. But it was not just a building; it was a home for a vast range of living plants incapable of surviving outside in the English climate. Some were unique, many were rare and the problems of conserving the collection over the years of restoration were stupendous. Everything had to be moved out. Great palms that had taken a century to

reach the roof were felled, smaller specimens transferred to holding houses, duplicates donated to other botanic gardens; a key concept was to propagate so that no essential genetic material was lost. Anyone who has known the Palm House in all its manifestations since the 1950s cannot fail to rejoice in the present scene; greater age in this case having brought a youthful vitality that could not have been imagined.

Not only has the physical structure been renewed, giving this tropical forest in the north better light and heat than ever before but cultural techniques have moved forward marvellously as well, especially in the areas of composts and pest and disease control. Species of mealybug, red spider, aphids, white fly and thrips both native and exotic had always found the conditions to be insect heaven and gardeners waged continual war against them. Sprays in such a vast space could only ever be of

LEFT The splendid symmetry of the Palm House profile: the west door here is framed by a pair of Trachycarpus fortunei , the only palm generally hardy in Britain.

ABOVE A close-up of the eastern door of the Palm House, with elegant glazing.

local effect and even in the 1950s insecticidal smokes were in their infancy. The traditional remedy was to burn piles of tobacco (obtained from Customs and Revenue's impounded contraband stock – by a happy irony Kew had provided the seed back in the 1870s for much of East Africa's vast tobacco industry) and whilst it was always very exciting to start the conflagrations (damping flames to smoke in the innermost areas and retreating backwards to a door) the horticultural incendiaries invariably staggered out red in the face and coughing prodigiously. Not all the pests were so susceptible. Nicotine became replaced with smokes of DDT and various organo-phosphorous compounds. These were hailed in the 1960s and 1970s as the answer to gardeners'

prayers, only to eventually be shown as even more dangerous to users, with the additional problem that most pests built up resistance to them. Ever more noxious substances poured from the chemical industry in an attempt to find the best solution.

Today's mainly biological controls are both more environmentally satisfactory and effective. Thieves are set to catch thieves; larvae of parasitic wasps and other predators are released and though they require regular boosting it is hoped that an acceptable balance becomes established as, more or less, occurs in the wild. When particularly recalcitrant pests occur modern, less lethal, insecticides are used as targeted treatment and part of integrated control.

Climate control is assisted by the current planting arrangements which form mixed rainforest communities with herbaceous and shrub layers under the controlled shade of canopy trees. The groupings are geographical with South America in the centre block (where some especially tall palms from other regions are, out of necessity, also grown) with tropical Africa in the South Wing and Asia, Australia and the Pacific Islands in the North. Automatic mist sprays and humidity controls have added to the ability to provide what is – though the biggest at latitude 52 degrees north – a tiny encapsulation of these floristic regions which are so vital to the continuity of life on this planet. The Collection provides living plant material for research and study at Kew itself and other academic institutions and to the public gives pleasure and food for thought at every level. Literally at every level – visitors may climb the fifty-one spiral iron steps to the gallery to experience a monkey's-eye view of the forest canopy. They may also go down below ground, where for decades sweating Victorian stokers shovelled coal into roaring furnaces, to the modern Marine Display which offers more native habitats and plant and animal interactions.

A crystal palace in all but name. Magically floodlit, the Palm House floats above the water guarded, it seems, by a dozen golden lions – the Queen's Beasts transformed from their daytime Portland limestone.

Although the Palm House was especially vulnerable to decay because of the need for high temperatures and humidity, not surprisingly, Kew's other great conservatory, the Temperate House, was also badly run down by the mid-twentieth century and for the same reasons – age, lack of maintenance and depredations in the War. It had to be closed to the public in 1970 when glass and masonry began to fall; on days of high wind it became a hard-hat zone for staff working within. A comprehensive restoration was completed and the restored Temperate House was opened by the Queen in 1982.

As with the Palm House, while maintaining historical and architectural validity and appearing externally both bright and beautiful, the restored Temperate House had experienced a real renaissance. It will be recalled that it

LEFT In the Temperate House a pair of staircases take visitors to a balcony at canopy level. Their spiral forms reflects the tree-fern alongside.

ABOVE Temperate House roof-lines lead to the Pagoda towering above Cedar Vista.

had been built stage by stage, the north wing not until 1899 – almost forty years after the main block – and hence it had never appeared fully of a piece. Now statues and urns along the cornice were renewed or replaced, while improved glazing and ventilation together with a new heating system vastly improved growing conditions. Many species took on a new life, and South African Proteas flowered there for the first time. The opportunity was taken to rearrange the collections on phytogeographical lines; Asiatic plants in the north wing (the *Vireya* rhododendrons are particularly exciting), the Americas and Australia in the main block, and South African and Mediterranean species in the south wing and octagon. The great Chilean wine palm was, fortuitously, in its correct region, so it remained, shrouded in polythene, while the work went on around it. Raised from seed (on the tree they are like clusters of tiny coconuts the size of

walnuts) in 1846, just two years after Sir William Hooker was appointed Director, it is probably the biggest tree under glass in the world.

It was not just Kew's great buildings that were in need of physical restoration and plant collection renewal after the Second World War; the grounds needed similar attention. Not only had the lack of staff during the period of hostilities and subsequent years of austerity taken their toll but public attitudes to what were

Decimus Burton's Temperate House begun in 1861 but was not completed until 1899. It has all the components of a great eighteenth-century country house with its central block, balanced wings and linking octagons. Its design is strangely conventional after the soaring originality of the earlier Palm House.

considered pubic places had changed. More was expected. Traditionally Kew had resented any claims to right of entry – as the battles over opening hours attest – and perhaps one can read the erratically imposed one penny entrance fee from 1916 onwards to be an extension of this; little was demanded from the visitor who could therefore demand little in return.

It was fortunate that a new Director, (Sir) George Taylor, appointed in 1956, caught the mood of the times and realised that if Kew were to flourish it needed friends and supporters from all segments of society. Coming from the Natural History Museum where he had been its Keeper of Botany, he was a keen gardener and an academic botanist who had led plant collecting expeditions to the Himalaya and elsewhere. His wide-ranging ambitions for Kew came at a suitable time. The bicentenary was only three years away and with a celebratory royal visit in view a number of projects were underway – the Rose Pergola through the Herbaceous Ground (now called the Order Beds), copious planting of native

BELOW The Queen seems often to be at Kew in line of duty – to open this or inaugurate that. How suitable therefore that the newly restored Kew Palace should be the venue for a family party to celebrate Her Majesty's eightieth birthday.

RIGHT The gently curving Rose Pergola was constructed and planted in 1959. It adds structure and form to the otherwise herbaceous material of the Order Beds – by their nature out of sight in winter - and a feast of colour and scent in summer.

woodlanders around Queen Charlotte's Cottage, an extensive Heather Garden, Rock Garden extensions and so on. The Orangery was restored to its original role. All this work coincided with the Ministry of Agriculture setting up an inquiry into Kew's roles and *raison d'être*.

The Ashby Visiting Group (its Chairman Sir Eric Ashby, Vice Chancellor of Queen's University, Belfast) can be likened to that Lindley/Paxton study of a hundred years earlier. Again, a changing world had caused doubt to be cast upon existing institutions; were their traditional roles still valid, should they change and if so how? The Ashby Group submitted its report in 1958 but it was a further twenty-six years before its major recommendation – that of giving the Royal Botanic Gardens, Kew independence from direct government control – was implemented. Under the National Heritage Act, 1983, The Ministry of Agriculture (subsumed under Defra), which had had ultimate control throughout the century, passed responsibility of the Gardens to a new independent Board of Trustees with effect from 1 April 1984. Such innovation was by no

means a new idea. Even before Lindley and Paxton were brought in, the then Woods and Forests Department had mooted it and both Hookers pursued the idea; now as a non-governmental grant-aided institution it is in charge of its own destiny.

Another long-mooted hope became fulfilled. It had always been realised that certain groups of plants did not succeed in Kew's thin river-gravel soil – that the world's most prestigious botanic garden was formed on this particular site was rather more accident than design, and the land does have some natural disadvantages. These problems were compounded as London's atmospheric pollution and industrialisation across the river at Brentford took its toll on already stressed plants, especially conifers. Additional sites were sought and in 1924 the National Conifer Collection (now Bedgebury National Pinetum) was set up, in association with the Forestry Commission who owned the land at Bedgebury in East Sussex. It was laid out by Kew experts both to test species as potential timber crops and to demonstrate their ornamental and landscape potential. Any visit

The late-sixteenth-century façade of Wakehurst Place in Sussex. The house and 500 acres of land were donated to the National Trust in 1963 and leased to Kew two years later.

today, as the trees mature, attests to the visual effectiveness of the rides and clumps as laid out amongst established woodland seventy years ago. But still it was not an ideal solution.

There were flirtations with the Duke of Northumberland across the river at Syon – who could provide more land but only of the same quality – and with Major Dorrien Smith in the Isles of Scilly. There at Tresco the climate makes a garden like no other in Britain, like an extension of the Temperate House at Kew with the lid off. While there would be no surprise at flowering proteas there it was hardly a convenient location.

The Ashby Committee was still sitting when a much more appealing possibility turned up. Wakehurst Place is a great country estate on the High Sussex Weald about 50 miles south-east of Kew. Its then owner, Sir Henry Price, was concerned for the future of the elegant Elizabethan house, its gardens and wider estate. Negotiations with the National Trust led to its donation to the Trust, supported by a generous endowment. Acceptance by the National Trust gives inalienability to the property; it is safe for all time – always a major consideration for the donor – but it also means maintenance into the foreseeable future, with historic buildings an unpredictable drain upon resources. The Trust is also concerned, for cultural as well as economic reasons, that wherever possible an estate finds a role and earns its keep in a manner consistent with its historical integrity and traditions. Ownership by the Trust began in 1963 and the lease of Wakehurst Place – the house and towards 500 acres of land – to Kew two years later seemed a marriage made in heaven. The National Trust is relieved of much of the maintenance while retaining ultimate control – and the working farmland – while Kew is able to build upon already significant plant collections in a site extraordinarily different from the original Royal Gardens.

The story of any national institution develops in parallel to the story of the country itself, the ethos of the times interpreted and acted upon by statesmen on the world stage and by institutional heads back at home. Kew's intimate connection with the monarch in its early

days, with ministers of the crown, with an expanding empire (indeed being instrumental in such expansion) and government at all levels exemplifies this. If it were possible to show Kew's progress in graphic terms the line would be generally upward with a few serious blips. The national graph would be similar. Now, however, perhaps the integers have changed. The move to grant-aided independence might be seen as a release from direct government interference but of course it is no such thing. While freedom offers the ability to succeed it also provides the opportunity to starve. There is also a danger that economic considerations can start to impinge upon an institution's choice of research projects and published papers. With full annual government subventions no longer the case, funding this complex institution is an ongoing concern.

It might be thought that government at its higher levels, leaders of the country, with all the professional advisers, background materials and clear facts available to hand, would be able to take a more considered view. But it must be conceded that a cost/benefit analysis directed at such a multifarious institution as a botanic garden is not easy; in various ways, as has been shown, justification is a problem that has haunted Kew throughout its two centuries of life. It is not even very surprising. At any great estate in straightened circumstances it is the gardens that are first to go; the early signs being the decline of the boundary walls and fences; owners understandably trying to keep the roof from leaking. Government in charge of a country does the same.

Professor Bell, Director of Kew from 1981 to 1988, had to fight the increasingly fierce political mantra of 'if it doesn't pay for itself, chop it'. How can the Palm House recoup its costs, as was initially demanded? How does anyone compute the value of this property, its buildings, its trees, and its land? How much does a ten-storey scarlet pagoda cost these days? What price an orangery? There is, fortunately, a positive side to most change if only that it provokes thought. Dr Johnson's oft-quoted dictum about the prospect of being hanged on the morrow concentrating the mind wonderfully does have a certain

ghoulish truth and certainly the change to Kew's governance has made change and development more obviously ongoing activities. Kew did not go into retrenchment mode; in fact the 1980s were a period of encouraging developments, some long on the drawing board. The dramatic Palm House reconstruction has been described; the Princess of Wales Conservatory and the Sir Joseph Banks Centre for Economic Botany (between Kew Palace and the Herbarium) were built, with the latter opening in 1990. The museum by the Rock Garden that William Hooker had converted from King George III's fruit store became the formal base for the School of Horticulture and was officially opened in 1990. All these developments provoked royal visits, emphasising yet again, even in a less deferential age, the significance given to this unbroken strand of Kew's history.

It is not without significance that both Directors Sir Ghillian Prance (1988–99) and Sir Peter Crane (1999–2006) spent a proportion of their early careers in North America, at the New York Botanical Garden and the Field Museum in Chicago respectively. In the USA central government funding is not the norm; scientific and cultural institutions vie for grants from foundations, charitable bodies, local government departments, commercial interests and individuals. Since the 1980s such sources have become increasingly important in Britain. But traditions and tax concessions are different; it is unlikely that a well-wishing individual would fund, not once but twice, a major greenhouse restoration as Mrs Enid Haupt did, at a cost of millions of dollars, of New York Botanical Garden's huge Palm House.

The concept of such major institutions 'earning their keep' with various semi-commercial activities in addition to their primary scientific and cultural work also crossed the Atlantic. In North America it had become a normal part of any such institution, whether

The Sir Joseph Banks Building, though not open to the public, can be seen behind the Nash Conservatory. It houses the Centre for Economic Botany, a major concern at the Royal Botanic Gardens since the eighteenth century.

opera house, art museum or botanic garden, to promote a series of supporters' groups – the Curators' Circle, The Director's Circle and so on – committed to financial contributions at different levels. There is, of course, a concomitant progression of 'perks'. These groups organise fund-raising activities that relate to the *raison d'être* of the institution. Thus, a botanic garden might offer plant study tours, lecture series, plant sales and art exhibitions; probably all of these. Additionally, public auditoriums are part of any major visitor centre in the States, enabling botanic gardens to become a focus for the local and wider community. It is salutary to compare such current trends to the animosity to public involvement as expressed by Kew's nineteenth-century directors. And while the situation hardly changed for much of the twentieth century, eventually it had to, as survival was at stake.

In 1990 two initiatives were launched by Sir Ghillian Prance in response to the changing world: the Kew Foundation and Friends of the Royal Botanic Gardens. Originally separate, the two organisations were merged into one on 9 December 1994. Its role is to raise support for research programmes, garden maintenance and regeneration as central government grants decline. Equally important, it encourages the public's active involvement with the Gardens, the scientific work and the conservation work abroad. The general public often, at first glance, see Kew as a particularly upmarket park. Not only are there the usual park's beds of brilliant annuals (though throughout the country less than there used to be because of the same wave of 1980s economies that threatened to hobble Kew), there are the extensive woodlands and shrubberies and glasshouses of all sizes sheltering plants from all over the planet. And the plants are labelled. This is a window on the natural world, easily visited but not, perhaps, so easily comprehended. The work of Foundation and Friends helps members to comprehend and engage with the different strands that together form the Royal Botanic Gardens, Kew.

The developments of the last few decades exemplify two parallel convictions concerning the importance of Kew both as a place and of its work. The first can be

expressed through a line from an old hymn, 'live this day as 'twere thy last'; in other words, provide daily maintenance in trust for posterity. Without continual care – handed on from person to person, generation to generation – irreplaceable heritage (especially the living plant collections) could be irretrievably lost. The second is the belief that the knowledge inherent in the Living Collections, the Herbarium holdings and the written material generated from them has the potential, if suitably shared, to benefit Mankind. This, in essence, is the curatorial justification for all museums; they are not only accumulation of artifacts rich and rare, humble and domestic, they illuminate and preserve a people's culture. And they help to move culture forward if their significance can be suitably disseminated and shared.

As we saw in Chapter Five, the establishment of a museum at Kew in the 1840s was entirely befitting for the Victorian age of collections and discovery. But one only has to read Wilfred Blunt's jolly *In for a Penny* (which one could still do in well after its publication year 1978) to realise that such collections were no longer considered exciting phenomena. Mr Blunt nonetheless enjoys himself hugely, at one point commenting, 'there are things in bottles that would turn a man's stomach against pickles for a fortnight'. And in many ways one is sad to see such places all around the country as redolent of their age as the collections they proudly housed, now mainly dispersed. Only the ground floor of Decimus Burton's custom-built museum is still used as such, and has become very much a place of its time – as indeed it always has. Today's modish interactivity is a complete contrast to the old, wonderfully dotty, heterogeneous hotchpotch in mahogany display cases quietly waiting to bore or inspire, amuse or repel. Now you are invited to touch the screen, lift the flap and fill in the questionnaire. It is difficult for the museum – however inherently interesting the displays of healing plants, scents, and the story of rubber are – to compete with the living plants outside.

From the urn at the end of the Broad Walk, Kew's first custom-built museum is lit by a low sun against a stormy sky.

ABOVE Special seasonal displays are mounted every year at Kew. Amongst the most spectacular are the amazing diversity of autumn gourds and pumpkins, while in winter the Princess of Wales Conservatory becomes a bejewelled Aladdin's cave, full of orchids of every colour and form.

This is why, unfortunately, the museum is apt to be used as a wet afternoon add-on when one should make a frequent half-hour visit when still fresh. Then the extraordinary diversity of plant products, those of the past and those of huge economic value today, can give inspirations to viewing the Living Collections. Hooker's criterion for objects to be collected and shown is quoted there. They should be, he said, 'either eminently curious or in any way serviceable to man'. The wreath of blue water lilies from the coffin of the Pharaoh Rameses II, dating from 1200 BC and the sample of cotton cloth sent by James Brooke the White Rajah of Sarawak in 1850 are certainly that.

Not only economies but also the acceptance that there are other places whose museological role is more central caused Kew's ethnobotanical and ethnogeographical materials to be rationalised. The desire to show and share collections has led to the Natural History Museum, the British Museum and others now displaying some of Kew's materials. All is catalogued and available for study, so that knowledge of how certain plants were once used (along with where and by whom) and might be effectively used again is not lost. The belief in the usefulness of such knowledge – and the belief has been fully justified – led Sir Joseph Banks and the Hookers when directing collectors abroad to insist that such information be gathered. It occurs again and again on the labels of their herbarium sheets.

Such reaffirmation of any major botanic garden's *raison d'être* – the employment and exploitation of plants for the benefit of mankind – sensibly brings this part of Kew's story into current focus, but with a very different emphasis. The very word 'exploitation' has connotations that need to be left behind or at least put into context. The process was not all take and no give, although many early settlers in new lands would attest to that. All we might sensibly say to defuse an argument that has simmered for centuries is that we now have greater knowledge on which to base judgments that cannot fail to affect peoples and countries and continents. Exploitation need not be an unacceptable word if it is coupled with the key concepts of sustainability and conservation. These two concepts are at the core of what Kew stands for today and their importance are emphasised by Kew's maxim: all life depends on plants.

There is a further modern slant on museological concerns which is known modishly as interpretation. At its simplest level plant labels are that. If you know the language each plant's name, country of origin, serial numbers and date of planting can be read. Beyond individual labels, informative panels around the gardens describe special collections and put them into context. Similarly the seasons are celebrated by putting on extra (often wonderfully extravagant) displays of, for example, orchids in February in the Princess of Wales Conservatory or gourds and pumpkins in the Waterlily House cleared for the purpose in the autumn. Individual plants of note such as the historic *Ginkgo* and scholar tree from Princess Augusta's original botanic garden have their own interpretation signs. All are concerned to stress the significance, the beauty and the diversity of the world of plants.

RIGHT Unique plants deserve their own interpretation. Autumn – gold leaves of the primitive conifer *Ginkgo biloba* and (below) *Amorphophallus titanum*, the titan arum, which flowered for the first time outside its native Sumatra in 1889. Every few years the vast corm can be persuaded to push up its 5-foot high spathe. The smell is famously disgusting.

THE GARDENS TODAY
The Plant Collections Up Close

Woodland and Wild Gardens

I N THOSE MAGICAL ACRES around Queen Charlotte's Cottage, the native Surrey woodland – give or take a couple of exotic conifers – predominates. It's a traditional country cottage in a traditional country scene; straight out of Thomas Hardy, perhaps. But we know this scene borders on pastiche, an eighteenth-century idyll, contrived for a queen and set down in the wildwood. Under the native oaks, ash and birch a classic English ground flora has built up or survived. Presumably it never quite went away during the early Georgian menagerie years and the area of today's famous bluebell wood with its attendant grasses, bachelors' buttons, wood avens, self-heal and so on – all plants for which John Gerard botanised around London and wrote up in his 1597 *Herball* – has gone back, literally, to its roots. In our cliature can be very forgiving and hates a vacuum. As with all plants in all habitats, these woodlanders have adapted to a specific lifestyle that is reliant on the availability at the right time of those essentials of plant growth – light, moisture, warmth, air and nutrients. There is seldom much problem with the latter two but for the other essentials, given the huge dominance that forest trees exert, smaller plants have to make do with what little they can get.

The growth pattern of bluebells (*Hyacinthoides non-scripta*) is a perfect example of successful adaptation to habitat, as the sea of blue at flowering time testifies. Go to Queen Charlotte's Cottage in midwinter (though not Christmas Eve and Christmas Day, the only days in the year when Kew is not open) and already the fresh green

Queen Charlotte's Cottage in spring is surrounded by unfolding beech leaves above the bluebells, like something from a fairy tale. This is the rural idyll that Queen Caroline and the princesses enjoyed as a refuge from the formality of court life.

BELOW One of Britain's favourite plants. In England it is bluebell, in Scotland wild hyacinth; its unmistakable habit resembles a bishop's crosier or, in Edward Lear's spoof *Nonsense Botany*, *Manypeeplia upsidedownia*.

RIGHT Traditional cleft oak fencing leads visitors through Queen Charlotte's Cottage grounds under fresh spring leaves, with wild cherry, *Prunus avium*, in full flower.

spears of bluebell leaves are pushing through the ground. With the leaves off the trees, light conditions, even though it's winter, are as good as they'll get. And under the trees' protective canopy the worst of the winter cold is ameliorated: growth is slow but sure, boosted by food reserves stored in the bulbs beneath. Thus, in Geoffrey Chaucer's words, 'When that Aprille with his showeres soote/The droughte of March has pierced to the roote' not only are people ready to go on pilgrimages to Canterbury but plants leap into growth. In woodland they must be quick before the light is cut off by the trees' expanding foliage. The bluebells must expand their own leaves,

photosynthesise to build up the bulbs for next winter's food store, send up flower-spikes, encourage pollination and set seed. By July they are ready for a six-month rest below ground.

In temperate woodlands throughout the world a wonderful array of beautiful plants employ similar strategies to succeed in these same conditions. The trees that comprise the overhead canopy are different – oaks and hickories in North America, magnolias and maples in the Himalaya, for example, but they are exerting similar pressures on the plants beneath. Many of these forest-floor species are favourite garden plants and at

Kew the north-facing slope of the little artificial hill on which the Temple of Aeolus stands holds a wide selection. There is something in flower or of particular interest to see every day of the year. Woodlanders naturally nestle in deep leaf litter that has accumulated over centuries. To provide acceptable conditions Kew's thin and hungry soil has to be continually helped, so vast loads of leaf-mould and crumbly compost are added annually as winter top-dressing or incorporated into the ground before any new planting takes place. The wide-spreading roots of the canopy trees also take their considerable share and renewal is essential.

OPPOSITE AND ABOVE Not far distant in position but worlds apart in season. Views of the Lake demonstrate wonderfully the pleasures of the turning year, from winter minimalism to early summer lushness – here elderflower and yellow flags.

At the Temple of Aeolus a late, light snowfall disappears quickly
and within days wild daffodils carpet the ground.

LEFT Recycling is a current buzzword but gardeners have been busily doing it with compost heaps since Adam left Eden. Here, deep in the Arboretum, vast heaps of organic material from every part of the gardens are stacked, turned and turned again. A nutrient-rich crumbly compost is the best possible top-dressing for Kew's thin gravely soil.

RIGHT Contrasting leaf forms and silhouettes around the woodland garden below the Temple of Aeolus.

The Woodland Garden is not a garden for purists – plants are not arranged taxonomically (that happens across the way in the Order Beds) or geographically (as in the Rock Garden) but it is, of course, habitat specific: that is the point. The trees that make the woodland canopy are wide-ranging. One particularly interesting specimen is a huge black walnut, which in its North American home has a reputation for preventing the growth of other plants within its shade by exuding a chemical inhibitor from its roots. There seems to be no such problem at Kew where other things happily nestle up close.

Other noteworthy trees include one of the southern beeches, *Nothofagus obliqua*, which is native to Argentina and Chile and the Himalayan handkerchief tree, *Davidia involucrata*, perhaps Ernest 'Chinese' Wilson's most famous introduction. It's a dogwood relation with long fluttering white bracts hanging from the branches in June. Several trees are chosen for autumn colour, a festival that lasts here for many weeks. While the Japanese katsura tree (*Cercidiphyllum japonicum*) drops its ginger-pudding-scented leaves in October, the pair of Japanese coral-bark maples (*Acer palmatum* 'Sango-Kaku') remain clouds of butter-yellow for a further month and the *Acer davidii* is still summer-green. When at last it drops its leaves the pale stripes on its bark give winter interest. Best of all are the snake-bark maples, here making little more than a large twiggy shrub across the path, *A. pensylvanicum*, bright with Regency green-and-white-striped bark. It is satisfactory to think that George IV, when Prince Regent, might well have seen a plant of this; it was introduced to Britain in 1755, more than a century ahead of its oriental relatives.

A few rhododendrons indicate that the genus has a significant role in woodland gardens but this is not really their place: more and better are in Rhododendron Dell and especially, dramatically so, at Wakehurst Place. Other significant shrubs include *Mahonia* x *media* 'Charity', whose bright shuttlecocks of yellow bells enliven the end of the year, and *Corylopsis* with scented primrose 'catkins' in spring. Many magnolias might well have been included but they are elsewhere except for a fine specimen of the American swamp bay, *Magnolia virginiana*. Although it reached Britain long before the orientals (Bishop Compton was growing it at Fulham Palace in the 1690s) it has never become common in spite of its quiet charm; evergreen, with milk-white

LEFT Plants in the Woodland Garden. The first magnolia to be grown in Britain, the swamp bay (above) is seldom seen. It has one of the most delicious of all flower scents. A number of ferns provide lush green ground cover (middle). *Cyclamen hederifolium* (below) flowers in September without its marbled leaves; these follow and remain attractive throughout winter.

RIGHT *Cardiocrinum giganteum* is well named. This giant Himalayan lily can reach 12 feet high before opening its waxy fragrant trumpets.

OVERLEAF A grass path meanders through the Woodland Garden. A fine black walnut gives shade to woodland floor species from around the temperate world.

backs to the leaves and, for months, a progression of creamy fragrant flowers the size of pheasant eggs to whose olive colour they turn before falling.

The shrub layer is necessarily restricted in order to give pride of place to herbaceous plants, whose foliage is often as attractive as their flowers. As some go to rest others come into growth. Mediterraneans with marvellously marbled leaves – *Arum italicum* and *Cyclamen hederifolium* – appear in September as if they were responding to the autumn rains after a baking summer in a Tuscan cypress grove, a pattern which London's climate more and more resembles. *Cyclamen coum* soon follows and by January is in flower, gleaming rose and ruby amongst the leaf-litter. Several ferns are evergreen while *Matteuccia struthiopteris*, the shuttlecock fern, having lost its foliage even before the first frost, maintains charcoal-bronze fertile fronds throughout winter, like a marooned coral strand with the tide gone out. The bulb and tuber progression soon begins – rare species of snowdrops, anemones and hardy orchids – and goes on for months. There are lilies such as *Lilium martagon*, *L. hansonii* and that liliaceous monster from Himalayan hillsides, *Cardiocrinum giganteum*. The

immature plant displays attractive hosta-like leaves but the main show comes after the four to five years it takes to build-up its bulb. Then it shows off, shooting up a flower-spike up to 12 feet high within a couple of months. At the top it flaunts up to a dozen sweet-scented flowers. They are greenish white with purple stripes and look for all the world like those trumpets the angels are playing on the organ-case in King's College Chapel at Cambridge. With floral display over, upright seed pods the size of fat gherkins catch the attention until the following spring.

Less spectacular but no less arresting are the arisaemas, arum-relations with fingered leaves and cobra-hooded flowers often followed by spikes of scarlet berries. Their time above ground is strangely short: *Arisaema candidissimum* only appears at the end of June and is gone again by October. Not so the hostas, one of the commonest and most valuable garden genera, which provide lush foliage from May to October, bolstering this garden of rare delights.

The Order Beds

The early botanic gardens, as has been mentioned, were relatively small walled enclosures – a few acres at most – with plants grown in long narrow beds to facilitate observation and study. There were a few trees and shrubs if space permitted, though often they got out of hand when it was not known how big a new acquisition would grow; other shrubs and climbers were trained against the walls. This traditional pattern is still evident at Oxford Botanic Garden (founded in 1621) where, entering by the splendid Danby Gate designed like a Roman triumphant

Running between the Jodrell Laboratory and the Temple of Aeolus, the Rose Pergola bisects the Order Beds. Here, in the manner of traditional physic gardens, plants are grouped according to their family relationships, though it must be accepted that as research progresses these, and indeed some plant names, have to be changed.

arch, one is transported back into the seventeenth century. Much of the original layout remains *in situ*, as it does at the Chelsea Physic Garden, founded some fifty years later. There you can still ring at the students' gate in Swan Walk as you would have done in 1700.

The pattern was adopted at Kew by Princess Augusta and Lord Bute in the 1750s for her botanic garden, the enclosed cabinet of living curiosities in which strange new and rare plants were assembled. Here, John Hill began the compilation of the first *Hortus Kewensis*; the collection, dried herbarium specimens from it and the text becoming a mutually supportive triple-stranded way of taking botanical studies forward. Plants were grouped according to their uses or to their presumed relationships.

Princess Augusta's botanic garden is long gone and some of the actual site is now beneath the Princess of Wales Conservatory – hence the name. But that essence of grouping plants to facilitate comparison and study extends to much of modern-day Kew. With the gradual inclusion of the Pleasure Grounds and the acres along the Thames, trees have been able to be grouped family by family. This was a major preoccupation of both William and Joseph Hooker and that traditional pattern can still be enjoyed today with the Order Beds (to the north of the path that leads by the now-closed Cumberland Gate, round the back of the Temple Mound to Museum No 1). It is almost enclosed by the high boundary walls of Kew Road (with a collection of ivies growing on it) and that which screens the rock garden. To the north is the Jodrell Laboratory.

The land that is today used for the Order Beds was originally the Royal Kitchen Garden. Approximately a dozen acres in size it is easily twice the average size of early botanic gardens. More than 100 long beds 10 feet wide hold an enormous collection of mainly herbaceous species arranged by family. While its role is taxonomic the Order Beds can look stunning when in late summer great swathes of colour give the air of the prairies from which many of the species come. While some of the smaller plant families share a bed, others need more space. Such is the profusion of hardy herbaceous daisies throughout the temperate world (all told the *Compositae* (*Asteraceae*)

have around 25,000 species in 1,600 genera), the beds here can show only a representative collection of this amazing family.

Until a couple of years ago, the arrangement of the plants and beds was itself home-grown as it was devised by George Bentham – that prodigious taxonomist who wrote, among other things, the seven-volume flora of Australia as well as world monographs of several genera – and Director Joseph Hooker. Their joint publication, the *Genera Plantarum*, comprised the names and descriptions of all known genera of flowering plants arranged in a progression they adapted from earlier continental attempts at producing a 'natural' system of classification. Linnaeus's 'Sexual System', though revolutionary a hundred years earlier, was now recognised as artificial and mechanical, grouping plants as it did purely on floral parts.

With some relatively minor variations made in response to continuing studies, that arrangement of Bentham and Hooker (a binomial that is as botanically famous as Tate & Lyle or Laurel and Hardy in other fields) served Kew effectively for towards 150 years. But botany moves on and the Order Beds now demonstrate aspects of plants' family trees by an arrangement based upon genetic characteristics. Floral structures, leaf patterns and other morphological features, however visually similar and apparently diagnostic can seldom tell the whole story: that contained in the genes cannot be gainsaid.

While the Order Beds has this basic botanical function of demonstrating material from a living textbook laid out page by page in the soil from *Acanthaceae* to *Zygophyllaceae* (or would be if it were alphabetically arranged) it is also deserving of inspection from a horticultural point of view. A discerning gardener can pick out many highly ornamental plants well worth growing that will never be found for sale in conventional garden centres yet may be offered from seed in specialist catalogues.

Included in the Order Beds are the original wild species from which favourite garden plants have been bred and selected, North American *Aster* species which brighten autumnal state highways in New England, for example. These have given us the splendid array of Michaelmas

The heart of the matter. A peony species, its glowing petals enclosing a mass of saffron-like stamens. In China peonies have been used medicinally for hundreds of years, as well as being extensively hybridised and selected for garden worthiness.

daisies. The precursors of our common summer annuals can be found – petunias, marigolds and so on – often showing a delicate habit and poise that has been lost in the frantic breeding programmes obsessed with brilliance of colour and dwarfness. Others are species from which garden vegetables have developed.

At the south end of the Order Beds, one genus, *Paeonia* has been chosen to demonstrate this process of horticultural selection. It has its own family, the *Paeoniaceae*, closely related to the stonecrops. There are some thirty wild species mainly from Europe, Asia Minor and the Far East with just a couple in Western North America. *Paeonia officinalis*, as its name suggests, is a classic physic garden plant once used for 'the Epilepsy, Apoplexy, & all kinds of convulsions & nervous afflictions, both in young & old'. In fact, peonies are extremely poisonous; nonetheless the Chinese peony, *P. lactiflora* and the moutan or tree peony, *P. suffruticosa* are still being used today in traditional Chinese medicine for a wide range of complaints. These species have all been used and interbred to produce a stunning diversity of garden plants which can be compared here with their parents and also with exquisite species which often have a limited distribution in the wild. Several are island endemics, such as *P. clusii* from Crete, *P. rhodia* from Rhodes and *P. cambessedesii* which is confined to the Balearic Islands.

The high south- and east-facing walls and the borders at their feet are used for a number of note-worthy plants – not systematically arranged – that either need support or enjoy the protection afforded. At the corner where they meet is a fine evergreen with wide wavy leaves, white-bloomed underneath, with huge creamy bowls of flowers: this is the seldom-seen *Magnolia delavayi* from Yunnan. Near by is *Colquhounia coccinea*, a tall scarlet-flowered sage-like shrub from India. Worthwhile watching out for is the strange Mexican, *Amicia zygomeris*. Though sub-shrubby in the wild, here it starts from ground level each spring. By September it is 8 feet high;

each leaf has two pairs of leaflets which fold themselves away tidily at night, young ones protected by ear-muff-like stipules. Typical yellow broom-flowers eventually appear. It's a caricature of a pea, as if invented by Edward Lear for his *Nonsense Botany*. Nearby is the Brazilian *Feijoa* (*Acca*) *sellowiana*, a robust evergreen with grey felted backs to its leaves. Related to guavas and therefore in the myrtle family, it is grown commercially in California as 'pineapple guava'. It fruits only erratically at Kew against this warm wall, and these yellow-green banana-shaped pods are preceded by flowers with a central boss of scarlet stamens and four deliciously sweet crystalline petals. One must not get caught.

This is the border to visit in winter too; while *Zygomeris* has been cut down and *Colquhounia* is leafless, *Feijoa* keeps its leaves, clumps of the Algerian iris, *I. unguicularis*, are purple-bright from December to March and wintersweet, *Chimonanthus praecox*, wafts its perfume upon the chilly air.

The Grass Garden and Davies Alpine House

Only in the last few years have grasses become a frequent and fashionable part of garden design, except, of course, when rolled and cut as lawn – to be walked on not looked at. But now the diversity of habit, size, type of flower-spike and colouring, combined with animated tactile and textural qualities, brings them into innumerable garden schemes. Most follow designers such as Dutch Piet Oudolf or James van Sweden from the States, using swathes of grasses in company with herbaceous perennials to build up naturalistic if not natural associations that evoke the Eastern steppes or the prairies of mid-America.

Kew's Grass Garden long predates today's fashion. There was an extensive collection arrayed in beds of concentric circles back in the 1820s; grasses were an early botanical enigma. The present site, north of the Rock

Winter at Kew. Roses on the pergola have been pruned and the best growths tied in for next year's flowering whilst herbaceous plants in the Order Beds are cut down and divided as necessary. The ground gets a dressing of rich home-made compost. Even in snow Hamo Thorneycroft's *Sower* keeps to his task. This could well be a motto for Kew – the world of plants is never at rest.

OVERLEAF A low winter sunset brings the plumes of *Cortaderia* and spikes and tassels of a mass of different hardy grass species into prominence. Beyond are the triple flues of the Princess of Wales Conservatory.

Garden, was developed in 1963. Today its focus is the fine bronze statue presented to Kew by the Royal Academy in 1929. Sculpted by Sir Hamo Thorneycroft in 1886 and placed on a Lutyens plinth, *A Sower* strides forward casting his seed-corn with a sweep of his right hand as if straight out of the Biblical parable: 'A sower went forth to sow, and as he sowed some seed fell upon . . .'. At Kew all falls on good ground and behind and around him are the cereals or grains – though naturally no rice – that are the staple foods of most of mankind since early times: barley, wheat, oats and rye from the Old World, maize from the New as well as widespread subtropical millets and sorghums.

Four big corner beds hold a huge collection other grasses – *Gramineae* (*Poaceae*) is one of the largest families of flowering plants with about 675 genera containing 10,000 species strewn as if by some celestial sower throughout the world. Many are of vast economic importance; as well as the cereals think forage for farm stock, think sugar cane. At the back are clumps of *Arundo donax*, the giant reed of southern Europe so often used as a necessary windbreak against the Mistral in the Camargue and also in the Po Valley; at Kew it reaches 15 feet in a season. There are silvery plumes of *Cortaderia*, the so-called pampas grass, little lockets of quaking grass

Grasses, grasses everywhere. Not only do the beds hold a wide range of them but, of course, the paths between them are made of yet other species. The *Gramineae* (*Poaceae*) is one of the biggest plant families distributed around the world, succeeding in almost every habitat. It is probably the human race's early domestication of grasses, turning them into agricultural crops, that has enabled it to be so successful. The Grass Garden demonstrates the huge range of forms, annuals and perennials, all bearing aloft the typical inflorescence of small, highly-specialised florets.

(*Briza*) and *Chasmanthium latifolium*. All these grassy seed heads are products of variations on the theme of effective pollination by wind. There are a few clumps of representative bamboos but Kew's main collection of this great group of woody grasses has its own site over towards Rhododendron Dell. Tropical grasses can be found in several of the glasshouses: sugar cane, lemon grass and vetiver in the nearby Princess of Wales Conservatory and giant bamboo (*Gigantochloa verticillata*) in the Palm House, which is still not high enough to take its full growth. They can grow to heights in excess of 25 metres and at a rate of up to a metre a day.

Aligned on the Sower's stride is the revolutionary Davies Alpine House at the north end of the Rock Garden. From this angle it reminds one of an early nineteenth-century cocked hat of the shape that the Duke of Wellington wears on all his statues; from the side it's Sydney Harbour Bridge writ small. The first

As if beckoning us on from his Grass Garden, *A Sower* faces the Davies Alpine House. This unique design provides an energy efficient environment for growing high alpine or high latitude plants and others that are intolerant of an English climate and so cannot be grown outdoors. Its south door (right) gives on to a viewing platform that overlooks the Rock Garden and its pools.

LEFT ABOVE Sandstone blocks support raised beds at the north end of the Davies Alpine House. This continues the pattern of the Rock Garden itself with the addition of a roof and climate control for especially difficult-to-grow plants.

LEFT BELOW From the New World *Alstroemeria* (Peruvian lily) and white and yellow mariposa lilies (*Calochortus* species) enjoy the conditions provided.

RIGHT In the Rock Garden wild tulips and fritillaries from the eastern Mediterranean and Asia Minor, and erythroniums like diminutive Turk's-cap lilies – this is one of the American trout lilies – can be given the care they require. Later, perhaps they can be moved to the more rough and tumble conditions of the Woodland Garden to naturalise as if in the wild.

alpine house at Kew was built in 1887 and twice extended. It was a conventional narrow span greenhouse with gravelled benches down each side and a central path. The requirement then, as now, was to be able to display species from high altitudes that are unsuited for outdoor cultivation in the nearby Rock Garden. Many have bulbs as corms, or tubers as below-ground resting organs that need perfect ripening if they are to succeed. Difficult crocuses, tulips, irises and so on can be grown in pots plunged into gravel beds covered by glass lights to protect them, usually, not from cold but excessive moisture. They can be brought out for display when they are in flower. Many difficult high alpines from mountain screes and moraines that grow as tight cushions of minuscule leaves can be equally intolerant of damp. Others have evolved intensely hairy leaves as protection from desiccation on exposed mountains and rock faces and those too need protected cultivation.

The Davies Alpine House is light years away from that traditional design. It replaces a rather fine pyramidal structure completed only in 1978 that was in the way of a major Jodrell Laboratory extension in 2006. Techniques for the successful cultivation of especially difficult plants were learnt there, for example species from the High Arctic – which survive a nine-month permafrost winter followed by a sudden burst of summer light and warmth – grew on refrigerated benches where their native habitat could be to some extent replicated: Spitzbergen in Surrey, Baffin Bay-on-Thames. Less than thirty years on technology has moved forward markedly, and a sustainable, energy-efficient growth environment has been created. Its height causes air which has been naturally cooled in an under-floor labyrinth to be circulated around the plants like mountainside breezes. Its south door opens on to a deck overhanging a wide pool to be drawn out of the building and the Rock Garden proper with rills and terraces planted geographically, showing a vast diversity of upland species. There is floral interest here for twelve months of the year.

LEFT AND ABOVE There have been rock gardens of greater or lesser success at Kew since the 1840s, using a variety of stone on various sites. The current version inhabits a sandstone-lined valley between the Order Beds and the Princess of Wales Conservatory where a diversity of natural habitats can be simulated. Plants adapted to living on rock faces and arid screes, on moraines or moisture-rich alpine meadows, give interest here throughout the year.

The Queen's Garden

No doubt Mr and Mrs Samuel Fortrey had a garden on the north front of their grand new Dutch House when, as a successful City merchant, Fortrey moved his family to the country in 1631. There were horticultural Joneses to keep up with (not least Sir Henry Capel next door who, John Evelyn recorded after a visit, had 'the choicest fruit of any plantation in England'). The views from the windows and the pillared loggia at the back stretched to the river, the wooded eyots (islands) and the little village of Brentford on the other bank. But it was all rather elbowed aside a hundred years later when Sir Henry's old house was turned into the White House for Frederick, Prince of Wales and though the Dutch House later became Kew Palace it was always a refuge from, rather than a centre of, glittering court life. Its gardens were similarly low key.

Not until a partial restoration of the palace and a royal visit to Kew in its bicentenary year of 1959 was there any serious commitment to use the unconsidered area at the back, a potentially charming spot. It was provoked by typically acerbic remarks from the Duke of Edinburgh looking out from the palace on to superannuated allotments and ash heaps. The Director took up the implied challenge and Her Majesty returned ten years later to open the Queen's Garden, which at last put Kew Palace into a suitable and delightful context. Now that the house has been fully restored and is open to visitors that context can be properly appreciated, its domestic scale enjoyed from the house itself. From the front door a stone-flagged passage leads straight ahead, with small panelled rooms right and left, to that little loggia a few steps above ground level at the back. It is as if one has opened a seventeenth-century treatise on the art of garden-making and this is its frontispiece. Yew hedges left and right continue the house walls for a hundred yards, then curve inwards to form an apse. Five stone terms (classical busts that grow from their plinths), white against the yew's darkness, give an architectural

The Queen's Garden was opened by Her Majesty only in 1969 but it was consciously designed in the seventeenth-century manner to be in accord with the north front of seventeenth-century Kew Palace, whose little-pillared portico enjoys this view. Gravelled walks, formal box-edged beds planted variously with plants that would have been used at the time are all enclosed by high yew hedges. Italian terms, well placed against the yew – white on near-black – seem to look on approvingly.

RIGHT Lavender in the Queen's Garden.

BELOW AND OPPOSITE In May one of the most beautiful sights in all of Kew is the Queen's Garden laburnum tunnels that frame the Nosegay Garden. It is as if the legend of Danae and her shower of gold were made flesh – or actually flower.

frame. These terms, sculpted for Frederick, Prince of Wales in the 1730s, after a decidedly peripatetic life have found their perfect home. A parterre of geometric box-edged beds fills the space; they are planted with purple sage, lavender cotton and *Lavandula dentata*. Crown imperials thrust through in early spring. A Renaissance well-head makes a central feature with, beyond, a rectangular pool into which water splashes gently from a copy of Verocchio's *Boy with a Dolphin*.

Obviously, the Queen's Garden is a pastiche, a twentieth century take on a seventeenth-century ideal which Samuel Fortrey might have considered highly fashionable; to King George on the other hand it would have been very old hat.

For Kew it was quietly revolutionary, celebrating a form that long predates the Royal Botanic Gardens themselves. It takes the opportunity, therefore, to be 'not just a pretty face' but to tell two stories, one of a fashionable garden style almost entirely swept away by 'Capability' Brown and his followers of the landscape school, and one of a time when wild and common garden plants were considered to be a natural support to human existence, herbs in the widest sense of the word. This attitude remains valid today throughout Kew.

The Garden offers other pleasures. To the south, two sets of five steps at gaps in the hedge lead to a raised terrace walk which surrounds the apparently sunken

Views of the Nosegay Garden behind Kew Palace. In summer the beds are a tumble of cottage garden plants all of which were known to be popular in the seventeenth century. Their labels give not only their Latin and vernacular names but also references from those two contemporary classics, Gerard's *Herball* and John Parkinson's *Paradisi in Sole Paradisus Terrestris*.

Nosegay Garden (it is of course virtually at basic ground level), with an arched laburnum tunnel on three sides. The garden grows only plants that were cultivated in the seventeenth century and, as if leafing through a contemporary gardening treatise, labels add suitable quotations from Parkinson's *Paradisi in Sole Paradisus Terrestris* and Gerard's *Herball*, the expanded second edition of which came out just two years after the Dutch House was built. There is also a mulberry tree already taking on its typical impression of old age and a little courtyard with trained figs and vines.

North of the main garden and parallel to it is a wide flagged path shaded by pleached lime trees, making a

pair of hedges on stilts. They are underplanted with hardy cyclamen, whose pink flowers in August and September, then white and green marbled leaves till early summer give almost year-round interest. A fine stone urn and the statue of an epicene flute-playing youth in a fig leaf close side vistas and at the end of the lime alley a spiral path leads up a mount clothed with clipped box. From the blue and gilt ironwork gazebo at the top are views all round – through plane trees to where the towpath once made the river a vital commercial corridor and back across the Queen's Garden to the Palace. To the north-east are the modern Sir Joseph Banks Building and the Herbarium, buildings that are not generally open to the public.

It is worth wandering in that direction through the extensive plantings of native woody plants. Clumps of hazel demonstrate the once-important country technique of coppicing – where plants are cut to the ground successionally, usually on a ten- or twelve-year rotation, and the strong straight shoots arising from the base are

The white marble *Boy with a Flute* closes a side vista in the Queen's Garden on the river front of Kew Palace. Curving Dutch gables on the attic storey give the house it original name. They and the windows beneath are capped with pediments hinting at the formal classicism that was to dominate architectural practice throughout the eighteenth century and in which Kew is so rich.

RIGHT Small, fragrant yellow flowers of *Jasminum fruticans*.

OPPOSITE East of the Orangery is the Secluded Garden. Opened only in 1995 it is concerned to show how plants, in association with moving water the weather and the changing seasons, affect all our conscious senses. Not only sight but touch, hearing and smell are provoked. Only taste is missing.

RIGHT Small, fragrant yellow flowers of *Jasminum fruticans*.

used for tool handles, hurdles, chair splats and so on. Ash, sweet chestnut and other species also respond to coppicing, which remains an important tool for maintaining a rich herbaceous woodland flora. Here, too, are Britain's few evergreens, including fruiting yews full of quarrelling blackbirds in late autumn. By the Banks Building are two quiet moat-like ponds. The upper pond is animated by a playing fountain, from where water falls into the lower, which is so still as to be entirely covered in duckweed – an eau-de-nil carpet only momentarily spoiled by a coot or two paddling through.

Back towards the mount, railway sleeper steps lead to Kew's Bee Garden, also on a raised area. There are other colonies within the Gardens but the two hives here are home to a relatively quiet strain of bees bred in New Zealand so that visitors can approach closely and safely. The hives, one the traditional white pagoda-like design introduced in the 1880s and known as a WBC (after its inventor William Braughton Carr), are set back behind low wattle hurdles and a rosemary hedge and surrounded by acclaimed bee-forage plants such as borage, lavender and sage. Not surprisingly Kew's honey is extremely varied, coming as it does from an unprecedented range of flowers. Just how the bees go about their business can be seen in the glass-sided observation hive set up for children in Climbers and Creepers, south of the Palace beside White Peaks.

The Secluded Garden

The Secluded Garden is another of Kew's domestic spaces, a garden one would be pleased to own, flowing out from French windows perhaps or on from the lawn. It was Maggie Jencks who, as she and her husband Charles Jencks were creating their amazing 'Garden of Cosmic Speculation' in Scotland, determined to design within it a garden for all the senses including, as she insisted, 'nonsense'. Kew's essay on this theme does not intentionally cover that sixth sense but it is happily present to anyone with a spot of imagination. The elegant sculpture *Seven Slate Towers* by Daniel Harvey in the pleached lime rondel seems to oscillate with light as it drips water down layer by layer; here slate no longer offers protection from the wet but is its very producer. Natural plant forms can also lean towards the nonsensical; though if we accept, as we must, that organisms are ideally adapted to their habitats, even the most apparently bizarre have their reasons. Here in close-up (and hence even more extraordinary than across the Palm House Pond where it is more in scale) is *Gunnera manicata*, the so-called giant rhubarb. Stout prickly stalks 10 feet high support great webbed leaves – umbrellas for elephants! This is a plant of sub-tropical Brazilian swamps, settled in Surrey.

The basic four senses are continually provoked and

LEFT AND RIGHT Human lifespan seems almost transient when compared to trees. These, a still elegant maidenhair tree and an anthropomorphically crippled scholar tree, both knew Princess Augusta personally. Lord Bute obtained them for her from the Duke of Argyll's arboretum not far away at Whitton Park in Surrey.

RIGHT BELOW The wisteria, still flowering prodigiously every May, was originally planted on the east wall of Sir William Chambers's Great Stove, long gone.

each is encapsulated in a poem engraved on a plaque. Sight, for most of us, is so omnipresent that the miracle of its existence is inevitably taken for granted. The Secluded Garden concentrates the mind to make us see anew just as the low hedges of *Sarcococca* in the rondel offer sudden traces of sweet vanilla scent in February. The insignificant flowers have to be searched for. On those blessed days when the wind direction sends Heathrow's monsters another way, sound comes gently from a flowing rill and the whispers in the bamboo grove. Soft furry leaves, hard shiny cuticles and great water-worn boulders all offer tactile sensations for the sense of touch.

The Secluded Garden, which is planned as a linear progression – a royal progression of the senses – cleverly screen a service area. It is best entered from the south after marvelling at two of Kew's oldest inhabitants planted for Princess Augusta around 1760: the 80-foot-high maidenhair tree and, still in perfect health, the aged scholar tree, arthritically bent over its zimmer-frame of steel bars (though if you stand back you can admire its perfect bonsai proportions). Also worth

pausing by is a vast wisteria which has long outlasted William Chambers's Great Stove on whose east wall it once grew, and whose site it marks. These orientals evoke the intense celebration of the senses that Chinese philosophy and gardens exemplify.

At the far end of the Secluded Garden the path through the bamboo grove suddenly offers a view of another veteran tree, *Pinus pinea*, planted in 1846. This is the stone pine, the 'umbrella open' contrasting so dramatically with the 'umbrella closed' cypresses in the gardens of the Villa Borghese in Rome.

The Secluded Garden is a recent addition to Kew's pleasures. It is not a botanical collection *per se* – all of its plants grow in other places and other contexts within the Gardens – but is concerned to involve the visitor, contemplatively, in the diversity of plant forms. A small conservatory whose doors open silently on one's approach offers a further range of species that a little warmth permits – passionflowers, scented jasmines and so on. The conservatory has, on occasion, been used to host artists' works commenting on the world of plants. One show took Wardian cases as its theme. 'Treasure Trove', as it was entitled, assembled in a number of small reproduction cases plant-based artifacts from around the world; reminding visitors yet again, and necessarily, of man's dependence upon the vegetable kingdom.

The Duke's Garden

Behind Hamo Thornycroft's *A Sower* an old south-facing brick wall shelters the Duchess Border, which contains a splendid assortment of subtropical plants that certainly have no right to flourish at this latitude. It has been so for very many years but London's increasingly warm microclimate makes for further surprises. *Caesalpinia japonica* has long been resident, with huge heads of bright yellow in summer – only the seed pods that follow show it to be obviously a legume. Admiration should be tempered by the thoughts of blood shed by whoever pruned it in winter, as this is one of the most wickedly-armed garden ornamentals. Near by its South American cousin *C. gilliesii* sports great buttercup-like clusters with brushes of long red stamens to each flower. Once called *Poinciana*, it is closely related to the brilliant flamboyant tree, a common street tree throughout most of the tropical world and quite out of context here.

The Duchess Border is a progression of horticultural improbabilities showing how a protected site with well-drained soil can extend the boundaries of conventional frost-hardy presumptions. There are climbing daisies, mutisias, from Chile; *Sophora tetraptera*, which Joseph Banks collected on the *Endeavour* voyage and was chosen as New Zealand's national flower, Californian *Ceanothus*, Chinese *Pittosporum tobira* with its delicious scent of orange blossom and so on. But a botanic garden needs always to display more than just a wall of trophy heads, however exciting, so the front of the Duchess Border holds a definitive collection of lavenders. This is a far more extensive genus than most of us realise, happily content with a variation on the Gertrude Stein mantra of 'rose is a rose is a rose'. The three dozen or so species of *Lavandula* spread far beyond the Mediterranean where our common herb-garden plants are native, into the Canaries, India and Africa. One Kew botanist has produced the definitive study with a Cambridge colleague, *The Genus Lavandula* (Upson & Andrews, 2004), and many are grown here, some with untypical fern-like leaves and even un-lavender scents.

The Duchess's Wall hides the Duke's Garden. At first it seems to be a very different Kew, one might almost be in the garden of a well-heeled country rectory (almost inevitably today an 'Old Rectory'). The generous shallow bay window of its drawing room, the old London stock brick walls, the glimpse of St Anne's tower beyond, all harks back to a time of understated privilege, the house perhaps of a Trollopian Rural Dean. In reality, this was the home of Adolphus Frederick, Duke of Cambridge and

OPPOSITE The propped-up stone pine dates from 1846. Native to southern Europe, this tree species is the source of pine nuts, which are obtained from the big egg-shaped cones.

ABOVE With its broad bay windows giving on to swathes of flowers and wide lawns under mature trees, Cambridge Cottage has an aura of a particularly prosperous country rectory. A glimpse of the tower of St Anne's on the Green adds to that ambience.

LEFT In the Duke's Garden. *Magnolia* x *soulangiana* 'Rustica Rubra' (above), a fine selection of the well-known hybrid of two Chinese species; the hop hornbeam, *Ostrya virginiana* (below), with its bladder-like fruit clusters. Bishop Compton grew this tree at Lambeth Palace in the 1690s.

RIGHT As well as offering a fine show for much of the year (hellebores are a winter treat), The Duke's Garden is used to show how Kew's thin sandy soil with low rainfall can manage with minimal irrigation.

youngest son of King George III; only the *porte cochère* added to the front of the long low house on the Green hints at royal grandeur. The Garden is dominated by a tall black pine; to the east are fine examples of the Persian ironwood (*Parrotia persica*) and *Magnolia* x *soulangiana* 'Rustica Rubra'. *Parrotia* is a witch hazel relation with fuzzes of red stamens in late winter and often superb autumn leaf colour. Across the garden, sheltering a summer house, is a North American tree known there also as ironwood (indicating again the need for clear botanical nomenclature), *Ostrya virginiana*. The fruit clusters look like hops but the green catkins, already well developed by November, indicate its hazelnut relationship.

This corner is now a Gravel Garden, sponsored by Thames Water, to demonstrate how economy in water use does not necessarily lead to uninteresting planting. On the contrary – here are plants from the Mediterranean maquis and other dry areas, some with silver aromatic leaves and many grasses. There are also spring and autumn bulbs, which in the wild avoid the heat of summer by retiring to resting organs below ground. Interpretive panels in the summer house emphasise saving water, watering wisely, choosing suitable plants and using soil mulches. HRH would surely have approved. He was one of those people, happily uninhibited by the conventional social sieve between brain and mouth, thought and utterance. At Matins in St Anne's across the road one summer Sunday the Vicar

offered prayers for rain: 'Oh God, my dear man,' said the Duke loudly, 'How can you expect it to rain with the wind in the East?'.

The inner garden around Cambridge Cottage capitalises upon the sheltering walls, and the current planting emphasises tropical-looking foliage: bananas, tree ferns, the South African *Melianthus major* and others. Visit here in summer as many of these are wrapped-up in winter. In the main garden around the lawn are wide herbaceous borders with swathes of early flowering hellebores under the *Parrotia* and with peonies complementing the magnolia. Opposite, the high-summer border becomes a palette of blues with delphiniums, agapanthus and catmint; then follows the oranges, reds and russets of autumn.

This chapter has discussed some of the most significant garden areas of Kew, but while moving from one to another of these others unfold to be enjoyed in their season, for instance the Lilac Garden, the Azalea Garden, Rhododendron Dell or the Cherry Walk. Throughout its broad acres Kew's generic collections of trees and shrubs, though some are now more fully represented in the more encouraging environment of Wakehurst Place, demonstrate the diversity of temperate woody plants that succeed in Britain's climate. These are living textbooks for botanists, gardeners, artists and all who visit to meet the world of plants. They are a multi-layered, many-textured resource, assembled over three centuries and still evolving.

Alfred Noyes's unexciting little poem 'Go down to Kew in lilac-time (it isn't far from London)', especially when it appeared on the District Line trains, used to raise visitors' expectations unnecessarily. Lilacs were never a speciality. However, today's Lilac Garden is both a treat for the nose and eyes as well as demonstrating – with suitable interpretive panels – the origins and breeding developments of a popular genus over 150 years.

241

⟦8⟧

ENQUIRY INTO PLANTS
Science on the World Stage

N O BETTER HEADING for this chapter can be found than the title Theophrastus coined for what was the first work of plant classification in Western literature, developed 300 years before the birth of Christ. In *Enquiry into Plants*, Theophrastus, pupil of Plato and Aristotle, described towards 500 plants noting resemblances and differences. 'Inquiring into plants' encapsulates precisely the role of Kew's scientific wings – the Herbarium, Jodrell Laboratory, Library and Archives.

As we have seen, in the nineteenth century Kew led the world in taxonomy and systematic botany; with Bentham and Hooker on the spot and Darwin and others in support this is not surprising. But plant physiology and chemical-based research trailed behind continental universities. To begin to correct this imbalance the original Jodrell Laboratory, privately donated, was built in 1877. The one-storey brick and tiled building with a bay window in the front, as Ray Desmond records, 'could easily have passed for a municipal branch library or working men's institute'. Nonetheless in the eighty years before it was replaced a number of acclaimed plant scientists laboured there with significant achievements in 'pure' theoretical botany as well as the more practical aspects that came from learning how plants, as well as pests and diseases, work. Research into such biological interactions continues to be a major part of the current laboratory's thrust today and is of international importance.

The original 1877 building was demolished in 1963 and the rebuilt laboratories were opened in 1965. The latest incarnation of the Jodrell Laboratory is still at the north end of the Order Beds but it no longer looks like a branch library. Following a generous contribution from The Wolfson Foundation, a new wing (the Wolfson

The first bespoke Herbarium wing was added to Hunter House on Kew Green in 1877. The elegant ironwork of the spiral staircase extended originally around both balconies. Thousands of pressed plant specimens are stored in the white-painted cupboards.

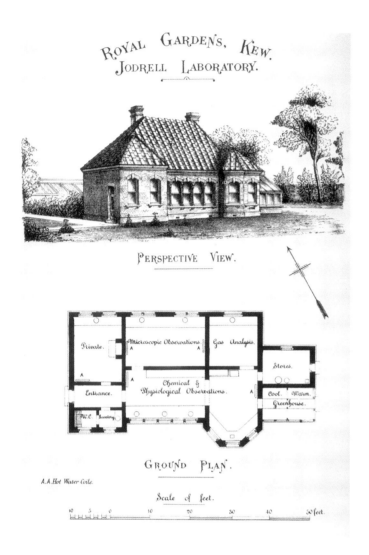

ROYAL GARDENS, KEW.
JODRELL LABORATORY.

PERSPECTIVE VIEW.

Private. *Microscopic Observations.* *Gas Analysis.*

Stores.

Chemical &
Physiological Observations.

Entrance. *Cool. Warm.*
Greenhouse.

W.C. Lavatory.

GROUND PLAN.

A.A. Hot Water Coils.

Scale of feet.

ABOVE The first Jodrell Laboratory was opened in 1876 and, like the near-contemporary Marianne North Gallery, was the result of private largesse.

OPPOSITE Kew's Colin Clubbe leading a vegetation survey in Anegada, one of the British Virgin Islands.

Wing) has been added, which opened in 2006. It's now a huge L-shaped building, five times the size of its first 1965 rebuilding, with a lecture theatre, meeting rooms and laboratories equipped to inquire into almost every aspect of plant science. With some seventy research staff the Jodrell has one of the highest concentrations of experts working on plant and fungal diversity anywhere in the world.

The Jodrell's five interrelated sections are ultimately concerned to understand as fully as possible plants as interactive organisms. Such work leads to their use by man and to vital aspects of conservation, ultimately the base-role of botanic gardens since early times but in very different ways. The Jodrell takes this base-role to hitherto unchartered levels of sophistication.

Certain sections may appear to the non-specialist to be merely of esoteric interest – the world of the music-hall absent-minded professor. Yet all lead to deeper understanding of evolutionary development and the relationship between organisms. The Micromorphology Section has floral and wood anatomists and palynologists who study pollen as a diagnostic feature. Systematic botany today has a vital molecular dimension using DNA sequencing to trace origins. Geneticists follow trails in cytology (cell science) in wild plant populations, leading to their conservation. Mycology is now also within the fold as the latest research demonstrates more and more how fungi – from moulds to mycorrhiza – are intimately involved in the lives of higher plants. Fungal identification is notoriously arcane and here too modern DNA research is contributing its knowledge.

These bands of scientific inquiry seem to coalesce in the laboratory's Sustainable Uses of Plants Section which incorporates the Centre for Economic Botany as well as a Biological Interactions group. This continues a line of inquiry that stretches back to the laboratory's foundation; when the unsolicited offer came from T.J. Phillips-Jodrell, Joseph Hooker saw that it would promote the study of 'the effects of blights, insect ravages and diseases of plants', and such concerns at home and abroad have been pursued ever since. Today's emphasis, however, takes on a poacher-turned-gamekeeper undertone very different from the insistence on ever-more lethal chemical cocktails that characterised most twentieth-century plant protection programmes. Not only do these have adverse effects upon other possibly beneficial organisms and the environment as a whole but they also seem to encourage the target species to build up greater and greater resistance. Now, by analysing plants from a pest's perspective it becomes possible to discover and support the host's natural defence systems. Many natural pesticides of plant origin are being investigated.

The Sustainable Use of Plants research team isolates and identifies plant chemicals and demonstrates their use. The projects chosen are problem-based and have a wide geographical focus. They vary from problems facing small-scale farmers in Africa to extensive studies of high-potential plant families. In the *Labiatae*, for example, extracts from *Salvia*, *Rosmarinus* and *Mentha* have been shown to have major medicinal applications and this is leading to further investigations focusing on an extensive range of British flora. Significant species do not have to be from 'far-away places with strange-sounding names'. Britain's own herbal heritage, still widely used before the introduction of the National Health Service in 1945, is currently being documented while it is still in the memory of people living today. 'Ethnomedica, Remembered Remedies' is a collaborative project with the Chelsea Physic Garden, the Eden Project in Cornwall and the Natural History Museum which focusses on collecting information from elderly people before it is too late. Odd facts have emerged, for example that the use of dock leaves to soothe nettle stings is an almost exclusively a British remedy.

Wherever the geographical focus, the key questions remain the same: how are wild plants used? Can traditional uses be improved upon? Are the resources – the plant populations that could provide a desirable product, medicine, food, fuel, timber – sustainable? Who derives the benefit – the indigenous population or multinational conglomerates? Who decides? Answers can be glimpsed through the words of Sir Peter Crane (Director 1999–2006), who emphasised the moral duty of organisations such as Kew to share their global resources with 'the broadest possible public and to connect (their) scientific efforts to important

issues that people care about'. In an effort to do just this Kew has developed many different 'outreach' initiatives.

One such initiative is KLARF – the Kew Latin America Research Fellowships Programme, which provides fellowships to scientists from specially targeted countries in South America, providing them with the opportunity to learn the importance of new scientific methods for studying the use of plants in everyday life. It is vital, of course, that such training does not just produce academics for developed countries but practical experts who will return home and work in their field. One North African success story is Tunisia University which, after receiving training and direct help from Jodrell staff, set up its own botanic garden with a supporting herbarium and seed bank in the coastal town of Monastir. These facilities enable research to be carried out on the medicinal and

other uses of the country's indigenous plants. Plants have endless potential and the stated remit of these Jodrell teams is to maximise the beneficial roles that plants can play in society. At the same time sustainability and habitat conservation are never forgotten. This is the ultimate credo.

New laboratories filled with staff undertaking high-tech research can all sound modishly 'cool Britannia'. Yet it must be realised that however 'cutting-edge' today's research is, it is part of a continuum that goes back to Kew's earliest days and the documented plant collections such as William Aiton's *Hortus Kewensis* or Joseph Banks's herbarium specimens from the *Endeavour* voyage. The subsequent accumulation of species in cultivation and

specimens preserved was principally concerned with identification, as has been discussed, and the writing of floras of whole swathes of the developing world. Perhaps the colonial origin can now be taken as read, as a function of the age, and concentration can be shifted onto the facts and practicalities of two centuries of intense plant study. The ever-growing Herbarium remains central to Kew's work and, as with the Jodrell Laboratory, a central ongoing strand of its research is to build a clear view of the family trees that demonstrate plants relationships. This supports both conservation and applied research into plant products.

From the ground floor of the original Hunter House Herbarium the serried shelves of pressed specimens

behind their labelled doors spread upward and outward as further wings have been added. A new extension, a £15 million project, is the latest but glimpses of the past can be found in the present; the office of today's Keeper of the Herbarium, for instance, is still in an elegant panelled room off the fine early ninteenth-century staircase hall. The Keeper leads a daunting staff of around thirty taxonomists who between them cover much of the world. Regional Teams concentrate on African Drylands, Tropical America, South-East Asia and so on. Other teams cross all geographical boundaries by concentrating their work on the systematics of families within the two parallel divisions of flowering plants that we all learnt (even if getting no further) at school – the

OPPOSITE AND ABOVE From this elegant eighteenth-century room in Hunter House the keeper of the Herbarium leads a daunting team of specialists whose researches will have effects far into the future. Busts of earlier botanical luminaries keep watch.

monocotyledons and the dicotyledons. Obviously, such is the multiplicity of plants and habitats that not every area or every family can be the subject of research; informed choices have to be made. Much research – and this is where the Jodrell Laboratory's molecular and anatomical research supports Herbarium taxonomy – now focusses upon relationships between genera within the same

family. If one plant is known to be valuable in some way it is likely its relatives will also be of use and thus the building-up of family trees – known as phylogenetic classification – is vital. The relatively small, mainly tropical *Meliaceae* family is a logical choice to work on phylogenetically. Although the family contains only approximately fifty genera it has economic and ecological importance way beyond it size. There are oil-seeds, edible fruits and many important timber trees including mahogany, as well as species used medicinally for their biologically-active compounds.

As a resource for such work Kew is unparalled. The Herbarium now holds seven and a half million preserved specimens and the number increases annually by tens of thousands as new surveys, especially those in hotspots of endemism, are conducted. The age of plant discovery is by no means over. Two recent expeditions in Bolivia produced over 13,000 collections and surveying small area within Western Cameroon's major ecological reserve led to the discovery of a number of species hitherto unknown. Species new to science join the 400,000 'type' specimens, those unique individuals which have been classified and named for the first time. The scientific name and the formal plant description are duly published and each new type specimen is stored in the collection, available for study and comparison for all time.

Kew's Herbarium and Library have long attracted visiting scholars and students from all over the world as much valuable research work is collaborative. Modern technology, however, is making resources available without great expense of time or travel. This is particularly important to workers in developing countries, especially those in the tropics and subtropics, where the greatest diversity of life forms are concentrated. This great biodiversity is threatened by

Herbarium sheets are dried, pressed and carefully mounted plant specimens available for comparative study. They may be centuries old but retain – apart from flower colour and scent – all the attributes of the living plant which modern microscopical investigation can reveal.

human development and there are few local information resources to help support conservation strategies and sustainable development. The traditional floras that Kew has been publishing for years are an invaluable resource but are inevitably both expensive and bulky, so alternative ways of widely disseminating this knowledge are being developed.

One of these developments is the production of field guides, which are now published in addition to major floras. These practical guides are as scientifically rigorous as the traditional floras, but unlike them are specifically developed to be user-friendly, aiding easy plant identification in the field, even by non-experts. They fulfil a need that is the modern parallel to the need of the early travellers and collectors in the eighteenth century in that they provide a key with which to identify, record and understand the land's wealth. Armed with that knowledge, local workers can promote sustainable use of the flora alongside conservation of the habitat.

Another development is the digitisation of both new and previously published material, enabling material to be searched for and consulted online. All thirty-two published volumes for the *Flora Zambesiaca* have now been digitised with 27,000 plant names listed in a searchable online database. It is planned to use the same technology for other major floras currently only available in print. The size of these projects can be glimpsed when it is realised that in the whole of Britain there are less than 1,500 native plants which have been gradually collected, collated, named and classified over 500 years whereas the *Flora of West Tropical Africa* contains towards 7,500 species, *Flora Zambesiaca* (once completed) will contain 10,200 species and the *Flora of Tropical East Africa* will contain 12,500 species. Time is not on their side.

Eventually it will not be necessary for botanists to either send material to Kew for comparison or travel there to work in the Herbarium, even when they need to consult diagnostic type specimens. Several major projects to digitise these vital reference points have begun. The African Plants Initiative is an international collaborative project which continues to grow in size. At the moment it involves forty-five botanical institutions representing twenty-three countries. The project will make around 70,000 of Kew's type specimens available electronically, courtesy of generous funding from the Mellon Foundation. Once complete, the collaborative database is expected to include approximately 300,000 specimen records. This unique undertaking can be seen, like priceless paintings looted in times past as trophies of war, as repatriation of cultural material, accumulated in scientific institutions worldwide since the age of exploration and now returning from whence it came and to where it is most needed.

The Richard Spruce Project focuses on a different continent, and is a salutary story of the past resurrected in support of the present. Richard Spruce was one of the explorers of tropical South America searching for new species of *Cinchona* for quinine production, 150 years ago. He was the first explorer to provide herbarium material for Kew of *Hevea brasilienisis*, commercial rubber. The project is a joint collaboration between Kew and the Natural History Museum, funded by the Mellon Foundation. It locates Spruce's specimens from within the Kew and Natural History Museum collections, and makes the collections and journals available online. The first phase (2002–5) focused on Spruce's collections from Peru and Ecuador.

The other reference collection that supports the Herbarium is Kew's Library and Archives. One of the world's foremost botanical libraries, it holds over 300,000 works from the earliest incunabula to current ongoing publications in print and electronic formats, alongside substantial collections of letters and private papers, plant drawings, watercolours, prints, paintings and photographs. The library compiles a bibliographic database, available online and in print – *The Kew Record of Taxonomic Literature* – which lists the most important new publications (since 1971) relating to the taxonomy of flowering plants, gymnosperms and ferns.

The written word is in turn supported by a vast array of plant illustrations. The Marianne North Gallery has already been described – a treasure house of exuberant plant portraits. But while many are wonderfully evocative depictions of plants in their native habitat – and therefore scientifically valuable, for it is possible to compare the condition of those habitats today – they were never intended as botanical reference points. Work produced specifically as botanical illustration, to aid in the identification of plants, is both an art and a science careful to delineate the whole plant, often with additional magnified diagnostic features. The Library Collection contains approximately 200,000 of these often supremely beautiful plant drawings, watercolours and prints.

The importance that Sir Joseph Banks ascribed to this aspect of botany and his paying the salary of Francis Bauer has been mentioned. When William Hooker

Miss Marianne North presides over some of her life's work – hundreds of portraits of plants painted in situ in several parts of the world. The habitats that this intrepid Victorian traveller recorded 150 years ago can be compared with their condition today as an aid to their conservation.

HORTVS

NITIDISSIMIS OMNEM PER ANNVM SVPERBIENS FLORIBVS

SIVE

AMOENISSIMORVM

FLORVM

IMAGINES

QVAS MAGNIS SVMPTIBVS COLLEGIT

VIR CLARISSIMVS

D. D. CHRISTOPHORVS IACOBVS TREW

REIPVBLICAE NORIMBERG. PHYSICVS SENIOR &c.

IPSO VERO ANNVENTE

IN AES INCISAS VIVISQVE COLORIBVS PICTAS

IN PVBLICVM EDIDIT

IOHANNES MICHAEL SELIGMANN.

NORIMBERGAE, TYPIS IOHANNIS IOSEPHI FLEISCHMANNI. MDCCL.

Der das ganze Jahr hindurch

im schönsten Flohr stehende Blumen-Garten,

Oder

Abbildungen

der lieblichsten

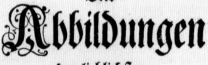

Blůmen,

von dem

Hochberühmten Herrn D. Christoph Jacob Trew,

der Republic Nürnberg Physico Seniore 2c.,

mit vielen Kosten zusammen getragen,

auf Deſſelben Genehmhaltung aber in Kupfer gestochen, und mit ihren natürlichen Farben vorgestellet

herausgegeben von

Johann Michael Seligmann.

Nec tam sidereo fulget Thaumantias arcu:
Quam nitidis hilares collucent foetibus horti. Columell.

Nürnberg, gedruckt bey Johann Joseph Fleischmann. 1750.

came to Kew he had been editor of *Curtis's Botanical Magazine* for some years and he brought Walter Fitch, its main artist, with him to Kew from Glasgow. Similarly to Banks and Bauer, Hooker paid for his services for forty years. By this time Fitch had drawn (and for the last half of his career engraved) over 2,500 plants, rare or entirely new to science. His paintings now form part of the Library Collection. Not surprisingly, in its almost two and a quarter centuries of continuous publication the *Bot. Mag.*, as it is colloquially called, has had some worrying times; happily its text is still edited by senior Kew staff and is published quarterly – the oldest continually published botanical magazine in the world.

Kew has promoted, commissioned and collected both written and illustrated reference works throughout its existence, making them available to scholars and research workers. But there is the same concern as with the herbarium materials, of ensuring access and availability to a worldwide readership. The same answer is provided – digitisation. This has been achieved in a spectacular fashion with the eighteenth-century *Hortus Nitidissimis* (the start of its polynomial Latin title) of Christoph Jacob Trew. This prosperous Nuremburg doctor and amateur botanist commissioned plant portraits from all the best flower painters of his time, notably, Georg Dionysius Ehret, and as its parts were published between 1750 and 1786 the *Hortus* gradually grew as if it were a real garden. As a periodical very few complete volumes exist and probably none in perfect condition. The digitisation is an amalgam of those owned by Kew and the Natural History Museum with a few plates from the Arnold Arboretum in America. Funding was once again generously provided by the Mellon Foundation. Thus an ideal *Hortus Nitidissimis* has been compiled and, at the click of a mouse, *The Flowering Garden in Perfect Bloom* . . . can be summoned up from the middle of the eighteenth-century. There are all the favourite spring bulbs, some of lost cultivars such as the lovely lilac-coloured double hyacinth 'Gloria Mundi', roses, lilies and even a passion flower. The website quotes Sacheverell Sitwell who, writing about such treasures just fifty years ago, lamented how:

> locked away in museums . . . are beautiful and quite unknown albums of flower drawings that are in prison as it were, and only visited at rare intervals by a mere handful of amateurs and students. This hiding away . . . is, apparently, insurmountable and an obstacle to the general appreciation which will never be overcome.

The quotation comes from *Great Flower Books: 1700–1900,* which Sitwell brought out with Wilfred Blunt (author of *In for a Penny*) to make available through reproduction the botanical treasures that exist. Ironically, even that publication has now become an expensive collector's item. The potential of websites such as that hosting the *Hortus Nitidissimis* offers hope that – although still involving enormous time and expense – Kew's historical Library can become a part of its 'outreach' programme.

OPPOSITE The cover page of *The Flowering Garden in Perfect Bloom*, in which Jacob Trew published plant portraits commissioned from the finest botanical artists of his time. Few copies exist and these are in libraries available only to scholars, but now, unimaginable only a few years ago, it is accessible to anyone online.

❧ 9 ❧

KEW PALACE
Let's Call on the King

A S PART OF THE BUILD UP to the 2002 inscription of Kew as a World Heritage Site (other designations include such disparate places as Angkor Wat, Fountains Abbey and the Niagara Escarpment in Canada – a bit of which is in Ontario's Royal Botanical Garden) a full-scale Site Conservation Plan was commissioned by Kew from a firm of outside consultants. They worked with Kew staff to gather together all possible information and evidence about this extraordinary site from the earliest times – Mesolithic and Bronze Age artifacts have been found in the river near by – to the latest greenhouses such as the new state-of-the-art Davies Alpine House. It is accepted that the Royal Botanic Gardens Kew is the world's premier botanic garden and an international centre of excellence for the study of plant diversity – that is its job. That such work takes place in a setting of national historic significance emphasises its uniqueness. While constructing its future, Kew cannot avoid caring for its past.

Kew's landscape can be seen as a palimpsest; layers of the past can be glimpsed through the present, they are seldom swept away entirely as is often asserted.

LEFT The south front of Kew Palace, neglected for years and once even hidden behind the White House, has now received the acclaim and restoration it deserves to welcome the public.

RIGHT Sir Peter Crane (Director 1999–2006) proudly shows Kew's designation as a World Heritage Site.

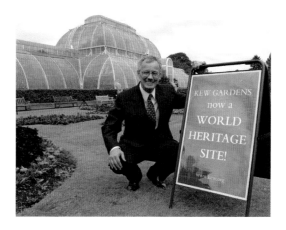

Remnants, for instance of some eighteenth-century Bridgemanic features, remain and are used or adapted. Yet, when it comes to houses – or in the case of Kew, palaces – historically the normal story was to pull down and rebuild. The same is true for many great estates throughout the country: contemporary comfort for the owners is apt to win over concern for the past. Many royal dwellings at Kew have come and gone: Richmond Palace, Richmond Lodge, the Queen's House, the White House, the Castellated Palace, all were demolished in their turn. Only the first is not entirely lost. In this context, survival of the Dutch House is positively miraculous and as such deserves special care, now administered by Kew's partners, Historic Royal Palaces.

The completion of the Site Conservation Plan, with its emphasis on the uniqueness of the place and the conservation recommendations that flowed from it, propelled the designation of 2006 as Kew's Heritage Year. Although there is no end to the maintenance of such a portfolio of buildings and further research will probably add to maintenance demands, the situation today is remarkably rosy. We are apt to look back with longing to some golden age long gone but, as this book shows, that is not always justified. Today, the prime nineteenth-century icon – the Palm House – stands wonderfully restored and is fully matched by the Princess of Wales Conservatory and Davies Alpine House, icons for the current age. These heritage buildings proclaim Kew's status as a unique

LEFT A charming contrived conversation piece by Philip Mercier. Here in 1733, ostensibly in front of the Dutch House (now Kew Palace) Frederick, Prince of Wales plays the cello, accompanied by his sisters Anne and Caroline. Princess Amelia listens to the right.

RIGHT The King's Dining Room at Kew Palace. It was in this room that King George's doctors cornered him and placed him under restraint when it was believed he was mad.

botanic garden. Kew Palace reveals to the visiting public another important aspect of Kew's history, its royal past.

The Palace's reopening, after a decade of intensive work to the building itself and an entire rethink of its presentation to the public, formed a central part of the Heritage Year celebrations. A tour of the Palace offers another dimension to the enjoyment and understanding of the Gardens as a whole. With careful research into the planned route that earlier visitors took around the grounds, it is now possible to come out of the front door of Kew Palace as a latter day royal (or more likely a servant in attendance) and walk through the estate, down towards the Pagoda – even today it beckons intermittently through the gaps in the later plantings – and then on to Queen Charlotte's Cottage; an authentic eighteenth-century experience.

The restored Palace is shown, as far as possible, as it would have been in around the year 1805, when it was in frequent use by the King and his family. Of course, 1805 is also the year of Trafalgar – a suitable bicentenary to celebrate as the restoration neared completion. Admiral Nelson's victory over the combined French and Spanish

fleets on 21 October of that year ensured Britain's supremacy of the trade sea-lanes on which its power depended, ensuring too that the colonial vision of the King and Sir Joseph Banks for the royal gardens could continue unhampered. For the next fifteen years, in spite of the King's bouts of illness and eventual removal to Windsor, Banks maintained the momentum. He could call upon His Majesty here as we, in more than virtual reality, can today.

Extensive research has enabled the Palace to be displayed as the royal family knew it and lived their surprisingly simple domestic life. It gives an authentic insight into Georgian taste and style, wonderfully enhanced by audio 'radio play' in some of the rooms of conversations overheard – as if they had been soaked up by the panelling 200 years ago, and now the walls can speak.

Entering the front door and turning left into a little anteroom to the library gives an immediate *coup de théâtre*. For there is King George III himself, in the form of an entirely realistic life-mask modelled by the famous Madame Tussaud. This vision seems to follow as one moves into the other ground floor rooms – the King's

ABOVE The Queen's Boudoir, or 'sulking room'.

library, dining room and the breakfast room. In here is an amazing survival, a dolls' house, only recently repatriated from a New York antique dealer's storeroom. It appears that the house was originally given to one of the princesses who, once she had grown out of it, redecorated it in the style of Kew Palace and gave it as a present to the daughter of the captain of the royal yacht. Here too is Philip Mercier's amusing painting *The Music Party*.

There are vestiges in several rooms of Samuel Fortrey's original seventeenth-century house but the staircase hall off the flagged front-to-back central passage is still exactly as he built it in 1631, as is the plaster work in what became the Queen's boudoir on the first floor. Elegantly hung and furnished, the Queen's boudoir was also known as the 'sulking room' (the elegant sounding word *boudoir* having come from the French verb *bouder*, to sulk), not for incubating bad temper but for gentle feminine retirement and lady-like work – painting, embroidery and so on.

ABOVE The Queen's Bedroom.

The adjoining drawing room still has Mr Fortrey's grand chimney-piece but is otherwise the height of Regency taste (a dangerously emotive rather than factual phrase in this house, as the Prince of Wales did not actually begin his decade as Prince Regent until 1810). It is small for a room central to the history of Britain, the empire and the world. In 1818, when the King was blind and irretrievably ill at Windsor and Queen Charlotte was only months from death, a dual wedding took place. The Queen had fifteen children but still, with no legitimate grandchildren, the succession to the throne of England was unclear and action was necessary. Two royal Dukes did their duty and married. The Duke of Clarence's (William IV to be) bride did not help but Princess Victoire of Saxe-Coburg, who married the Duke of Kent, had a daughter, Victoria, a year later. The rest, as they say, is history.

The Queen died in the chair that can be seen in her bedroom next door. After her death, the Palace was closed and much of its furniture was dispersed. Only a resident housekeeper lurked in one corner while the rooms quietly kept their memories. The house was seldom used over the next sixty years and by the 1880s its future was uncertain. In 1896 Queen Victoria agreed to sell the Palace to Kew Gardens and it opened in part to the public as a museum in 1898.

On the second floor the range of smaller rooms have been conserved but not restored and it is fascinating to see the clues left in the two princesses' bedrooms, and those of servants, indicating their original decoration and use. From this height views to the south take in the expanse of the remains of the White House Great Lawn, the Orangery and on into the Living Collections. Below to the north is the Queen's Garden, that charming formal seventeenth-century pastiche, the garden that Samuel Fortrey never had.

It will have been noticed that there has been no sign of a bedroom for the King. His private apartments were in a low wing, now pulled down, on the west side of the Dutch House. Of this nothing remains but the Site Conservation Plan does emphasise that the remaining early buildings glimpsed through the trees and half-hidden behind garden walls are of significance. What is now called Kew Palace Flats and used for staff accommodation was originally the kitchen and some of the domestic quarters of the White House itself, whose demolition they have survived. Below, unchanged and unconsidered for two centuries, are splendid Georgian kitchens with their ovens and spits and all the best culinary equipment of their age. Kew has much history to offer yet, much still to be researched in detail. The hope is, as has been so successfully achieved in the Palace itself, that it can be opened and interpreted to visitors. If it can be definitely shown, as seems likely, that this is one of William Kent's ancillary buildings designed as he was building the White House, Kew's architectural heritage rating would gain yet another star or two.

Winter emphasises the formal bones of the Queen's Garden. The pleached hornbeam hedge-on-legs, yew hedges and box-edged beds repeat the seventeenth-century plaster-work patterns on ceilings inside Samuel Fortrey's house.

10

BEYOND THE MILLENNIUM
Conservation in Action

O VER THE CENTURIES, millenarians of different persuasions – depending how they interpreted the dates – have gathered together in expectation of the imminent end of the world or some equally cataclysmic event. In Britain, the year 2000 was marked around the country by rather different celebratory events: festivals and the opening of numerous public buildings, from village halls and cricket pavilions to major museums. Not all, as evinced by the Millennium Dome in East London, have been of conspicuous success. However, two very dissimilar high-profile millennium projects have gone from strength to strength and perhaps ironically have overtones of those traditional millenarians. These are the Eden Project and Kew's Millennium Seed Bank Project (MSBP). While projections of doom are made, instead of passively awaiting the cataclysm, these are attempting to prevent it. The key, of course, is the vital part that plants play in the maintenance of a healthy planet.

In Cornwall the Eden Project is a dramatic stage-set of futuristic greenhouses and gardens designed to demonstrate to a visiting public the centrality of the world of plants to our very existence. The message is communicated through displays of plants in simulated natural habitats from tropical rainforests to Mediterranean maquis. It is thus a botanic garden in all but name – but one without any historical hang-ups and preconceptions. It tells the story of our dependence on plants and comes to the inevitable conclusion: conserve or die. Within its first half-dozen years over 8 million people had passed through the doors and, it is hoped, learned the lesson.

Palms, cycads, gingers and bananas combine to give the feeling of an authentic bit of rainforest under the curving roof of the Palm House. It does, of course, need continual care and maintenance.

Kew had a similar millennial vision: the development of a global seed conservation network, capable of safeguarding wild plant species. Throughout its history Kew has been concerned with conserving its own collections, but from the start of the 1970s onwards it has become increasingly involved in international conservation. Perhaps the most well known element of its conservation work is the Millennium Seed Bank at Wakehurst Place. The proposal for the MSBP was submitted to the Millennium Commission in 1995 and approved that same year; heralding the time when need, knowledge and ability had come together sufficiently to make a significant impact on species and habitat loss.

Since pre-history man has known that collecting and storing seed is a way of providing for the future – while conversely the consumption of seed-corn is an age-old prophesy of doom. But how long will seed stay viable and what conditions help it? Back in 1969 a unit was set up in

Like a row of Dutch barns in a futuristic farm-yard, the Millennium Seed Bank at Wakehurst Place houses laboratories with cold rooms below which already store seeds of the whole of the British Flora. By the year 2010 seed of 10 per cent of all the dryland plants of the world will have joined them.

the Jodrell Laboratory to examine longevity of seeds stored in controlled conditions. It moved to laboratories installed in the mansion at Wakehurst Place five years later and the now internationally acclaimed Millennium Seed Bank Project is its natural and highly expanded successor. It's a bit like buying rare wine *en primeur* and discovering the best cellaring conditions with tastings – in this case germination tests – being carried out at regular intervals.

The years around AD 2000 have been something of a watershed for Kew and for plant-based institutions across the world. At last the wider international community has taken some notice of what they have been saying for years – that natural habitats are under serious threat from human activities, and that many plant and animal species are in danger of extinction. And that it matters not only to the species directly affected, to a little local human population and to a worthy conservation lobby but to the world as a whole. International altruism has never been Mankind's strong point so notice is particularly taken when national interests are at stake.

It had long been accepted, though without any deep concern, that whenever there is a highly organised society, Man's activities take their toll of the land and the natural resources on which it developed. The classic examples are famous: the Fertile Crescent of the Middle East supported rich cultures for millennia; North Africa was the bread-basket of the Roman Empire feeding its armies across Europe. Desert has now taken over. Of all the lands that supported the lost civilisations of the distant past only that miraculous strip of Egypt replenished every year by the flood-silt of the Nile has maintained its fertility as a lifeline for the people.

In Britain, early industrialisation, when it was little more than a cottage industry – iron-foundering in the Weald of Sussex and woollen manufactories in the Cotswolds – doubtless changed the countryside considerably but after they moved on a gentle oceanic climate and a small peasant population, demanding little from the land, enabled the natural world to regroup and reform over a couple of centuries. These are now considered areas of natural beauty and the vernacular industrial buildings that remain are part of our cultural heritage. The effects of the extraordinary success, in economic terms, of the later industrial revolution further north were less benign. The after-effects in social and environmental terms are still being felt and fought over.

Similar examples can be found throughout the industrialised world; the prosperity and power that such activities engender are a source of envy to those countries without the resources or technical knowledge to fuel them. But as with political revolution, the longer ago a country industrialised, the better. Countries that became prosperous through early industrialisation and indiscriminate exploitation of resources, national and imported, now worry with comfortable hindsight that emergent powers such as China and India are determined to follow suit. Injunctions from the prosperous West to 'take care' and 'watch out' are naturally not greeted there with much enthusiasm.

Any account of a modern botanic garden cannot fail to be cognisant of such social history, especially an account of one whose foundation and history are an intimate part of Britain's development as a great industrial and colonial power. For while the Royal Botanic Gardens were instrumental in moving crop plants around the world, demonstrating, for example, how successful rubber and cinchona and oil palms could be in Ceylon or Singapore to support a prosperous and increased population, they were at the same time endangering the native flora they were equally concerned to protect. It was an irony not lost upon even the early travellers. Kew historian Ray Desmond quotes a visitor in Ceylon recording as long ago as 1844 that 'Botanists of future time will look in vain for many of the species which their predecessors had recorded in the annals of science as natives of the island'. 'Dead as a dodo' – referring to the flightless endemic bird of Mauritius made extinct by 1690 – is a graphic phrase lightly used that has ever-increasing currency.

Throughout this story there have been parallel strands with different but mutually supportive motives. There is the image of the classic botanist, collecting, naming and classifying: assembling knowledge apparently for its own sake, studying plants because they are there. One thinks of Linnaeus, of George Bentham and numbers of herbarium and laboratory scientists who make up the academe of botany. Alongside are the enthusiasts such as Banks or the Hookers who have national aspirations to put botanical discoveries to use. (Directors today have little choice; how else can they promote their institutions to get the necessary funding to run them?) Then there are the horticulturists who tend and propagate the Living Collections – a group late in receiving recognition as a contributory part of the whole. The interrelationship of these strands is no longer doubted and it is the call of conservation and the sustainable use of plants that has brought them together.

Conservation should not be seen as a negative concept – a don't use, don't do directive. While there are internationally accepted evolutionary hotspots of extraordinary biological diversity, which it is fully agreed should be conserved at all costs, it is equally now realised that such conservation cannot be arbitrarily imposed upon the nations on whose territory they lie. Areas of importance are found throughout the world, even in so highly populated a country as Britain – Wicken Fen in Cambridgeshire, Wystman's Wood in Devon or the remnants of the Caledonian Forest, for example – but the hottest of hotspots are found in the world's tropical rainforests. The concern here is not only to conserve what is known to be there but also to permit the scientific study of what has not yet been identified. It has been asserted that towards 40 percent of the world's biota is to be found in the canopy of tropical forest regions, much of which is yet to be classified.

Island floras are also especially vulnerable. These little outposts of land have often developed a unique and mutually interdependent flora and fauna – such as those that Charles Darwin famously described in the Galapagos Islands. While happily balanced if left alone, these miracles of adaptive evolution are dangerously vulnerable to outside interference. Until the Age of Discovery – Europe's sudden explosion of exploration from the fifteenth century – many such places were like the Garden of Eden before day six – untouched, inviolate. It is difficult to conceive of such a considerable and familiar island as Madeira being uninhabited as it was when 'discovered' by Henry the Navigator's ships in 1419. It is also difficult to imagine its unique virgin forests almost all reduced to ashes to clear the land for its first farming.

Man's depredations, a conscious and inevitable result of settlement, are to some extent understandable. Worse has been his introduction of exotic animals: goats and pigs intentionally as a food source, rats by accident. *Opuntia* (prickly pear) and kudzu vine are comparable invasive plant species introduced by accident or unfortunate design. In all cases the historic balance is upset, the natives cannot compete against the invaders and are pushed to the edge of, if not over, the cliff of extinction.

The analogy is not fanciful; while we cannot always know what has been lost (dodos are sad exceptions) studies of many island floras have revealed tiny populations of endemics, literally hanging on to cliff faces that even the most athletic goat cannot reach. Islands, it must be realised, do not have to be surrounded by sea and there are other once isolated areas where an endemic-rich flora is under similar threat.

The International Union for the Conservation of Nature and Natural Resources (IUCN), founded in 1948, can be seen as a significant precursor to a number of conservation-concerned initiatives designed to bring the international community together to appreciate the effects of man's activities on a global scale. Kew became involved with the IUCN's work in the 1960s, when Ronald Melville, a retired member of Kew's staff, was invited to become a member of the IUCN's Species Survival Commission. Aided by Kew's resources he compiled a list of those flowering plants and gymnosperms (conifers and cycads) proved to be in danger of following the dodo to extinction. Published in 1970 as the *Red Data Book*, it caused consternation around the world when it initially estimated that some 20,000 plant species were at risk. This is now feared to be a serious underestimate.

Through the work of the IUCN, an important Convention was established: the Convention on International Trade in Endangered Species of Wild Fauna and Flora (CITES), which came into force in 1975. CITES aims to ensure that international trade in endangered species does not threaten their survival, and it covers everything from ivory poaching in Africa to the collection of rare cacti in Mexico. CITES-listed animals or plants may not be legally traded as wild taken specimens without documentation to show their provenance. A CITES export permit is required from the country of origin and a CITES import permit from its destination plus, of course, a phytosanitary certificate. Plants (and animals) regarded as especially threatened are listed in Appendix One. For such species permits are much more strictly controlled: the slipper orchid genera *Phragmipedium* and *Paphiopedilum* are listed in this Appendix. Not surprisingly this is something of a mysterious world for Customs and Police Officers who

are directly faced by illegal trade in wild products and each year Kew hosts a training course on the Convention for such staff.

International cooperation in conservation matters developed in the last two decades of the twentieth century with the usual progression of conferences, memoranda, papers and signed agreements, some more effective than others. But the Rio Earth Summit of 1992 marked a truly significant step forward with the resultant Convention on Biological Diversity (CBD) having being signed by 190 parties (168 countries). The Convention has three main goals: the conservation of biological diversity, the sustainable use of its components and the fair and equitable sharing of benefits from the use of genetic resources. However, it is worth bearing in mind that responsibility for implementing the CBD rests with signatory nations and there is, therefore, a danger of worthy intentions not being followed through. At the Rio Summit, Britain announced an initiative that funds projects which put UK biodiversity expertise to work

Young leaves unfurl on an oriental maple. It will flower, fruit and the ripe seeds be whirled away on the wind to reproduce the species elsewhere.

with local partners in countries rich in species but poor in resources to implement the goals of the CBD. The Darwin Initiative, as it is called, is funded through the British Government ministry Defra. As of 31 March 2007, the Initiative has supported 458 projects – an investment of around £60 million. The distribution of funding reflects the Initiative's investment in the most threatened biodiversity hotspots, mainly in Africa and Asia. Grants are relatively small, with a typical project lasting for two or three years: matched funding sources are expected and thus there is collaboration between the parties. Many projects have all the hallmarks of Kew's expertise – the production of field guides, local keys and database management plans for reserves and threatened habitats and species, fieldwork training for local people and so on.

OPPOSITE In modern agricultural fields scarlet poppies (*Papaver rhoeas*) are seldom seen amongst the corn. But seeds shaken from the 'censer' type capsules can stay dormant for decades until cultivation on field edges or road sides provokes germination. In turn a new generation is able to set its seeds.

While the ramifications of Kew's conservation concerns can be followed across the world – each of which would make a book in itself – perhaps the biggest initiative of all has been set up at home, at Wakehurst Place. The opening of the Millennium Seed Bank (MSB) could well claim to be the ideal millennium present. The project itself had been running for several years in advance of the Seed Bank's formal opening by HRH the Prince of Wales on 20 November 2000. It has the potential, should civilisation as we know it continue so far, to still be earning its keep at the next millennium. It is the ultimate conservation project – so far.

One of the most extraordinary aspects of flowering plants is their sophistication in sexual reproduction. There is no end to the diversity of pollination methods through wind, water, insects, birds, slugs in the case of aspidistra and even mice with some South African proteas. Then there are the adaptations to spread the resulting seeds far and wide – the elegant parasols of dandelion, sycamore's helicopters, explosive impatiens, fleshy fruits designed to be eaten, and hooks and glues and various forms of natural Velcro. Every seed carries the full genetic complement of its species whether it be dust-like as in begonias and orchids or the two kilogram monster coco-de-mer from the Seychelles. Conceived, developed, ripened and dispersed; the whole sequence is exquisitely programmed to reproduce its race in the habitat for which it is adapted. Thus it's 'all systems go' it would seem: germination now. But the time may not be right – wrong season, no rain, too hot, or too cold. There may be no space. And so another range of techniques has evolved to permit a Sleeping Beauty-like dormancy, which is broken only when changed conditions make success more likely: some day the prince will come. We are delighted when after years of disappearance spectacular shows of annual poppies and corn marigolds appear on a bit of newly turned land. They may have been waiting ten or twenty years for just this stimulus. In Australia wattles (mimosas to us) and other natives only germinate after a forest fire when open ground is thus made available. Every species has its individual road to success.

The phenomenon of seed dormancy is a conservation tool of the greatest importance: collect seed, store it and bring it out when needed. Of course it is not that simple. We all know that seeds left in the potting shed drawer will lose their viability, some quickly (there's just no point in sowing the other half of that packet of parsnip seeds left over from last year, they're as good as dead) while others last several years. The role of the MSB is to collect seed and store it in conditions which ensure its viability. The Seed Bank is another of those nice concatenations where the past – here the estate of a 500-year-old country house – is host to a future planned to last at least as long.

Behind the sandstone mansion is the custom-built seed bank building. Its series of long Dutch-barn-like arched roofs give a feeling of a futuristic farmyard. Inside are laboratories, offices, seed cleaning rooms, drying chambers and the freeze-rooms kept at a constant −20°C. Visitors can see staff through the glass walls in conventional white lab coats or hooded parkas and it is obvious who works where.

RIGHT In the laboratories at the Millennium Seed Bank seeds are cleaned, dried and stored at −20˚C. They are tested for viability on arrival and this will be repeated throughout their storage lives.

The project costs up to 2009 are £80 million. It received its initial grant from the government's Millennium Commission (whose work has now been taken over by the Big Lottery Fund) with a supplementary grant in 2003. Major contributions from the Wellcome Trust – a leading medical research charity – and Orange Plc are reflected in the names of the building and its public exhibitions area. Kew's Foundation and Friends, charitable trusts, businesses and individuals have also been significant contributors. It seems set, like Kew's great buildings of the nineteenth and twentieth centuries, the Palm House and Princess of Wales Conservatory respectively, to be an icon for our times. Architecturally striking both inside and out, it takes the botanic garden role in a new direction. Traditional collections, traditionally cultivated had always maintained a conservation ethic (even if the word was not current) in that propagation could increase plants to be sent around the world and even, if need be, back to their countries of origin. But the presumption was that plants were safest behind high walls, where they could be carefully overseen by expert gardeners and made easily available for study by resident botanists. This is classic off-site conservation, which requires continual intervention of one sort or another. The contents of the MSB can, of course, permit this and indeed over time seeds will be extracted regularly from the cold stores for germination viability tests. But the real benefit of the Seed Bank is that it acts as an 'insurance policy' against extinction of species in the wild and provides options for their future use far into the future. Collected seed is already being used by the MSB and its partner organisations to re-introduce presumed extinct species to the wild, as was the case with interrupted brome grass in the UK, or to re-vegetate degraded land, as with partner projects running in Burkina Faso and Kenya.

Encouraged by the early success of seed-storage experiments a decision was made to collect and store seed of all members of the British flora. Part of the MSBP, the UK Flora Programme begun in 1997 and was substantially complete by 2000. As of November 2007, 96 per cent of the UK's wild flora had been collected. The remaining 4 per cent (sixty-eight species) either do not produce seed, produce seed that cannot be conventionally stored, or are

LEFT In the Millennium Seed Bank an insulated parka can be necessary on even the hottest day.

too rare to collect from without risking their survival, although efforts continue to collect from such species. Britain is the first country to have harvested and preserved its botanical heritage, a boast helped by our relatively restricted species list. Translate this on to a world stage and the project becomes frightening and almost overwhelming. What should be collected? What is the most at risk? What is most worthwhile? With 80 per cent of the world's plants still un-investigated for possible medical uses, for example, these are not easy questions to answer – especially because choice of some also implies rejection of many others.

Target species for collection are selected by local partners so they reflect their needs and interests. Once these broad objectives have been outlined the MSBP helps its partners identify and locate the exact species for collection. Partners often choose to base their collecting on endangered *Red Data Book* species, endemics (those species restricted to a given habitat) and those valuable to local economies. These latter by their very nature are apt to move into the other categories at the same time. Other partners choose to focus on collecting species useful for land restoration, which may

include widespread species. The key aim is to collect 10 per cent of the world's wild flowering plant species (totalling 24,000 species) by 2010. There is a particular focus on dryland areas (arid and semi-arid regions), chosen because nearly a fifth of the human population – over a billion people – live in such areas and are directly dependant on the plants that grow there. By mid-2007 the MSB held around 20,000 species, covering every continent.

Partnership projects are central to the overall project. Many, but not all such projects are in developing countries. Partnerships are not just for seed-collecting activities; research, training and other capacity-building elements are included in the projects. Each project is based on a legally-binding agreement that complies with CITES and CBD regulations and collections are shared between the country of origin (with help given in collecting and storage methods, often through the Darwin Initiative) and the MSB. By raising the capacity of local botanical organisations to collect and conserve seeds of their own flora these Kew-led partnerships are designed to half the feared loss of plant species. By 2005 collaborative project partnerships had been

ABOVE A batch of incoming seeds, from one of over 100 international partners, is opened in the initial drying room at the Millennium Seed Bank, Wakehurst Place.

developed in eighteen countries from China to Chile, from Madagascar to Mexico.

Collecting cannot take place without an authorisation permit from the land owner/manager. In many cases there are also formal legal procedures that must be followed. A typical collecting team comprises four collectors representing two institutions. They make, on average, three collections per day, while travelling widely across the region. Local partners usually have the knowledge needed to find the plants; otherwise information from Kew's herbarium sheets is used. This will have been recorded by the original collector, possibly many years before. Once at the location a plant needs to be identified by the collectors, who use regional field guides and checklists to aid identification. Then the location is assessed, the key consideration being whether or not the location holds enough plants with developed seed. The last check is a cut test to estimate the number of damaged or empty seeds in the fruit or capsule.

With these preliminaries taken care of the seed can be harvested. A range of techniques, adapted to the dispersal characteristics of the seed, are used to harvest the seed manually. Seed is taken from at least fifty individual plants (to ensure a wide genetic sample) at random. To protect the species' existence in the wild no more than 20 per cent of the available seed is harvested. In addition to the seed, the collectors also take a plant sample, known as a voucher specimen. Finally, comprehensive field data is recorded – an essential record that may need to be called upon at any point during the collection's existence. In all, this is an extremely exacting process.

Collected seed and its data are sent on to the seed bank as soon as possible, as storage in incorrect conditions can damage seed viability. If the collection has taken place in a partner country, the collection is sent to their seed bank for processing and storage, with duplicate collections being sent on to the MSB. Collections from the UK are sent straight to the MSB.

Once safely at the seed bank every collection has to be cleaned and visually checked. The checks are unable to tell us whether a seed might germinate, but they can indicate that the seed will not germinate. And they are crucial in order to ensure that the collection can be turned into living plants, the first step in any subsequent habitat restoration. The checks are carried out using either x-ray analysis or a cut test. Following this the size of the collection is determined. The seeds are then transferred to the drying room; a carefully-controlled zone where the temperature is kept between 15–18°C with 15 per cent relative humidity. Once the collections have been dried (and tested for dryness) they are packaged, ready for long-term sub-zero storage in the vaults.

But what is the timescale? It is now established that over three-quarters of all plants produce 'orthodox' seeds that can be dried and stored at low temperatures for decades and even centuries. This is the type of seed stored at the MSB. For the rest, however, further research is providing other means. Ultra-low temperature techniques are being developed to store these 'recalcitrant' seeds. Cryopreservation (a process now routinely used to store reproductive cells of animals and humans for artificial insemination) is a storage technique in which the material is put into tissue culture and treated with chemicals that help to reduce the averse affects of both freezing and dehydration. The moisture content of the cells is then lowered and they are frozen and stored in liquid nitrogen at a temperature of –196°C. It is believed that such techniques can keep organisms in suspended animation and capable of being revived after hundreds or even thousands of years. The MSBP is a member of the Cryopreservation Network, a European project set up to establish a network of scientists with expertise and interest in the technique, with the aim to establish efficient cryopreservation procedures.

These techniques, of course, are not an end in themselves but a part of Kew's central mission to restore endangered species to a flourishing natural habitat. The challenge does not end with successfully freezing viable seed – eventually healthy adult plants need to be produced from the deep-frozen source material. This takes the story back to Kew itself.

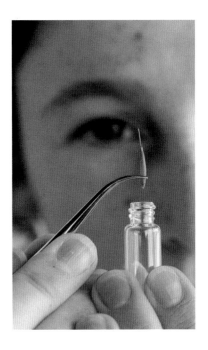

ABOVE The billionth seed to be collected for the Millennium Seed Bank Project, from *Oxytenanthera abyssinica*, a drought resistant species of African bamboo. A very useful plant, its natural habitat is under increasing threat; it sets seed only once every seven years.

LEFT While most orchids can be propagated vegetatively by conventional methods, stock can be increased only slowly. Modern *in vitro* techniques for germinating the miniscule seeds and vegetative micropropagation are used for saving endangered species. These methods are also central to commercial orchid production and have turned many orchids from collectors' rarities into common house-plants for all to enjoy.

The Micropropagation Unit was originally set up as a support to the Gardens' Living Collections to ensure the continuity of species that were difficult to propagate by conventional methods. It is based upon *in vitro* techniques first developed in the early years of the twentieth century for growing orchids from seed. Orchid seeds are minute, only a few millionths of a gram in weight – just an embryo and a single layer of protective cells. Their food reserves are inadequate to nourish germinating seeds and are supplemented by symbiotic fungi which provide additional nutrients. In the wild only a tiny percentage of the clouds of dust-like seeds will develop successfully. In the laboratory, however, seeds are sown on sterile nutrient medium in flasks or petri dishes containing the necessary symbiotic fungus or a combination of the nutrients that the fungus would naturally supply. Orchids can also be multiplied by vegetative micropropagation in which small pieces of tissue from a mature plant, only a few cells in extent, are provoked into reproduction. Obviously, all these techniques require carefully controlled light and temperature and exacting laboratory conditions. Micropropagated tropical orchids, now on sale in every garden centre in the land, attest to the commercial use of *in vitro* techniques.

Kew's successes with orchids include thousands of seedlings of Britain's rarest orchid, the lady's slipper (*Cypripedium calceolus*) – some of which are now flowering back in their natural habitat – and some 400 other species, seventy-five of which are of conservation importance, being grown in the laboratory. The techniques are now being employed to save more of the world's rarest plants including the bottle palm (*Hyophorbe lagenicaulis*) from Mauritius, Easter Island's *Sophora toromiro* and representatives of almost all the taxonomic plant groups from mosses and ferns to trees.

A classic case is that of café marron (*Ramosmania rodriguesii*). Only one plant remains in the wild on the island of Rodriguez, a speck of land in the Indian Ocean a thousand miles off the coast of Madagascar. Plants from cuttings grown at Kew have produced the first recorded fruit. Seed germination has resulted in young plants to add to those raised vegetatively for repatriation to the island. Further viable seed is now also stored in the MSB. Why the fuss about a single species that could well have disappeared without trace? At one level there is a botanical parallel with that resonant line from John Donne's *Devotions*, 'any man's death diminishes me, because I am involved in Mankind ...' At the basic utilitarian level café marron is related to *Cinchona* and *Coffea* and many of its relations have valuable alkaloids. It too may be of economic value in ways yet unknown.

Through the Millennium Seed Bank Project and Kew's Micropropagation Unit, this work can be seen as the ultimate long-stop in conservation terms. When negative news seems to be the norm from so many parts of the world its is heartening to learn how the apparently esoteric world of botany contributes practically to the betterment of populations far from Wakehurst's archetypal English scene in the High Weald of Sussex and those royal gardens on the banks of the Thames.

11

KEW IN THE COUNTRY
Wakehurst Place

THE IMPORTANCE of the Millennium Seed Bank to Kew's scientific mandate and to world conservation has already been described. The surprise, perhaps, is that this revolutionary international project grew out of early trials and experiments into seed dormancy and storage firstly in the Jodrell Laboratory and then in makeshift laboratories in a quiet historic house in the depths of rural Sussex. Visitors to Wakehurst Place today, having emerged from the extensive but unassuming entrance building – the Visitor Centre – see at once the long arched roofs of the Millennium Seed Bank stretching away in perspective below them. Away ahead and to the left, through the trees, are two or three cupolas and an array of high chimneys. Here, no doubt, is the conventional country house scene with which Britain is wonderfully blessed. This, certainly on a first visit, is a good way to go. But as the path leads on it becomes obvious this is no normal country estate. The range of mature trees is more than usually wide, the new planting is extensive and, fortunately, everything is labelled – name, country of origin, accession number. The private estate has become a botanic garden with its plant collections fully integrated into scientific programmes of the Royal Botanic Gardens, Kew.

It is now almost half a century since Kew signed its lease from the National Trust, to whom the estate had been bequeathed by Sir Henry Price in 1963. He and his wife were keen gardeners and they had succeeded Gerald Loder (later Lord Wakehurst), who had bought the estate in 1903. He was one of a family of great gardeners. High Beeches and Leonardslee are other famous Loder gardens. Only an hour or so away, depending upon traffic on the dread M25, Wakehurst Place could

A walk on the wild side at Wakehurst Place, affectionately known as Kew in the Country. There are 180 acres to explore.

hardly be more different from Kew: it's over 400 feet above sea level (while the Thames is still tidal up to Teddington) with an annual rainfall of 32 inches (Kew has around 20 inches). There is an extraordinary diversity of terrain here with hills and valleys offering all aspects while enviable soil gives growing conditions that exactly follow the requirements recommended in every traditional gardening manual, 'a deep rich loam, well-drained yet retentive of moisture'. How covetable; no wonder things do well.

The landscape reveals a century of acquisitions: the trees, shrubs and enthusiasm for Southern Hemisphere species in Gerald Loder's time were continued by Sir Henry Price. New species and even new genera flowed in from famous plant collectors – from Ernest 'Chinese' Wilson, Reginald Farrer and Frank Kingdon-Ward in the Himalaya and Harold Comber in temperate South America. Careful records and notes were kept of acquisitions which show that in 1908, only five years after Loder bought Wakehurst Place, the garden had around 3,000 species and cultivars. Sixty years on, when the early plantings had matured, the diversity was daunting and it was wonderfully apparent that here was a garden offering almost all the attributes needed to extend Kew's collections. Rhododendrons and conifers flourished as they never had in the thin soil and polluted atmosphere of suburban Surrey. All that had to be done, perhaps, was to continue in the same way while providing the necessary facilities for public access on an ever-increasing scale. By the early 1980s the plant count had more than tripled that Loder list.

All looked set fair for the future until the night of 15 October 1987 when the worst storm since 1703 swept across southern England. At Wakehurst, 15,000 trees were blown down, flattening plants beneath. Damage at Kew itself was serious but here it was cataclysmic and it

The ambience that only maturity can give. A group of slow-growing Japanese maples cluster around the pond while walks lead onward through botanical plantings that began early in the last century within an already established landscape.

ABOVE The restaurant, situated by the traditional early eighteenth-century stable block, is an invaluable meeting place before or after walking the grounds.

OPPOSITE Nearby, these two great redwoods with their buttressed trunks are an indication of the arboreal riches ahead.

seemed as if the place could never recover. A second severe storm occurred two years later causing further casualties. Now, approaching twenty years on, few signs of the scale of the tragedy can be seen. Indeed, while clearing the chaos and propagating rare plants so shattered that they would never regenerate by themselves, staff made a virtue of necessity by re-grouping the collections to reflect current knowledge of phytogeographic relationships and to enhance the flow from one area to another. The vital first impression from the Visitor Centre is a part of just that.

Approaching the house one sees that those glimpsed cupolas are on a fine early Georgian stable block, its yard now comfortably glassed over as home to an inviting, recently refurbished restaurant, named The Stables. A stop here is likely to be necessary; there is a great deal to see. Tables are set outside to the south where huge sequoias that survived the great storms hint at the plant pleasures to come. Every year one of these becomes a beacon for miles around when, ablaze with lights, it is turned into a towering Christmas tree. Skirting the

Britain is blessed by its wealth of historic country houses open to the public. At Wakehurst Place a couple of rooms contain furniture donated and left behind by Sir Henry and Lady Price while the rest is used to support Kew's work. Gabled doorways and stone transomed windows still give this courtyard a feeling of warm domesticity.

side of the house where a little door bearing the date 1590 on its lintel leads to the original chapel, an opening in a high yew hedge suddenly gives on to the flagged south terrace. Three storeys of warm Ardingly sandstone tower above, with the gables carrying an extravagant array of carved finials. Although appearing to be of the period, this is a mid-nineteenth-century romantic recreation made when the wings of the original E-shaped façade were shortened. The main door is usually open and there are temporary exhibitions among some surviving furniture from the Prices' time.

But it is the garden that calls. Unlike Kew itself, which is an amalgam of many parts and periods, Wakehurst holds together as a domestic setting, despite its size. This contributes enormously to its charm. The south front gives on to the terrace, the terrace to wide formal lawns, which in turn meet beds of shrubs and small trees flowing onwards down the slope where the canopy of tall trees, half lost in the contours, form the backdrop. The glinting water of the Mansion Pond to the south-east is the inviting start to what could be a considerable walk with innumerable choices, all of interest.

ABOVE Steps from the terraces of the house lead out in several directions into the collections. Specimen trees, here in autumn array, take the eye; all are carefully labelled and documented.

OVERLEAF 'England, their England.' The south front of Wakehurst Place from the Mansion Pond. There is no indication that this is no longer a private country house but a part of a significant scientific institution.

LEFT Just coming into leaf the towering swamp cypress (*Taxodium*) by the Mansion Pond contrasts with more conventional evergreen conifers beyond.

ABOVE A tapestry of dwarf rhododendrons and other shrubs in the Tony Schilling Asian Heath Garden frame a view back to the house.

It is vital to take a guidebook map. The full estate is almost 500 acres in extent of which the gardens make up less than half. The rest of the estate is part-commercial woodland managed for charcoal production (marketed as Bar-B-Kew fuel!) timber and Christmas trees; all of these aspects contribute to public education programmes. More significantly, what is called the Loder Valley Nature Reserve surrounds the northern end of Ardingly Reservoir, which extends southwards towards the town. With its steep-sided valleys, (known locally as 'ghylls') wetlands, woodlands and open meadows this is one of the most diverse reserves in the south of England and it is managed with great care to conserve its native plant and animal populations.

The gardens comprise the core of the estate and may, very loosely, be likened in shape to a sort of squashed bagel – a rich surrounding to a central hole – the hole in this case being private land used as grazing for cross-bred red deer, hence the essential high fence that can be occasionally seen. Thus, starting at the Mansion Pond, one takes a 2½-mile clockwise circuit with, of course, temptations being continually placed in one's way as this path or that leads to yet another particularly spectacular planting.

Until the 1987 tempest the pond was backed by forest trees sheltering Gerald Loder's great Rhododendron Walk. Almost everything was shattered and clearance left utterly different conditions; areas that had been in dappled sheltered shade were now in full sunlight and exposure. It was decided to use the land to demonstrate mountain terrains; fortunately Kew's Curator in charge of Wakehurst had worked and collected in the Himalaya as the UK Advisor to the Royal Nepalese Government at their Godavari Botanic Garden, and so knew first-hand that type of terrain. The Tony Schilling Asian Heath Garden is the result, a managed ecological planting of the high Himalaya inevitably concentrating upon dwarf small-leaved rhododendrons, the heather equivalent there. It can be spectacular in May.

Below, a small rill flows down a valley known as The Slips to a trio of ponds whose banks are planted with an extraordinary range of small trees and shrubs, the ground carpeted with early spring bulbs and later wild flowers. Keen gardeners will discover memorable specimens of *Stewartia sinensis* (named by Linnaeus for Lord Bute, Princess Augusta's advisor in that first Kew botanic garden), *Pieris*, *Corylopsis* and *Magnolia*. In summer swathes of moisture-loving herbaceous plants surround the ponds – meconopsis, hemerocallis, astilbes and so on. A particular feature is made of cultivars of *Iris ensata*; the Japanese water

ABOVE AND RIGHT The Slips is a whole valley garden in its own right. Three ponds are linked by a tinkling rill, their banks clothed with fine mature magnolias and dogwoods. Aquatic and water-margin plants give interest and colour from May to October.

iris has been cultivated in the Far East for centuries, the wide flat flowers often appearing on screen and scrolls. Here, unusually for a botanic garden, is a wide range of horticultural cultivars, many of which are new to Western gardens. A raised boardwalk winding through the irises to a couple of seats at the base of a natural amphitheatre is planted with Kurume azaleas and Japanese maples, emphasising the oriental theme.

All around are covetable plants. A sudden wave of perfume in winter and early spring announces big groups of *Daphne bholua*, a superb Nepalese species that can reach a dozen feet in height. These and numbers of large-flowered magnolias are recent additions. Other rarities survive from Gerald Loder's time such as *Quercus myrsinifolia*, an oriental evergreen oak with striking purple young leaves and *Persea ichangensis*, a Chinese avocado. Sadly without edible fruit, this is probably the biggest specimen in Britain, and produces self-sown seedlings from its shining blackberries.

Here the contours begin to be more extreme as the little stream from the pond cuts deeply into Westwood Valley. Following this on its southern side, paths drop down through relict ancient woodland within

ABOVE AND RIGHT The Iris Dell in the Slips. The boardwalk permits visitors virtually to wade through the plantings without, of course, in any way compacting the soil.

There are over 200 distinct species of iris strewn around the Northern Hemisphere in almost every possible habitat from arid mountain-sides to moist meadows. Even Britain has a couple, the dusky gladdon and – shown here – yellow flag. The Japanese water iris with its wide flaring falls has been bred and selected in the Orient for centuries.

which exotic plantings have been made over at least 150 years, accelerating through the first half of the twentieth century. This continues circumspectly, maintaining the very special ambiance. Extensive views to distant hillsides, further woodlands and, eventually, to glancing light on the waters of Westwood Lake completely epitomise the concept of 'in the depths of the country'. By the lake is the Seeboard Field Study Centre and the entrance to the Loder Valley nature reserve.

To remain more within the garden proper, paths must be followed across the stream and back towards the Mansion, or westwards to continue the full circuit of the Estate. Mature plantings of rhododendrons demonstrate dramatically that the genus is not just a blaze of floral glory for a fortnight but offers, species by species, the unusual leaf forms and textures and often superb coloured bark of a year-round attraction as well. The contorted pink-purple trunks of a planting of *Rhododendron decipiens* are especially fine; interestingly this appears to be a natural hybrid between *R. falconeri* and *R. hodgsonii*, both of which Sir Joseph Hooker collected during his years in the Himalaya – a Wakehurst and Kew meeting point that long predates the lease of this land and their link.

BELOW The steep sides of Westwood Valley are traversed by zigzag paths. Towering native oaks give shade and shelter to exotic rhododendrons and other woodland species that come from the eastern Himalaya.

The Loder Valley Nature Reserve offers students a diversity of natural habitats for observing and studying both plants and animals. It incorporates a branch of the Ardingly Reservoir – one of the biggest stretches of open water in the county – which is home to resident water birds as well as being an important stopover for migratory wildfowl.

On the north side of the valley a sudden high rock face hangs over an open dell. This has been planted as if it were a bit of wild high-mountain yak-pasture. Typically spectacular Himalayan herbaceous plants such as euphorbias, polygonums and hedychiums grow through suckering clumps of cotoneaster and prickly berberis, all species of those mountainsides, now a part of our garden scene.

Following on westwards through this Himalayan Glade the collections take up a suitably Western orientation. This is the New World in trees. First,

There are rhododendrons in flower at Wakehurst from January to August but late spring is really their moment. Some are dwarf shrublets from above the Himalayan tree-line whilst others are full-sized trees in their own right. The range of leaf-forms and colour add further dimensions. Bark texture also catches the eye.

however, a stop at the viewpoint with picnic tables and benches overlooking Westwood Lake, where gusts of wind animate the water-surface seen through the trees far below. Then it's on to a long valley meeting Horsebridge Wood and, successively, Bethlehem Wood, Bloomer's Valley and Coates Wood. As Horsebridge Wood is approached (continuing the clockwise tour of the 'bagel'), the terrain is more open but punctuated by vivid exclamation marks of a half-dozen giant redwoods. They immediately proclaim the North American theme that flows forward. Other fine compatriots include *Abies bracteata*, native only to the Santa Lucia Mountains of California and *Calocedrus decurrens*, the pencil-slim incense cedar that grows from Oregon right down to Baja California. Out of context is a big Algerian fir, *Abies numidica*, with a tiny distribution on Mount Babor where it grows with Atlas cedars. Nearby are towering Douglas firs and long-leaved Mexican *Pinus patula*.

BELOW Cliffs of Ardingly sandstone overhang the Himalayan Glade. Plantings represent mountain vegetation – a mixture of tight shrubs and herbaceous plants that are adapted to life at 10,000 feet with hard winters, scouring winds and poor soils.

LEFT A viewing point with picnic tables, benches and interpretive panels high above Westwood Lake.

BELOW The path leads on through Bloomer's Valley to the Rock Walk, an almost continuous cliff of Ardingly sandstone, home to rare mosses, ferns and lichens.

As in the wild it is not all conifers; there is a big Californian laurel, *Umbellularia*, whose aromatic foliage is reputedly pungent enough when bruised to knock out careless sniffers, and new plantings of felt-leaved Indian bean trees. Half hidden behind old native yews appear further outcrops of Ardingly sandstone which develop into an almost continuous cliff-face along the edge of Bethlehem Wood. These outcrops, with their shaded, moist and protected conditions, provide so perfect a habitat for a unique community of ferns, mosses, liverworts and lichens that the area has been designated

ABOVE The long grassy needles of Mexican *Pinus patula* sway in the gentlest breeze.

LEFT Mature Wealden woodland becomes the nursery for the developing collections of exotics, geographically arranged.

a national Site of Special Scientific Interest. Several of the species growing here are rare and the site is continuously monitored for changes that might endanger them in any way.

Coates Wood is at the north-eastern tip of the whole Wakehurst Estate; while retaining the splendid views back down the valley the plantings concentrate upon Southern Hemisphere trees, especially *Nothofagus* species – the southern beeches from Chile, New Zealand and Tasmania. This is one of Kew's several National Collections here.

The whole circuit is completed by paths that cross the 'isthmus' to the privately-owned central farmland and emerge close to the Millennium Seed Bank. Of all Kew's scientific buildings, this is the one most available to public scrutiny. The design, with its wide central atrium bisecting laboratories and work areas on either side, is specifically arranged to involve all of us; epitomising Kew's modern mandate to promote understanding and appreciation of the world of plants. With interactive displays, a wide range of changing interpretive material and examples of the extraordinary diversity of seed forms, this is a visit in itself. It is given a strange immediacy by the fact that the scientific staff are there, through the glass walls, getting on with their vital work, apparently unfazed by being part of the 'visitor experience'. The MSB should certainly not be left as a final add-on to the Wakehurst visit when feet are tired

LEFT Towering redwoods, *Sequoiadendron giganteum*, at the beginning of Horsebridge Wood. They announce the New World theme of subsequent plantings.

RIGHT ABOVE Soft furry leaves and heads of foxglove-like flowers of North American *Catalpa*. The subsequent seedpods give it the name Indian bean and they hang on distinctively throughout winter.

RIGHT BELOW Not many Southern Hemisphere trees are fully hardy in Britain but Wakehurst holds the National Collection of southern beeches, *Nothofagus* species.

and minds already brimming over; it deserves our full attention. Perhaps it's restaurant first and MSB for afters. But that, of course, takes us back to the Mansion and on the other side are gardens yet unseen. The choice is considerable; better still is to come back tomorrow – buy a season ticket on the way out and you can come back again and again.

The great attraction of Wakehurst Place for Kew was the opportunity it provided for Kew to extend its documented collections of plants that needed better soil conditions than the Kew site could provide. Inheriting a huge collection of mature trees from all over the world and shrubs, especially rhododendrons, offered Kew a distinct advantage. The two great storms, though causing dreadful damage and the tragic loss of unique specimens, provided clean-slate opportunities to change the emphasis from private garden to scientific institution and public facility with less compromises in arrangements having to be fought over. These aspects of the collections, in addition to interrelated concerns for the rich native wildlife of the area, can be appreciated by a circumnavigation of the Estate. Naturally, it will take a number of visits, season by season and year on year, to understand the full complexity of the place.

A rather more unlikely inheritance was the accumulated result of Gerald Loder's passion for plants from the Southern Hemisphere. With even the extreme tip of New Zealand degrees closer to the equator than southern England it is not surprising that most of New Zealand's flora is on the edge of, or beyond, the expected level of frost-hardiness here. Certainly, in the early twentieth century it was considered eccentric, if not foolhardy, to try it anywhere except in the extreme south-west. Nonetheless, a formidable collection of species was built up which encouraged their cultivation more widely, so that today hebes, olearias, *Abutilon vitifolium* and many other Antipodeans and Chileans flourish around the country. Still uncommon are members of the uniquely Southern Hemisphere family, the *Proteaceae*, and here can be found the dramatic vermilion Chilean fire-bush, *Embothrium*, and *Telopea*, the Tasmanian waratah. Kew's building upon Gerald Loder's work, helped perhaps by the effects of climate change, are giving a new emphasis to Wakehurst's Southern Hemisphere Garden. Again, with great care being taken not to alter its visual impact, demonstrably geographical groupings are being built up in line with current phytogeographical research.

Closer to the west front of the house is the Winter Garden, which helps to integrate the Southern Hemisphere Garden into this part of Wakehurst Place. While there is much of winter interest throughout the Estate – diverse evergreens, the coloured bark of birches and maples and the tracery of deciduous trees – this

Close to the Winter Garden is the 'Monocot' Border. Monocotyledons (meaning 'one seed leaf') have typically long narrow leaves, always distinctive in the garden scene. All our spring and summer bulbs belong to this group.

particular concentration in its sheltered site is understandably popular with visitors. Close planting enhances the scents of wintersweet, *Mahonia japonica* and *Daphne bholua*, while carefully contrived plant associations show that, regardless of weather, spectacular effects can be achieved. Black-purple stems of *Cornus alba* 'Kesselringii' shoot up through a white heather ground-cover; *C. alba* 'Sibirica' is brilliant scarlet and, standing in pools of golden winter aconites, the effect is positively heraldic.

To the north, high walls protect the Monocotyledon Border which is a high-summer *tour de force* of red-hot (and yellow-hot and even white-hot) pokers; ginger lilies (*Hedychium*), alstroemerias, crinums and so on. Many of these are South African. Behind these walls are the sort of

LEFT AND ABOVE Wide mixed borders surrounded by high stone walls maintain a domestic air close to the house. The permanent plantings are enlivened by spring bulbs – here exotic-looking fringed tulips – and summer annuals.

enclosed gardens that might be expected to flow out from a great country house like rooms without ceilings, luxuriantly furnished. The Sir Henry Price Walled Garden celebrates the generous donor who gave this marvellous place to the National Trust. Filled with the sort of sophisticated cottage garden plants for which Sissinghurst Castle is renowned, it also follows the Vita Sackville-West/Harold Nicholson directive of 'the maximum formality of design with the maximum informality of planting', and is a cornucopia of colour from spring to autumn.

Here, and in the adjoining Pleasaunce Garden, the high walls are furnished with climbers and trained shrubs that enjoy the added warmth. *Clematis balearica* hangs out its freckled cream bells throughout winter, Chilean *Berberidopsis* drips with redcurrant-like flowers and rare desmodiums and indigoferas recall the Duchess Border back at Kew.

These spaces, with views of the stable and kitchen cupolas and Elizabethan chimneys towering beyond the warm sandstone walls, succeed in retaining a private country house ambiance from which the rest of the gardens naturally proceed. That these now hold botanical collections of international significance does not interfere with the delightfully domestic atmosphere that starts at the open front door. Wakehurst Place is more than a convenient extension to Kew; it offers more to its annual half-million visitors that anyone could have imagined when the Royal Botanic Gardens came down to the country in 1965. While maintaining and building upon its uniqueness there is no doubt Wakehurst exemplifies Kew's byline – Plants, People, Possibilities. There are increasing numbers of the first two of these and, it would seem, no limit to the last.

The Sir Henry Price Walled Garden celebrates the donor who gave Wakehurst Place to the National Trust. He surely would have been happy to know that his estate has moved forward so dramatically under Kew's aegis.

᪥12᪥

BRINGING IT ALL TOGETHER
Plants, People, Possibilities

T HE ROYAL BOTANIC GARDENS, KEW, were proclaimed a World Heritage Site by UNESCO from its Paris headquarters on 3 July 2003. The report of the World Heritage Committee stated that

> This historic landscape garden features elements that illustrate significant periods of the art of gardens from the eighteenth to the twentieth centuries. The gardens house botanic collections (conserved plants, living plants and documents) that have been considerably enriched through the centuries. Since their creation in 1759, the gardens have made a significant and uninterrupted contribution to the study of plant diversity and economic botany.

This book has been at pains to emphasise Kew as a continuum – its past has supported the present which continues to build upon it. It is frequently lamented that Mankind fails to take lessons from history. Here lessons have been taken, and the UNESCO inscription celebrates the fact. It gave great satisfaction, not only to people at Kew Gardens and in Government who put the highly complicated proposal forward, but also to local societies and specialist groups who are all part of Kew's community today.

This is a concept that has expanded enormously over the last couple of decades. When these lands were a royal estate, a country retreat for the monarch and his family, as are Sandringham and Balmoral today, some little public entry was permitted. Ownership was understood and no more was expected. But

Within Kew's unique landscapes a number of permanent sculptures are displayed and enjoyed throughout the seasons. In 2008 these were joined by the biggest exhibition of works by Henry Moore that London has ever seen.

when, from the 1840s, the national botanic garden concept was vigorously promoted in order to gain parliamentary approval and public funding, it opened doors metaphorically in ways that were resisted in literal terms. William and Joseph Hooker and their immediate successors saw Kew's community in a very limited way – the scientific staff, the gardeners as menial support and, as associate members, visiting botanists from comparable institutions around the world. Anyone else got in the way. We have seen how the 'Kew Wars' broke out as the public demanded access to a public facility; with various treaties and armistices being intermittently signed an uneasy peace was reached. But the authorities were always frightened – and with some reason – that unlimited access would lead to the demand for more and more summer bedding at the expense of botanical collections and that the place would become just another popular park.

Yet at the same time, as William Hooker's museum enthusiasm shows, there was that clear Victorian belief in the power of education to raise the aspirations of the masses. The public should be admitted during regular, restricted hours (without bank holiday brass bands as some had attempted) and the wonders of the world of plants would work its civilising effects. And in many ways, through a century of imperial expansion which Kew had done so much to promote, through two cataclysmic world wars and unimaginable social changes, this did occur. As early as the 1880s visitorship had exceeded a million a year; Kew had attained the status of a permanent Great Exhibition to which everyone came. It became accepted as a national institution of which the nation was justifiably proud, even if it didn't understand what it was about or anything much of its activities on the world stage. It didn't seem to matter, Kew brought the world to 'us'.

Two very different factors combined to change the attitude of a century's calm acceptance of the status quo. The first was the emergence of the conservation movement as a national and international force in which Kew took a leading role. The second was Kew's change of governance and separation from direct parliamentary rule. The concept of community had to change dramatically if the institution were to continue to be acknowledged as a botanical leader in global terms. Support had to be rallied from every facet of the wider public in ways that were positively revolutionary in British botanic gardens. It is worth repeating that recent Directors have spent part of their careers in North America where cultural and scientific institutions, even those of national renown, are expected to raise much of their own funding. As with university alumni, membership at different category levels – the Director's Circle, the Curators' Club – depending upon the amount of financial contribution is cultivated as carefully as the Living Collections themselves. Volunteers of various persuasions are vigorously solicited. Once considered a decidedly un-British way of running such institutions (and still rather resented in some quarters) it is a pattern that has crossed the Atlantic to great effect. It has had to.

In 1990 both the Kew Foundation and the Friends of the Royal Botanic Gardens, Kew were set up in this pattern, though in a somewhat more restrained British fashion. Originally conceived to bridge the gap caused by declining government grant, the Foundation and Friends of the Royal Botanic Gardens, Kew (as it was named after its merger) works today to raise revenue that helps Kew to fulfil its ambitious science and conservation plans. Government grant is currently static, but the challenges of climate change and biodiversity loss that Kew is working to address are urgent and increasing. The Kew Foundation is concerned that people should understand and support what Kew (and by inference botanic gardens worldwide) is committed to pursue. It is community-building in the broadest sense.

The Kew Foundation targets grant-funding bodies of all sorts – government and EU sources, charitable trusts, city and international business institutions – which can be persuaded of the value of supporting specific plant-based research projects at home or abroad. As with much university research today the individual scientist or the relevant laboratory team must be able to convince potential funders of the real value of a project. At Kew, for instance, a Jodrell team will produce a carefully explicit proposal, with a scientific summary that is understood by lay Foundation members. Greater detail is examined by the team's peers. In combination – whether for an expedition to a distant hotspot or for an extension to facilities in the laboratory – a funding proposal is prepared by the Kew Foundation and the potentially effective connections made. All funding bodies, from small family trusts to multinational businesses with a charitable arm, are continually besieged by supplicants and thus the promulgating role of the Foundation is vital. So too is the ability of all staff from the Director onwards to communicate the message. In financial terms the Kew Foundation is clearly successful. Over £10 million was raised in the financial year ending 31 March 2007 to support projects not funded by conventional grant aid; the Millennium Seed Bank remains its flagship project. Sponsorship of specific parts of the Living Collections is an increasing trend and provides a rare sense of ownership to the sponsors.

It should not be thought that by comparison the Friends of Kew association is of merely parochial concern. This is community-building on an impressive scale. With towards 10 million people within easy reach the potential is clearly enormous – encouraging to fundraisers and to the ethic that drives the institution. Membership offers a number of 'benefits' in return for an annual donation – the magazine, free entry to a dozen or so botanic gardens around Britain as well as to Wakehurst Place and Kew itself, a lecture programme and so on. For residents of London and much of south-east England with any interest in the natural world (and if the success of nature and gardening programmes on television is any indication this is a considerable proportion of the population) the invitation is compelling.

OPPOSITE Wigs, lace ruffles, top hats and tail coats, here the protagonists return just to check up: Sir William Chambers, Sir Joseph Banks and Sir William Hooker appear to approve the current scene.

Friends of Kew membership offers more than just the obvious benefits: many of Kew's conservation and research projects would not have been so successful without their support. Membership implies signing up to Kew's stated mission: 'to inspire and deliver science-based plant conservation worldwide, enhancing the quality of life.' This is serious stuff for a Friends organisation.

Perhaps to temper such millenarian thoughts the gardens and the great glasshouses are pressed into service to provide pleasure now, to bring in visitors who might well not immediately sign up to the mission or its message. Thus the Temperate House can transform into impressive private concert hall, its terrace ideal for summer jazz and fireworks. Private and corporate events run throughout the year in this and other Kew heritage buildings.

The grounds are ideal for exhibitions of sculpture. There are already permanent works by, amongst others, Hamo Thornycroft and Eduardo Paolozzi. A DNA-inspired double helix designed by Charles Jencks is sited by the new Wolfson wing of the Jodrell laboratory. For six months from September 2007 – with

ABOVE A floodlit Temperate House forms the spectacular backdrop to a popular summer concert welcomed by hundreds of visitors.

RIGHT The monumental scale of Emily Young's work is ideally suited to a wide woodland glade. The 2003 exhibition of her work – classical warrior heads struggling from their marble blocks and silk smooth figurative forms – left this *Wounded Angel* behind.

ABOVE The Princess of Wales Conservatory holds Kew's wide-ranging collection of tropical orchid species. Every winter they become the centre of an orchid festival that brings in splendid displays of modern hybrids.

RIGHT One of the twenty-nine works by Henry Moore, backed by sculptural *Gunnera* leaves, is seen against the Palm House. This was part of the hugely acclaimed exhibition in 2008.

BELOW AND RIGHT Like a dream-launched gondola at carnival time in Venice, this boat has yet to negotiate the buoys. For Grand Canal read Palm House Pond. This is the work of American glass sculptor Dale Chihuly whose work was highlighted in 2005. During the exhibition the Temperate House octagons held chandelier-like assemblages of writhing stems and translucent bells.

a single great piece which arrived early as an advance guard – Kew hosted a major exhibition of works by Henry Moore, arguably the most significant sculptor of the twentieth century. A collection of twenty-nine pieces on loan from around the country was brought together for the first time. Nearly all officially belong to the Henry Moore Foundation, who curated the exhibition, but many of these are usually sited around the country, at, for example, the Yorkshire Sculpture Park, Harlow Town and the Fitzwilliam Museum in Cambridge. Opera-goers welcomed Glyndebourne's *Mother and Child* which was able to come up from Sussex out of festival-time.

Enthusiastic critics viewing Moore's *Reclining Figures* against the Palm House, the *Goslar Warrior* in front of Doric-porticoed King William's Temple and others closing Kew's tree-lined vistas saw Moore anew in these utopian landscapes as an archetypal English romantic. No such show had ever taken place in London and it wonderfully emphasised to visitors Kew's role as a place where the arts and sciences meet. Each illuminates the other.

Seasonal events have become an expected part of Kew's social calendar. A month-long orchid festival takes place in the Princess of Wales Conservatory every February with vast quantities of plants in flower clothing the pillars and filling spaces between the

Kew is concerned to encourage the next generation of visitors and to help children enjoy and understand the natural world. A slide inside a vast 'pitcher plant', a child-sized badger set, and a giant stag beetle in its home are graphic exercises in relationships.

permanent collections. Illuminated at night the effect is particularly stunning. For much of 2005 several glasshouses took on a reversal of name as they housed glass, extraordinary multi-coloured glass installations by the renowned American artist Dale Chihuly. Inspired by natural plant forms, these spread into the grounds and even across the Palm House Pond. Lectures, films and glass-blowing demonstrations in the Nash Conservatory splendidly demonstrated the idea of Kew as the arts and sciences meeting place. This is

also inherent in the wide-ranging programme of adult education courses. Botanical illustration, plant photography, aspects of horticulture, natural history, and country crafts use the collections, resources and expertise at both Kew and Wakehurst Place.

Communities cannot be built without considering the next generation, and several new projects especially welcome families and children. Close to Kew Palace, the big greenhouse that was built as a safe haven for tropical plants when the Palm House was restored has

The Wildlife Zone in the south-western part of the Gardens. A wooden observation hut overlooks the dipping pond. Local schools helped with design of the pond, its planting and features, including a wooden model of a dragonfly.

very bravely been designated 'Kew's Play Zone for Kids', called Climbers and Creepers. The Victorian Directors may be thought to be revolving in their graves but again, of course, it is the plant conservation message writ large and writ differently. Plant–animal interactions become personal for children when next to a case with living insectivorous plants there are human-sized models of *Dionaea* and *Drosera* leaves to be activated, and when the mouth of a 6-foot-high pitcher-plant becomes a slide and the person is its prey. Clearly for young visitors the whole concept is a garden of earthly delights. With the glad cries on entry and roars of rage at being eventually dragged away the place could well be named Screamers and Yellers. A mixture of families and infant-school groups make this not a place for quiet contemplation.

At the other end of the Gardens further child-based activities have been developed in the Conservation Area around Queen Charlotte's Cottage. In only 40 acres a surprisingly varied range of wildlife habitats have been established – open and closed canopy woodland, scrub and bramble thickets, grassy meadow, hedgerows. There is an old gravel pit and a new pond with a dipping platform

BELOW The lofty magnificence of the Xstrata Treetop Walkway, opened in 2008. A permanent structure, its ingenious design is based on a Fibonacci numerical sequence, often found in nature's growth patterns.

for visiting school-groups. Wildlife observation for such urban children is made graphic by a loggery to encourage stag beetles and a human-sized crawl-in badger sett where children can relate to the real wild badgers that are known to have flourished in this area for forty years.

In 2003 and 2004, a temporary Treetop Walkway constructed here gave visitors both young and old a unique experience, literally a bird's-eye view of the world. Because they are a permanent backdrop to the lives of most of us – even of unreconstructed townies – trees are apt not to be appreciated as living things; the biggest organisms we can see, great grey whales not withstanding, on the planet. Yet take to the canopy like the most intrepid tree surgeon with a vertiginous 18-metre drop either side of the (safety railed) Walkway and this begins to be brought home.

From the roof of a little bit of our English deciduous woodland it is possible to make the leap of imagination – times three or four – to the tops of Amazonian rainforests, Californian redwoods or Australian gums, that is almost impossible from normal ground level. It also provoked amazement, as the interpretive

BELOW A mature deciduous tree floodlit to show both its architectural strength and the delicacy of its detail. This is a vast living organism that we admire for its beauty and marvel at as a miracle of plumbing.

RIGHT AND BELOW In our relatively northern latitude it makes sense to help the darker days and encourage people to realise that the botanic world of plants doesn't stop with the winter, even if it is lower key. A traditional carriage with its top-hatted coachman sits easily in Kew's landscape and the whirling carousel horses rising and falling on their spiral poles also evoke a gentler age.

OPPOSITE The seasons cannot fail to be celebrated by the annual miracle of an English bluebell wood as seen around Queen Charlotte's Cottage every May and enjoyed by thousands of visitors.

panels showed, at trees as miracles of plumbing supporting and supplying these vast organic structures with water and nutrients over possibly hundreds of years. The Treetop Walkway even had a classroom in the sky that could take school groups of up to thirty children.

It was all designed by Marks Barfield Architects, whose London Eye on the South Bank is London's most striking Millennium project. Architects like that would be the first to emphasise the importance of good foundations for any structure whether built of brick or steel or wood. Trees have theirs and the Treetop Walkway's height was emphasised by visitors being able to experience the vital subterranean workings of living trees. In the nearby Rhizotron relationships between soil, its myriad organisms and tree roots were shown. What we see as the arboreal canopy is virtually reflected in mirror-image within the soil. Walkway and Rhizotron in combination are an exciting and unique way of showing the wonderful world of trees and its importance to man and this planet. These features proved so popular that a permanent replacement, twice the length of the previous temporary structure, has been developed. This, the Rhizotron and Xstrata Treetop Walkway, opened in May 2008.

BELOW May Bank Holiday is a suitable time to recall those country crafts and sports that were once an integral part of rural life. With thatch and timber Queen Charlotte's Cottage in the background the fair looks entirely at home.

These family areas are also used as bases for seasonal festivities. Climbers and Creepers, with White Peaks café and shop to hand, concentrate on Christmas. A carousel, carriage rides, handbell recitals and a carol concert on the Palace Lawn are all hugely popular, encouraging visitors at a once unpeopled time of year. Their entrance fees are welcome and they may well go away with a certain subliminal sense of what the place is about when the merry-go-round stops. Queen Charlotte's Cottage grounds are the site for May Bank Holiday activities. This annual Woodland Wonders Festival celebrates the country crafts that belong to just such an area of English bluebell woodland. There are demonstrations of hedge-laying and charcoal making; willow-workers and bodgers sell their wares and heavy horses perform traditional forestry work. Again the intention is to build a wider public and encourage diverse use of all parts of the Estate.

In bringing these activities together Kew has taken to using a nice alliterative masthead byline – Plants, People, Possibilities. It's an apparently simple association that can also be seen as a conjunction of words and concepts to take the traditional botanic garden roles into new worlds. The statement that all life depends on plants would appear such a truism that it hardly needs to be repeated: even the most remote tribes though they may know nothing of the role of gaseous exchange or taxonomy would have no doubt that plants are central to their very existence. And that the plants, from forest trees to lowly ferns and mosses, are an indivisible part, with the mammals, birds, fish and insects, of the environment which they share. And those, of course, are only the bigger components in an extraordinary complexity of interrelated life forms. They are the easier aspects that we can comprehend, however superficially – at least we can see them. Beyond are microscopic worlds of bacteria and fungi that are also a part of the whole.

Plants, People and Possibilities is therefore an over-arching mantra that admits to no boundaries in the search for knowledge of the world of plants and its benefit to mankind. Knowledge is power, runs the old adage, to which the corollary is that is can be a force for good or ill depending upon the motive and upon its use. How encouraging, comforting even, that in an age obsessed, as we are led to believe, with the twin idols of instant gratification and consumerism that today's botanic garden ethic is the exact obverse of that coin. It is especially encouraging that the moral imperatives of that ethic have evolved, as the story of Kew has shown, out of a consumerist race no less vigorously pursued (just less immediate in a pre-electronic age) in the economic pursuit of plant products across the world. It *is* possible, it seems, to learn from history.

BELOW The May fair often includes falconry displays with a range of birds of prey flying freely from, and back to, the wrist.

Looking to the future: Whither Kew?

T HIS BOOK has been planned as a part of wide-ranging celebrations to mark the 250th anniversary of the founding of the Princess of Wales's little botanic garden, which the widowed Princess Augusta began to plant in 1759. It certainly was not intended to be, two and a half centuries later, a tract for our times. But, *faute de mieux*, that is rather what it has become because Kew, building upon its history, is so much of our times.

Such a celebration is also a commemoration, not just of one person – though here the Princess is bound to be a focus – but of an age. Although 1759 can seem incredibly distant from our current world of the twenty-first century, it is central to what presaged so much modern thought. This was the 'Age of Enlightenment' where in the arts and sciences, in philosophy and politics, in technical inventions and innovations, revolutionary developments spilled out on all fronts.

This was the age of Mozart and Haydn, of Voltaire and Gibbon, Hales (he of *Vegetable Staticks*) and Lavoisier, Hume and Adam Smith. It was also the age of Hogarth's Gin Lane, Tyburn and Bedlam – not all was elegance and politesse. It was an extraordinary melting pot, one that could not but have its effects upon the King, the Court, the Country and upon Kew.

We have seen how the Princess's botanical enthusiasms drew upon traditional sixteenth- and seventeenth-century physic gardens for her garden's layout and the arrangement of her plants. Within a dozen years it was beginning to burst at the seams as the fruits of a rapidly expanding world (Joseph Banks, it will be remembered, came back from Captain Cook's *Endeavour* voyage in 1771) produced more and more botanical treasures. But its subsequent international standing could never have been even guessed at.

It is natural for anyone with the vision and the means to garden on any scale to expect that their creation will continue into the future. When we plant a tree we must accept that its lifespan will far exceed our own and indeed we should plan for this fact. Yet gardening is the most difficult art-form to predict; its materials live and grow; they die. They are at the mercy of the weather and even, in our own time, of discernable changes in the whole pattern of climate. All of which makes maintaining gardens for future generations an extremely problematical process. It

The soaring arch of the Davies Alpine House at the north end of Kew's Rock Garden. The spider's-web-thin glazing bars ensure the maximum amount of available light, necessary for high alpine plants.

is sometimes suggested that our current concern – obsession even – of keeping up or restoring 'heritage' gardens such as Vita Sackville-West's Sissinghurst and Lawrence Johnston's Hidcote (to mention just a couple from the dozens that surround great houses owned by the National Trust, other conservation bodies or hereditary owners) is misconceived. The external forces, say the pragmatists, are too redolent of the story of King Canute. Gardens are by their very nature transient and should be allowed to be so.

These, however, are gardens made solely for pleasure. They are aesthetic statements of their time, which also, usually, give intense satisfaction to their makers *in the making*. As we have seen, this is how the gardens at Kew began. But royals are apt to possess a stronger sense of dynasty than mere commoners (though few had it more obsessively that Ms Sackville-West – how she would have loathed the Ms!) and might well expect their creations to persist. Perhaps there is a distant whisper of the Divine Right of Kings still drifting from the shrubberies.

What they could not have envisaged is the manner in which these gardens have persisted and evolved over 250 years from fashionable pleasure grounds and *ferme ornée* and the random, albeit surprisingly extensive plant collections, into an internationally renowned centre for the study of the world of plants. This story of Kew has shown how such a phenomenon has come about, by design, by foresight and even by sheer luck, with the right person being in the right place at just the right time. It could well be that Kew is in such a situation today, being led by a Director of vision whose passion is restoration ecology; good fortune certainly, but not merely luck. His thoughts resonate through much of this final chapter.

We can follow, therefore, through Kew's fascinating progress, three centuries of British history. It has been fashionable in recent times to decry the centuries during which these little offshore islands became an unparalleled world power. But at last, with memories of empire dissipating, it is possible to discard some of those politically correct cries of embarrassment and look back with more balanced judgments. Altruism, of course was never an overriding imperial motive and few today

would consider reasonable Lord Curzon's assertion that 'the British Empire is under Providence the greatest instrument for good that the world has seen'. But then he *was* the Viceroy of India, and hence, perhaps not entirely disinterested.

Kew's story, as has become apparent, parallels many aspects of Britain's story on the world stage and we have seen how the institution has contributed to it. Celebration of that first botanic garden's founding here has encouraged us to follow Kew's progress and to celebrate that as well – its ups and downs, its pros and cons – and to see it, with perhaps less equivocation than with the British Empire as a whole, as the force for good that Lord Curzon claimed. Princess Augusta and Lord Bute and those who have followed, though they would have been surprised at what such a seed grew into, have reason to join in the party. Such a moral dimension is not commonly considered.

What now? Whither Kew? These are questions that Kew's staff and the interrelated scientific community are vitally engaged with. For its work is concerned with no less than the survival of our planet as we know it and the human race upon it. When Kew's first botanic garden was planted with the products of an expanding world only strange millenarian sects ever predicted the end of this world. It was certainly not the expectation of scientists. On the contrary they were the realists wresting Mankind, as they thought, from the shackles of medieval belief and myth. 'The true and lawful goal of the sciences,' wrote Francis Bacon as far back as the beginning of the seventeenth century, 'is none other than this; that the human life be endowed with new discoveries and power.' The inherent optimism in that age-old claim still fuels the work that lies ahead. Whether optimism dare foresee a future on the scale of the anniversary being celebrated is a moot point.

What can be done by Kew and members of the worldwide botanic garden community is to join with other bodies and movements – scientific, political and lay – to communicate to all who will listen the problems facing our world and, within their area of expertise, offer possible remedies. It may be palliative care but it is truly constructive. Where, in the previous times, Kew's major role was to support trade and the prosperity of Britain and its dominions, its role today is stated as 'serving the needs of the world community'. Here, of course, plants and – with increased knowledge of their mysterious world – fungi are becoming ever more important. Here lies the key. Conservation of natural habitats, supported where necessary by cultivated collections and seed banks, protects biodiversity and emphasises the sustainable use of those elements on which man is dependent.

Behind the scenes in the Orchid Nursery. Epiphytes grow in hanging pots or on slabs of bark, terrestrial species more conventionally on the benches. High temperatures and humidity are essential for their success.

Kew's current mission statement – 'To inspire and deliver science-based plant conservation worldwide, enhancing the quality of life' – is perhaps overly modest. Ultimately, in the broadest sense, the world of plants permits life: without plants we die. 'All flesh is grass,' cried Isaiah with alarming prescience.

While such resounding phrases can be fully justified and their concepts applauded there is a danger of bombastic overkill. We can only take a certain amount of doom before switching off and shrugging metaphorical shoulders at such apparently intractable problems, which are worldwide and at least in part manmade.

So it is the practicality of Kew's activities that offers rays of hope 'amid the encircling gloom', to use Cardinal Newman's only too evocative phrase. This book has shown how Kew increasingly uses its accumulated

knowledge and expertise to address in practical ways many aspects of global problems and to broadcast that knowledge on all fronts.

Botanic gardens today can well claim to be the most accessible of scientific institutions: however apparently esoteric the research being pursued in the Jodrell Laboratory or the Herbarium it can be shown to have direct relevance to the world of nature. And the Living Collections are the window to much of this. The sometimes critical dismissals given to the concept of 'pure science' – though there probably is no such thing – do not apply here in any way. This is not a haunt of self-indulgent boffins. Alexander Pope, who lived just up-river from Kew and knew Princess Augusta, famously asserted that, 'The proper study of mankind is man'. He, philosopher, poet and gardener might well accept a misquotation today that 'the proper study for mankind is plants'. And Pope might have been amused to find his *Essay on Man* rather than *The Epistle to Burlington* used to celebrate Kew Gardens.

It has been repeatedly emphasised that Kew's primary purpose today is the conservation and enhancement of those aspects of significant natural and cultural heritage both within its own curtilage and the wider world. Over 200 staff members are involved in research and some of the most exciting areas have already been described. Emphasis has also been given to the dissemination of the work pursued and on its being shared with whomsoever it can benefit. This is Kew upon the world stage, an aspect of ever increasing importance.

The 250th anniversary also celebrates locally the place that is Kew; it may well have been designated a World Heritage Site in 2003 but that was no aspic moment, when Kew stood still self-satisfyingly contemplating the activities and possessions of its famous past. Nor does it now. Just as its scientific programmes continually move forward, knowledge building upon knowledge, so too do its lands and the projects pursued upon them. 'Kew Gardens' is virtually a copyright binomial that attracts its millions of visitors who come to feel its history, to experience the wider world by travelling through its plant collections of the temperate outdoors and the tropical glasshouses, and to enjoy the art and science of horticulture. This itself is to be celebrated; it is by the successful cultivation of an incredible range of plants that the general public knows Kew. When Kew Gardens station, as part of London's extending network of public transport, was opened in 1869 (though maddeningly not on the expected site) an increase in visitorship of over 100,000 sent a frisson of fear through the Gardens' establishment. The place would be overrun by the lower classes, fumed the Director, who were 'mere pleasure seekers ... whose motives are rude romping and games'. That battle for public access with extended opening times rumbled on for years but as can be seen from the wonderful series of London Underground posters dating back to 1908 what really encouraged people were the

Even before the swathes of *Crocus tomasinianus* open in earliest spring, school groups visit Kew as part of curriculum projects.

plants. Rude romping can happen anywhere but this was a place universally accepted as being special. The general public and Londoners in particular felt a sense of ownership. Everyone knew or knew of Kew Gardens and they came in their thousands.

The fear that democracy would lead to a mere proliferation of carpet bedding gradually subsided. Today the great Palm House parterre continues to amaze year by year – a *tour de force* of texture, colour and form that is a twice-yearly celebration of the gardener's art. But it is also conceived, like the more obviously didactic botanical collections, as a part of Kew's broad educational remit. The design team even has fun. In 2004 a cottage garden theme was chosen. The display – 10,000 plants or so – included decorative vegetables such as sweet corn, wigwams of runner beans and even scarecrows. As so often at Kew there was a glance back at history. Archival photographs show the whole Palm House parterre as one great onion bed, part of the war effort in 1918, producing a prodigious crop.

There are changing displays and changing emphases throughout the grounds as plants grow or become senescent and need replacing. Changes in the pattern of our seasons and an appreciable warming encourage other developments. *Cordyline australis* growing outside the Princess of Wales Conservatory and olive trees by King William's Temple would have been inconceivable less than fifty years ago when the present writer was a student there.

What plants to grow and where to grow them is the concern of a wide range of staff. Physiologists in the Jodrell Laboratory need particular genera and species to further their research; taxonomists in the Herbarium may want wide-ranging collections for comparative purposes. In addition, the continual demonstrative role of a national botanic garden presumes the cultivation of the widest range of plants that climate, facilities and space can encompass. Why grow them? Because they exist – this is the museological role which a civilised country is bound to offer its citizens.

Such a role encourages botanic gardens to have outposts that provide other climatic patterns and

LEFT The Palm House Parterre is a twice-yearly celebration of the gardener's art. Thousands of plants are propagated in the nursery and combined in splendid display.

ABOVE Daisies come in all shapes and sizes but their essential daisy-ness is always apparent – a central mass of tiny florets surrounded by insect-eye-catching petals. Thus they can be described as composite flowers and hence their family name – the *Compositae*. Here from Australia is the 'everlasting' *Helichrysum* and Mexican *Cosmos*.

different soils to extend the range. The Royal Botanic Garden, Edinburgh has an astonishing trio of satellites, utterly different from the home base. Dawyck in the Scottish Borders has greater extremes of temperature that promote brilliant autumn colour in its wide-ranging collections of trees and shrubs. Benmore in Argyll has towards 200 inches of rain a year (and midges to match) which many rare South American plants enjoy. Gulf-stream-washed Logan in the extreme south-west is like Kew's Temperate House without its roof.

As we have seen, Kew's sister garden Wakehurst Place has increased the diversity of Kew's collections, and these have been further enhanced by the setting up of the Castle Howard Arboretum Trust. Kew has become closely involved in this important Yorkshire garden to maintain and develop its collections of trees and shrubs, many deriving from Kew's expeditions. Including Sikkimese rhododendrons brought back by Sir Joseph Hooker and documented plants from expeditions of all the major twentieth-century collectors – Reginald Farrer, George Forrest, 'Chinese' Wilson, Kingdon-Ward and others – these are of considerable importance. New plantings in the developing Arboretum are made upon a historic site which parallels Kew in several ways, though on a vastly bigger scale.

Castle Howard is a great Vanbrugh-designed house, which, with its architectural landscape, is on a level of grandeur that equals Sir John Vanbrugh's better-known Blenheim Palace. As at Kew, strategically placed eighteenth-century garden buildings abound and far more have survived to catch the eye. Horace Walpole – Princess Augusta's neighbour at Twickenham – wrote of Castle Howard in 1772, just after her death, describing it as having 'the noblest lawn on earth fenced by half the horizon, and a mausoleum that would tempt one to be buried alive'. Again, as at Kew, and following soon after in 1850, William Nesfield was brought in to design a palm-house-like parterre to the south of the house. Kew and

Professional botanists, keen gardeners and family parties enjoying a day out are all members of Wakehurst's admiring visitors.

Castle Howard, it can be seen, have surprising parallels and today benefit mutually from what is far more than just a marriage of convenience. The appointment of John Simmonds as Castle Howard's Honorary Curator after his twenty-three years as Curator at Kew ensures this is so.

In addition to their ability through climate and soil – as well as the basic fact of more space – to extend the Living Collections in size and diversity, the sister gardens also have a public dimension. Wakehurst Place and Castle Howard are not mere outposts; they bring Sussex and North Yorkshire into the national botanic garden network. Membership and Friends groups involve the local communities in activities that promote understanding of the global issues that underpin the institution, as well as providing a focus for regional horticultural programmes. Newly built visitor centres provide a focus for such activities.

The ongoing dissemination of plant-based knowledge at these three gardens extends beyond the Living Collections by the public sharing of Kew's unique holdings of botanical art. It has been related how William Hooker, back in the 1830s when he was Professor or Botany at Glasgow University, employed the young Walter Fitch to illustrate *Curtis's Botanical Magazine*, of which he was editor. On coming to Kew, Hooker persuaded Fitch to join him and continue his role, working on the *Bot. Mag.* (as it is still affectionately known) for forty years and producing thousands of paintings. Subsequently Kew bought pre-Fitch *Bot. Mag.* illustrations and the work of his successors – representing most of the important artists of their times. These, together with innumerable gifts and bequests that have been made over the years, form an unrivalled collection of botanical art. Altogether there are over 200,000 illustrative items. But, with the exception of the extraordinary Marianne North Gallery, where that munificent artist gave not only the hundreds of paintings on display but also the building in which to hang them, this treasure trove has traditionally been a part of the Herbarium Library and Archives, available only to scholars and researchers.

Small exhibitions have been mounted in the Kew Gallery in Cambridge Cottage and have even been on tour abroad but there has never been a specific space to show Kew's artistic heritage. In time for the 250th anniversary, however, the first gallery in the world dedicated to botanical art is in place. This is a brainchild of Dr Shirley Sherwood who has long been a passionate advocate of this, if not neglected, certainly specialised oeuvre. The Shirley Sherwood Gallery of Botanical Art normally runs three exhibitions a year featuring material from the Kew Collection, partner institutions and the Sherwood Collection, with one exhibition based exclusively on the latter. The Link Gallery (which leads to the Marianne North Gallery) permanently displays items from the Sherwood Collection, on a regular changing basis. Thus what is in essence a trio of galleries now offers a stunning overview of the most significant botanical artists of the last 300 years.

The essence of botanical art is that the plants depicted are true to life, indeed the accuracy is often such that they actually appear to be alive – one can feel the texture of the leaves, the flowers seem still to cast their scent upon the air. Before the days of photography this was, of course, the only method of recording species new to science and encouraging their cultivation. The rather corny couplet on the cover of an 1845 *Bot. Mag.* gives the Victorian viewpoint:

> Nature and Art t'adorn the page combine
> And flowers exotic grace our northern clime.

The almost inevitable evanescence of plants in flower made it essential that an artist travelled with important voyages of discovery. The hugely talented Sydney Parkinson, who died on the way home from the *Endeavour* Transit of Venus voyage, is one of the most celebrated. Sir Joseph Banks had first employed him to paint plants at Kew in 1764; on the voyage he had completed 269 paintings and almost 700 sketches with notes and dried specimens enabling them to be worked up later. Botanical

The interiors of the Shirley Sherwood Gallery of Botanical Art; the central room (above) and the link gallery (below).

artists work in the same way today, from the growing plant whenever possible, yet producing amazingly 'living' likenesses from herbarium sheets as well. Dissections of flowers and magnifications of certain diagnostic features often add to their scientific value. From the hand of a master, these are true works of art, with which few photographs can compare.

Another recent extension of Kew's shared activities can be seen at the north end of the Order Beds. Ahead is the modern block of the Jodrell Laboratory, to the south a typical mid-eighteenth-century building in yellow London stock brick. Beginning life as the royal fruit store it become Sir William Hooker's 1848 museum and is now the education centre for Kew's renowned School of Horticulture. First-year students on the Kew Diploma

BELOW By the Waterlily pond is another eighteenth-century building. Starting life as the royal fruit store it became Kew's first museum, now it is the Education Centre for the School of Horticulture.

RIGHT Against its east side is the Kew Guild Garden, in which first-year students maintain vegetable plots to hone their practical skills.

course maintain individual vegetable plots to expand their practical experience. This activity used to take place out of sight behind the Herbarium; today's plots are part of a specifically designed garden adjacent to the school. It offers a contemporary take on the traditional kitchen garden. There are sixteen eight-metre-long plots; any space surplus to student requirements demonstrate green manuring techniques and a range of 'heritage' vegetable varieties. Historic varieties of fruit are trained in various forms along the surrounding fences while the garden pavilion holds interpretive material, notably about Stella Ross-Craig, one of Kew's most accomplished artists, who died in 2006 aged 100, and about the Kew Guild, the Association of members of Kew staff past and present.

A considerable bequest from Ms Ross-Craig to the Guild helped fund the garden. Characteristically she also left to Kew originals of some of her *Bot. Mag.* work, as well as the priceless originals of her famous *Illustrations of British Plants*. Examples of her work can be seen in the Shirley Sherwood Gallery and make an interesting link between two very different aspects of Kew's activities available to the public.

The Kew Diploma in Horticulture can be seen as yet another way for Kew to ensure that its huge range of expertise in the plant sciences and its resources – especially within the Living Collections – is widely disseminated. Though the formal education was pretty vestigial in the early years, former Kew students have been leaders in botanic garden and ornamental horticulture around the world since the early nineteenth century. Then, especially, new botanic gardens throughout the Commonwealth depended upon them.

Today's sophisticated course, recognised as at least first-degree level, combines practical work caring for the

LEFT AND RIGHT Students on Kew's Horticultural Diploma course come from all over the world. In their three years at the gardens they attend degree-level lecture series and demonstrations, travel on botanical field trips and visit other scientific establishments. But they are also involved in the practical plant-care of the gardens and experience the whole diversity of the plant collections outside and under glass.

Living Collections with a broad range of academic studies. This provides for a unique blend of science, horticultural technology and landscape studies. The tutors either themselves practice at Kew or hold senior positions in industry and vocational education. Kew's School of Horticulture is often described as a 'centre of excellence', and with reason. It is at the heart of international horticultural and botanical education, welcoming qualified students from around the globe. Kew's message, 'to deliver science-based plant conservation worldwide' is taken by all these young people who continue their professional careers with the coveted Dip. Hort. Kew after their names.

In trying to address that question 'Whither Kew?' it has been essential to emphasise the outgoing nature of the institution today. To some extent, this is a direct reflection of contemporary attitudes so different from times past. Sir Joseph Hooker fighting the Kew Wars to maintain strict control over public access in the 1870s (and his decidedly 'I'll show 'em who's boss' raising of the boundary wall in 1877) can be seen, with some generosity, as a rear-guard action to maintain standards. It can also be seen as petty insistence on maintaining an outdated status quo. It was certainly mirrored by official distain of the general public.

The twenty-first century, on the other hand, is obsessed by the call for accessibility and the involvement of almost anyone with almost anything. Not a radio programme is broadcast without listeners being bombarded with invitations to comment electronically or even, as a last resort, by letter. Much of this, it must be feared, is just cosmetic 'caring'. No institution, especially those funded in part by government, can disregard what might be called

LEFT AND RIGHT A botanic garden is bound to be a haven for animals as well as plants. Not all are native species: in addition to screaming flocks of ring-necked parakeets there are Canada geese and that other ubiquitous North American, the grey squirrel. Wildfowl both resident and migratory can be seen on the ponds. Colonies of bees are maintained, butterflies and moths also feed – here a rice paper butterfly on verbena flowers.

the mores of the moment, but its motives must be impeccable. Kew is no exception to this. Climbers and Creepers and other jolly japes for children could be put into a sort of modern 'bread and circuses' category just as any extension of carpet bedding in front of the Palm House was once regarded in similarly sinister terms.

This would be a misreading of Kew's commitment to openness and the sharing of its resources. The importance of botanic gardens in the service of plant and fungal conservation worldwide cannot be overestimated and any legitimate way of involving people and broadening their understanding and knowledge is valid. This fact is not new. The earliest physic gardens of the late Renaissance were concerned in their limited way – though 'cutting-edge' in the fifteenth century – to do just that. Plants were seen to be vital to human health and indeed existence. So to gather them together, to cultivate and propagate them successfully, to name, to classify and to disseminate the knowledge gained was a noble calling. The wilder claims of Paracelsian medicine have been lost along the way but the understanding of the importance of plants to man has never been in doubt. Where the life and health of individuals was once the focus, today it is the health of the planet itself that is at stake.

Plants have always been the universal providers for man's food, fuel, medicine, clothing, building materials and so on but they also underpin other forms of life. Their key role in the carbon cycle, however, adds an entirely different dimension. As major assimilators of carbon they are vital in moderating impacts of climate change and serious large-scale threats to their well-being are a threat to us all.

Kew promotes its public face to reach out and involve a sophisticated yet sadly complacent population with the current issues. From static interpretive displays to seasonal celebrations, from popular television series to lecture programmes, the Royal Botanic Gardens are concerned to share their heritage and their future with all. For everyone to accept the serious underlying message would be wise – if only from self-interest. This need not, however, detract from the enormous range of pleasures that this extraordinary place offers. The Gardens are a place of year-round beauty – of wide spaces, great trees, unlimited interest, and enormous diversity.

Within its high brick walls and bounded by Thames's ceaseless tidal flow, the Gardens, now further enriched by Wakehurst Place and Castle Howard, have been at the centre of British history through a dozen reigns. A vast empire, of which Kew was a significant part, has come and gone. Yet, in global terms, what goes on here has never been more important. In support of that work a major extension to the Herbarium and Library is newly completed, hot on the heels of an additional wing to the Jodrell Laboratory. Further plans are in train to enable Kew staff to work more effectively in the service of worldwide conservation and to encourage and involve an ever-increasing number of visitors. Ultimately, it is people who matter, from visionary leaders to every level of support staff, from internationally eminent scientists to casual tourists seeking an enjoyable day out but osmotically taking in some of Kew's message. This is truly a place where the arts and sciences meet – the linked avocations that show what it means to be human.

For 150 years everyone had to walk round the Lake to visit collections on the other side. Perhaps there is an apt symbolism in the elegant curve of the new Sackler Crossing that brings visitors more quickly to see and experience what is 'over there' within the world of plants.

Index

Picture acknowledgments

Photography by Andrew McRobb. All photographs and other illustrations © The Board of Trustees of the Royal Botanic Gardens, Kew except page 12 (© Joanna Jackson); page 22 (The Royal Collection © 2007 Her Majesty Queen Elizabeth II); page 232 (© Martyn Rix); pages 257, 258, 259 (Nick Guttridge © Historic Royal Palaces).

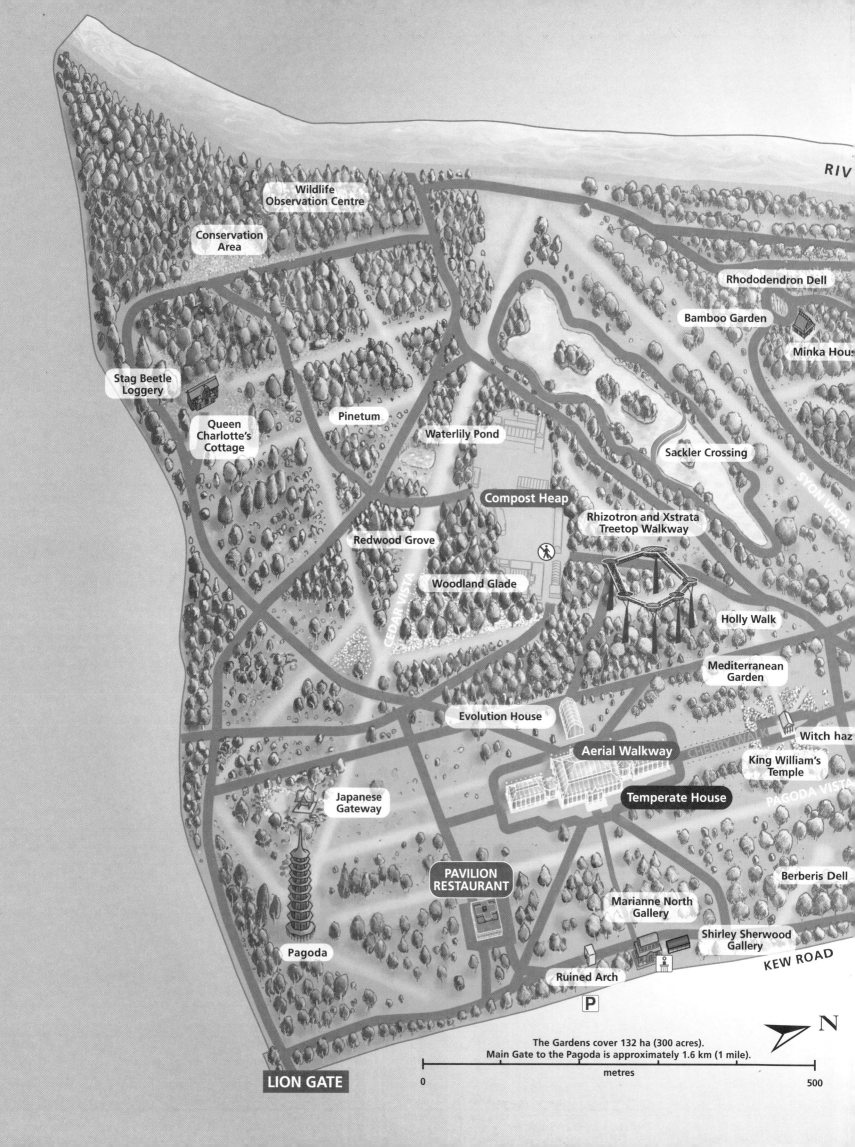

Wildlife Observation Centre

Conservation Area

RIV

Rhododendron Dell

Bamboo Garden

Minka Hous

Stag Beetle Loggery

Queen Charlotte's Cottage

Pinetum

Waterlily Pond

Sackler Crossing

SYON VISTA

Compost Heap

Rhizotron and Xstrata Treetop Walkway

Redwood Grove

Woodland Glade

CEDAR VISTA

Holly Walk

Mediterranean Garden

Evolution House

CHERRY WALK

Witch haz

Aerial Walkway

King William's Temple

Temperate House

PAGODA VISTA

Japanese Gateway

PAVILION RESTAURANT

Berberis Dell

Marianne North Gallery

Shirley Sherwood Gallery

Pagoda

Ruined Arch

KEW ROAD

P

N

The Gardens cover 132 ha (300 acres).
Main Gate to the Pagoda is approximately 1.6 km (1 mile).

metres

0   500

LION GATE